GREEK POLITICAL ORATORY

ADVISORY EDITOR: BETTY RADICE

A. N. W. Saunders was born in 1900 and educated at Rugby School, and later at New College, Oxford, where he obtained a first in Mods and Greats. He taught Classics first at Bradfield College, and later at Rugby, where he became Senior Classical Master. He retired from Rugby in 1965, and lived in Cambridge. He is also the author of *Imagination All Compact*, a book on the basis of art. He died in 1982.

GREEK
POLITICAL ORATORY

SELECTED AND TRANSLATED
WITH AN INTRODUCTION BY
A. N. W. SAUNDERS

PENGUIN BOOKS

PENGUIN BOOKS

Published by the Penguin Group
Penguin Books Ltd, 27 Wrights Lane, London W8 5TZ, England
Viking Penguin, a division of Penguin Books USA Inc.
375 Hudson Street, New York, New York 10014, USA
Penguin Books Australia Ltd, Ringwood, Victoria, Australia
Penguin Books Canada Ltd, 2801 John Street, Markham, Ontario, Canada L3R 1B4
Penguin Books (NZ) Ltd, 182–190 Wairau Road, Auckland 10, New Zealand

Penguin Books Ltd, Registered Offices: Harmondsworth, Middlesex, England

First published 1970
7 9 10 8

Printed and bound in Great Britain by
Cox & Wyman Ltd, Reading
Set in Monotype Ehrhardt

CONTENTS

INTRODUCTION

I. THE GROWTH OF ATTIC ORATORY

WHEN we speak of political oratory, we think first in terms of the great British orators of the eighteenth and later centuries, and of speeches in the House of Lords or House of Commons rather than of speeches in a court of law. It is therefore important to begin a discussion of Greek political oratory by emphasizing the fact that only a small proportion of the extant work of ancient orators was of this kind, consisting, that is, of speeches made in a constituent assembly and intended directly to influence political policy. In fact almost the only speeches of this kind which we still possess in Greek are the shorter speeches of Demosthenes, most of which are included in this volume, and a few ascribed to him, but now regarded as of doubtful authenticity. The great majority of extant Greek speeches are not deliberative, but forensic, that is to say that they were delivered in a court of law and aimed to secure the condemnation or the acquittal of an individual, as were Lysias' prosecution of Eratosthenes and Andocides' defence of himself against prosecution for impiety, which are both included here. This selection also includes two discourses of Isocrates, 'speeches' which were never actually delivered, but were published pamphlets employing an oratorical form and style. Greek prose literature sometimes adopted a convention of appearing in the form of speeches, like those of Isocrates, or of dialogues, like those of Plato. Finally, the speeches in this selection are preceded by a translation of the celebrated Funeral Speech, nominally of Pericles, which serves to represent a further division of Greek oratory, the epideictic, speeches made for public occasions. It is most unlikely ever to have been delivered at all as it stands, since it is part of the *History* of Thucydides. All these, however, share a markedly political content, and are closely associated with important political events or trends, and provide matter of importance for understanding political history.

All Greek oratory known to us is in the Attic dialect and was delivered or published in Athens. This of course is true of the great majority of Greek literature of the fifth and fourth centuries B.C. and is a fact which inevitably colours the views we hold of Greek life and politics. That oratory, like poetry, flourished in Athens can readily be understood. Athenian quickness of wit and tongue ensured it. It is not only in art, but in philosophy that Athens excelled. Nonetheless, there must have been speeches made by Spartans, Thebans or Argives, which are not preserved except for one or two which are given, changed, if not improvised, in the pages of Thucydides. But it must be remembered also that Athenian pre-eminence in speech must have been reflected in the choice of passages for reproduction by later centuries. The actual selection may have depended a lot on chance, or the requirements of rhetorical teaching, but it constitutes a judgement of posterity which, while it may have allowed some things of value to perish, did not preserve much of what was worthless. And the speeches which were so selected are entirely Athenian.

Nor is any Greek speech extant which belongs to an earlier date than about 417 B.C., the probable date of Antiphon's speech *On the Murder of Herodes*. This is in part due to the circumstances regarding publication, which will be mentioned below (p. 13). Addicted as they were to self-expr ssion, the Greeks seem not to have begun till then to write and record the speeches which were made, despite the enormous importance attached to the power to speak well. This is manifest from the Homeric poems onwards. Not only do we find s eeches given to historical persons in the work of Herodotus and Thucydides, but they appear as forensic, not merely dramatic, as early as the *Eumenides* of Aeschylus (458 B.C.), while the tragedies of Euripides show frequent signs of familiarity with speech-making both as a habit and as an organized art. Herodotus and Thucydides, indeed, used speeches in an original fashion, but it is unlikely that any of their readers supposed that the speeches in question had been delivered as they stood. They do, however, presuppose the habit of speech-making. The Herodotean speech, and after it the Thucydidean, presented ideas dramatically, in

8

the words of an orator who made or might have made such a speech on such an occasion. Such is Thucydides' *Funeral Speech*. Of a similar kind, too, is Plato's *Apology*, which purports to be Socrates' defence at his trial. Plato was probably present on that occasion, and in any case the general lines of Socrates' defence were no doubt well known. But Plato, as the great dramatizer of Socrates, may with equal certainty be supposed to have worded his defence in keeping with the rest of the picture he painted of him.

This last instance at any rate belongs to the fourth century B.C., but the true beginnings of Greek oratory are earlier. Prose is always later in the field than verse, but the rise of political freedom, especially in Athens, in the fifth century led to the realization that prose as well as verse could be developed as a literary form, and that human needs of expression covered wider ground in the pursuit of knowledge and the maintenance of civic rights. From this need arose what is called the Sophistic movement: the intellectual ferment of the fifth century had by the latter half of it been systematized in the hands of professional men of learning. They were in a sense successors of the early philosophers, such as Heracleitus or Pythagoras, and they met in the eager intellectual *milieu* of Athens. Men like Protagoras, Hippias, Prodicus and Gorgias professed among other things to teach and stimulate the art of speaking, both as one of a number of cultural subjects (Plato makes Socrates discuss with Protagoras whether virtue can be taught)[1] and as a practical technique of its own. Either part of this programme was expected to be of value both in politics and in litigation, to which Greeks were prone, and also to offer an inherent value in the improvement of education. It was perhaps most desired for its utility in a litigious community, and it is in this context that there arose the claim parodied by Aristophanes in the *Clouds* that the Sophistic training would 'make the weaker argument the stronger', while Gorgias in Plato's dialogue of that name is made to contend that the subject which he professes is the 'greatest and best of human concerns'.[2] These statements involve a claim to improve the citizen's ability to plead a case and

1. Plato, *Protagoras*, 324 seqq.   2. Plato, *Gorgias*, 451 d.

9

win it, but they were used as material for detractors, and can be seen behind Aristophanes' satire in the *Clouds*, and in Plato's many dialogues criticizing the Sophistic movement. The Sophists took fees for the tuition they gave, and in due course began to specialize in speech training. Some formed schools and composed a '*techne*', a rhetorical handbook, as Antiphon did. Jebb declares[3] that Greek oratory begins with Gorgias, Attic oratory with Antiphon.

Gorgias of Leontini in Sicily was born, like Protagoras, about 485 B.C., and is known not simply as a rhetorician. He led an important delegation to Athens in 427 to ask for Athenian assistance for his city. But it was probably his fame as a speaker which led to his nomination as a leader, as in the case of Teisias, who accompanied him. He is also known to have been chosen to speak at the Olympic festival of 408. He is in the sequence of Sicilian rhetoricians together with Teisias, the teacher of Lysias, and the reputed head of the movement, a certain Korax. Gorgias' claim to fame as an orator seems to have rested on skill in expression rather than on exposition or treatment of his matter. His influence is said to have extended in particular to Thucydides and Isocrates. The only continuous passage of his which survives is itself part of a funeral oration. It must be granted that it is tiresomely overloaded with symmetrical antitheses, and does not suggest great oratory. Nonetheless it can readily be understood that this style explains some of the peculiarities of the speeches which Thucydides includes in his narrative, and also the smoother antithetical method of Isocrates. And it was to Gorgias more than to any other, as we see in Plato's dialogue, that most early Greek orators of whatever origin looked up.

Born a little after Gorgias, Antiphon played a prominent part in the oligarchic revolution of the Four Hundred in Athens in 411 B.C., which is his claim to political fame (a fame, like that of Gorgias, due to rhetorical skill) and to which he owed his execution. But his extant speeches are not political in this sense. He was perhaps the first to do in Athens what Gorgias had not done (though Teisias did in Syracuse): that is, to organ-

3. *The Attic Orators* (introd. p. cviii).

ize a school and compose a manual of oratory. He was also the first professional writer of speeches, and thus the precursor of all the great Athenian orators. Greek orators did not deliver speeches for others, as Cicero did, but wrote them for others to deliver. Thucydides says that Antiphon never appeared in court except in his own defence in 411, with a speech extolled for its excellence, but in the event unsuccessful. His extant work is confined to cases of homicide, in which he seems to have specialized, and includes his four *Tetralogies*, sets of speeches in imaginary cases, two each for the prosecution and the defence. These bridge the gap between theoretical accounts of the needs of oratory and actual speeches in court. He was a pioneer in the practice and in the style of Attic oratory, writing, as did Thucydides, at a time which lacked a prose tradition. He is credited with many of the same characteristics of style as Gorgias, but his work seldom reminds one of Gorgias' existing remnants. Both are said to have played a part in the teaching of Thucydides, but except for occasional phrases Antiphon does not provide a strong resemblance to the speeches in Thucydides' history, though he too is given to brevity, symmetry and antithesis. These are characteristics which probably seemed to both writers to offer a method of bringing prose to the literary level of poetry.

From these beginnings, social and stylistic, Attic oratory rose and soon flourished. Of course Athenians had made speeches earlier than this, but they were probably extemporized. It is said that Pericles was the first to deliver a written speech in court, and it must be assumed that written speeches in the Assembly were a later habit. Pericles is described by the comic poets, Eupolis and Aristophanes, who refer to his lightning speed and persuasiveness.[4] But we have no record of his speeches except Thucydides' versions, nor of speeches by the famous demagogues, Cleon, Hyperbolus and Cleophon. In the extant speeches forensic oratory appears first, and most of the early examples were written for delivery in court. Two of these which are particularly concerned with political events are translated here, those of Lysias, *Against Eratosthenes*, and

4. Aristophanes, *Acharnians*, 531.

Andocides, *On the Mysteries*. The oratorical antecedents of these two orators are very different. Lysias learnt oratory from Teisias of Syracuse before coming to Athens. As an alien, however, he was not entitled to speak in court except during the brief amnesty after the fall of the Thirty in 404, when he delivered the speech against Eratosthenes. (See the introduction to the speech, p. 39.) Most of the rest of his work consisted of speeches written for others. He was, however, distinguished enough to be chosen to deliver the Funeral Oration at Athens (probably 392 B.C.) and a Panegyric Oration at Olympia (388 B.C.). Andocides, on the other hand, spent much of his life in exile, and there are but three of his known works of oratory, two delivered in his own behalf, and one in the Assembly after his acquittal. Jebb [5] calls him an amateur, which is not surprising since we know nothing of professional study in his instance. It is the occasion of his most important speech which makes it noteworthy. Indeed it concerns an earlier event than that of Lysias, though it was delivered later. Both, though politically important, are forensic in form. But the majority of speeches by Greek orators were on narrower and more personal subjects, like those of Isaeus, who enjoyed a special reputation as an expert in the composition of law-court speeches, particularly in cases of inheritance. Perhaps it is partly because of such narrow and individual aims that Plato regards oratory with such evident distaste and disparages it in a number of places. He calls it an art of spell-binding, and criticized its lengthy irrelevance,[6] naming Pericles the greatest of orators, because he learnt from Anaxagoras, and could fortify his art with philosophy.

There are also examples of epideictic speeches (the Greek word means speeches of display) delivered for particular occasions of importance. Mention has already been made of funeral speeches by Pericles, by Gorgias and by Lysias. The *Panegyricus* of Isocrates is in form of this kind. But with the exception of Andocides' speech *On the Peace with Sparta* we have no deliberative speeches from the Assembly till those of Demosthenes, the earliest of which was delivered in 354 B.C. It may be in part

5. *The Attic Orators*, p. 88.   6. Plato, *Phaedrus*, 270a, 271d,e, 272.

his eminence that secured his speeches from oblivion, but in fact the practice of publishing deliberative speeches does not seem to have begun much before his time and that of Isocrates. The speeches of litigants were commonly written from the later years of the fifth century B.C., when oratory developed in theory and practice owing to the habit of making handbooks of rhetorical theory, and the habit of 'speech-writers' (λογόγραφοι) composing speeches for clients to deliver. The publication of political speeches may, it is suggested,[7] have been begun by aliens, like Lysias, who were interested in politics, but not admitted to the Assembly, or due to private circumstances like those of Andocides, who seems to have published his *On the Peace with Sparta* by way of self-justification. These and the like may have led to the practice of Isocrates and Demosthenes. Demosthenes, indeed, may well have been the first to publish deliberative speeches already delivered in the Assembly. Such speeches may on occasion have been subject to alteration in the interval. This is suggested, for instance, by some passages in *Philippic III* whose genuineness has been doubted (see p. 249) as well as by the statement of Plutarch that comparisons were drawn between Demosthenes' extempore speeches and his written ones. In any case it appears that Demosthenes did publish speeches in his lifetime, perhaps to substantiate their political importance.

2. ISOCRATES AND DEMOSTHENES

Within these limits stand most of the Greek orators of whom we have knowledge, the Ten Orators, known to the first century A.D. in a list which became an established canon and thus ensured its survival. The list includes Antiphon, Andocides, Lysias and Isaeus, whom we have mentioned, the two great names to whom we now go, and in addition Aeschines, the great opponent of Demosthenes, Hypereides, Lycurgus and Deinarchus.

One, however, Isocrates, made still another use of oratory. He was full of talent, as Plato makes Socrates describe him in

7. See George Kennedy, *The Art of Persuasion in Greece*, p. 174 seqq.

celebrated passage at the end of the *Phaedrus*,[8] and had wide views about the Greek world and particularly his native Athens. But he lacked the voice and the robust temperament needed for active oratory. He therefore found his own niche as a teacher, and communicated his ideas as written pamphlets. But he did not practise either activity on the same lines as his predecessors. He was a teacher of rhetoric, yet one who was neither a mere theorist nor a mere exponent of technique, and therefore departed from the practice of writing speeches for imaginary situations, like Antiphon, because he regarded contact with real and vital questions as important. Yet he did not seek to achieve it by speaking. He was a sophist, as a man who took fees for teaching oratory. But in an early discourse[9] he makes a strong protest against sophists for making extravagant claims which they can never fulfil, for being oblivious of practical aims and for bringing discredit on genuine teachers – charges little different from Plato's. What he sought to instil into his pupils he called 'philosophy'; but it was not what Plato meant by the word. He regarded the Platonic pursuit of truth as too unpractical, indeed as humanly unattainable, while Plato grouped him with the Sophists, regarding them as tamperers with the truth rather than seekers of it. Finally he was a passionate admirer of Athens, but took no narrowly partisan view of her position in Greece, desiring to see her lead a united Greece against the Persian enemy whose attack had united her before. Isocrates was in fact a great liberal when liberalism was not the language of the day, and his political ideas were in advance of those of his contemporaries. As such he may be called doctrinaire or idealistic, and as such he differs from the great speaker of the day, Demosthenes.

Isocrates' pursuit of rhetoric made it into a general culture, almost a liberal education. He did not go quite as far as Cicero was to do[10] in depicting the orator as the ideally cultivated individual. But he did regard rhetoric not solely as a means to a practical end, success at law, but as a development of human

8. See George Kennedy, *The Art of Persuasion in Greece*, p. 279.
9. *Against the Sophists*, 12.
10. In *De Oratore, passim.*

powers by the study of the written or spoken word, the *log*
which would enable learners to improve their judgement of *a*
kinds of activities, specialized or otherwise. This was an educa-
tional system very different from Plato's and it is not wholly
surprising if the two men were alienated from each other. Whether
the tale of their enmity is true cannot be certainly determined.
Opposite views are entertained.[11] In any case we may imagine
that they differed considerably in temperament, as they did in
outlook. Plato scorned rhetoric, Isocrates believed in it, and
hoped to find in it a means to recover for Athens and for Greece
some of their old life and vigour. This was to be achieved by
teaching, and, no doubt, inspiring the young with the feelings
which he wanted to disseminate. This is the purpose which the
Panegyricus in particular was designed to serve, and in some
degree achieved. At least it greatly enhanced his reputation,
increased the demand for his services as a teacher, and launched,
if unsuccessfully, his campaign for the sinking of differences
and the solidarity of Greece.

This was not a theme which was due to his unaided invention.
In particular it had been put forward by his master, Gorgias,
on the occasion of his Olympic speech in 408 B.C., which has
been mentioned. But this Pan-Hellenism was suited to Isocrates' outlook and to the aims he was setting himself, to bring
his pupils to the highest attainments by means of the *logos*,
and to affect the trend of politics by exerting an influence on
the leading men. In the aim of Pan-Hellenism he showed an
exceptional insight into the needs of the age.[12] It may seem to
have needed no unusual penetration to realize the difference
between the atmosphere and the attitude maintained by the
Greeks in the defeat of Persia in 490 and 480 B.C. and after the
collapse of Athens during the Spartan hegemony. But in times
of declining community of spirit it is easier to confine attention
to narrow aims and the securing of narrow gains, than to go

11. cp. L. Robin in *Phaedrus* (Budé) and Laistner's edition of Isocrates'
Philip. One editor even takes the famous compliments on Isocrates in the
Phaedrus as a slight. The passage of course relates to a time when Socrates
was adult and distinguished.

12. See p. 28.

...nst the common view and seek a genuine broadening of .tlook. To have a real effect on public opinion and alter the attitude of the Greek states proved more than Isocrates could achieve. In the *Panegyricus* he had realized the need to unite them in attack on a common enemy, the same enemy, Persia, whose attack had united them in the great days of the past. With the stimulus of that aim he hopes that they will overcome jealousies about leadership and agree to accept that of Athens. This may have seemed somewhat naïve. If so, the feeling – that it was naïve – was part of the spirit which needed to be overcome. But it was not overcome. And whether or not he made overtures to other rulers (it is said that he approached both Dionysius of Syracuse and Jason of Pherae, but this is disputed)[13] the *Philip* shows him sufficiently disappointed of his previous hopes to feel that the only chance lay in finding a single champion who could rally the Greek states round his standard. For this purpose he saw a suitable figure in Philip of Macedon, clearly the leading single ruler in the Greek world after 350 B.C., and sufficiently integrated in it to appear acceptable.[14]

Yet never, or never until it was too late,[15] do Isocrates' aspirations appear to have been taken seriously. This was not principally because they did not appeal enough to Philip, nor because of the rise of Demosthenes, who took a different view. Better to say that it was due to the political state of fourth-century Greece, to which we shall revert, and to something in the character of Isocrates himself, which must have been partly realized by his contemporaries, and which makes us temper praise of a man who was ahead of his time, by calling him too little of a realist. The philosophers, according to Plato, must be the rulers, but they will never wish to rule. This applied to his ideal state. In the real world it seems doubtful whether they *can* ever rule, not merely through unwillingness, but through inability to make sufficient compromise with the actual. It is a charge made by Isocrates against the sophistic philosophers, and perhaps against Plato himself, as we have seen. Now it rebounds

13. See, for instance, Norlin, *Isocrates* (Loeb).
14. On Philip's ancestry see Isocrates, *Philip*, 32 and note.
15. i.e. after Chaeronea (see below, p. 25).

– on Isocrates; and we may speculate why exactly we feel r
be just, not only in relation to his ideas, but to his smoot.
unvarying style, so that we prefer Demosthenes, sensing that
greatness depends in part upon success.

Not that Demosthenes was greatly successful. Indeed he is
generally regarded as the patriot who could never induce a
declining state to surmount self-seeking and revert to action.
This is not wholly true. He was too great an orator to be always
unsuccessful, even though the times were against him too. He
is the culmination of this line of orators, the exponent of
political oratory in our original sense,[16] using his powers to sway
a political assembly and influence actual legislation. He saw the
truth, perhaps with a limited view, but without distortion or
wishful thinking, unless it was indeed unrealistic to hope for
any Athenian revival. If so, he was optimistic, where Isocrates
was doctrinaire or academic. In one sense the two men were at
one, in another far apart. Isocrates, like Demosthenes, had been
prepared to castigate Athens for her unwillingness to face
unpleasant facts. Demosthenes, like Isocrates, was inspired by
the past greatness of Athens, but he longed for her to recover it
in the world as it actually was, not as it might become. To
Demosthenes, Isocrates (strangely enough we seem to have no
record of contact between them) must have seemed to lack all
common sense in expecting concord among Greek states without
a strong motive for it, or Philip's unselfish abandonment of the
quest for power in Greece. But we can hardly fail to answer
the question which of them was right, and it will be asked again
at a later point.

Meanwhile we may make some assessment of Demosthenes
himself and of the claim of greatness that is made for him by
later Greek and Latin writers. Great oratory is not solely a
matter of style, but also of character. Whatever else Demosthenes was, he was a man of courage. He must have felt at his
best when he was wrestling with difficulty: with his own
temperament and physique, with his financial troubles after the
early death of his father, with acquaintances who found him

16. Here I omit reference to the numerous forensic speeches of Demosthenes, which do not appear in this volume.

ome, pompous and self-righteous (which he probably was) well as with an inert and complacent Assembly. What quali- es has his oratory which are lacking in the others of his day? Critics of the time of Cicero and later credit him with numerous stylistic features. Cicero himself dwells on his variety, subtlety, dignity.[17] But we have to wait for the writer wrongly known as Longinus to come nearer, with 'rugged sublimity', 'intensity', and finally 'stature'.[18] He was single-minded in his foreign policy, however double-minded he may have been called by his opponent, Aeschines, and showed, as perhaps no one else among the ancients could, the ability both to give lofty expression to a high cause and to make that contact with his audience which is the essence of practical oratory, and which Cicero describes under the word *'flectere'*, the power to influence hearers. We are not here much concerned with his private habits, except as they affect our view of him as an orator and a statesman. He may be accused of disingenuous, even dishonourable dealing on occasion; the personal rivalries which coloured his public relations with, for example, Aeschines, were sometimes sordid and his expression of them, worded in the normal fashion of the time, displeasing. We shall find this tendency in a personal speech, such as *On the Crown*, a forensic speech, but political in that it includes Demosthenes' assessment of his own career. It is too long for inclusion here, but it will reinforce the impression given by his speeches to the Assembly of an orator who can be called great for discarding popularity in a lofty cause. On the issue of success we must, in his case too, look more closely at the history of his time.

3. STYLE OF THE ATTIC ORATORS

In introducing a translation not much need be said of style. But some attempt has been made in this one to differentiate

17. *Orator*, 110.
18. *On the Sublime*, 34. The Greek word here translated 'stature' simply means 'size'. This treatise, previously attributed to an author named Longinus of the third century A.D., is now thought to belong to the first century A.D.

between individual characteristics, though it cannot be hoped that a translation will by itself make style or manner clear. Nor can style be entirely detached from character and conduct. Some mention has already been made of it in discussing the authors referred to. And style was of great moment to the ancients, particularly in the Ciceronian period and later, when analysis of the great treasure of Greek literature was prevalent. But, as with other critical study, the first to systematize it was Aristotle, and Cicero's own works on oratory and later the treatises *On the Sublime* and *On Style*[19] can still be reckoned as indebted to him.

The Ciceronian age made much of a controversy on the relative merits of the Attic style as represented by the best Athenian orators of the fifth and fourth centuries B.C., and the more florid Asian style, so called, which had developed since that time. We need not spend time in considering this, though Cicero devotes a little space to it.[20] But it is to Attic that he pays most attention, and to the differences within it. In this connexion Thucydides is mentioned, to distinguish his style from that of Lysias.[21] Cicero specifically says that Thucydides has no part in oratory, but that the speeches he includes 'contain so many remote and obscure passages as to make them barely intelligible'. The translator can only attempt a faint suggestion of this Thucydidean style, which is perhaps due to intense feeling packed into an antithetical style derived from Gorgias. It is as far as possible removed from the manner of Lysias. Ancient criticism of Lysias was no doubt based largely on the speeches he wrote for others to use in court, so that Cicero, for instance, denies him full grandeur of style, and Dionysius comments on his power of character-drawing.[22] The speech *Against Eratosthenes* is in fact fuller than most of Lysias, and shows that his plain and natural narrative could give place on occasion to more swelling oratory. But his most marked charac-

19. Ascribed to Demetrius of Phalerum (*c.* 300 B.C.) this work is now thought to belong to the first century A.D.
20. *Orator*, 25, 26.
21. ibid., 30.
22. Dionysius of Halicarnassus, 41.

teristic is his straightforward ease of statement, and the essay *On Style* follows Cicero in stressing his 'charm'.[23] The earlier orators were more practical in aim than Gorgias, and found that such an easy flow met their largely forensic needs. Andocides has it too, but his style suggests what is in fact true, that he was not at first a professional speaker; the present version has been composed with the feeling that ordinary speech touched with the colloquial might be nearest to the manner of the amateur.

Isocrates is a different matter. His methods were much more self-conscious. The author of *On the Sublime*, who was apparently no strong admirer of Isocrates, quotes Caecilius'[24] reference to Alexander as 'one who subdued the whole of Asia in fewer years than Isocrates took to write his *Panegyric* urging war on Persia', and later criticizes the *Panegyricus* itself for a long-winded passage sufficient to spoil Isocrates' point.[25] But Cicero points out, and we should remember, that Isocrates wrote with a view not to the 'thrust and parry of the courts, but to give pleasure to the ear'.[26] It is a polished style in which the antithesis he had learnt from Gorgias is ironed out, though it is still at times perceptible,[27] and in which period succeeds period 'with no less regularity than the hexameters in the poetry of Homer',[28] avoiding even hiatus as an undesirable roughness.[29] It is thus a style of more beauty than strength, reflecting perhaps Isocrates' personality and his own praise of a style which is as artistic as that of poetry.[30]

Demosthenes was universally upheld by Greco-Roman authors as the prince of orators, and has maintained that reputation

---

23. 'venustas', 'χαριεντισμός'.

24. A Sicilian rhetorician who taught at Rome in the time of Augustus.

25. iv, 2, and xxxviii, 2, on Isoc, *Panegyricus*, 8. But see Norlin ad loc.

26. *Orator*, 38.

27. See *Panegyricus*, 80, 84, for a passage which reminds us now of Gorgias, now of Plato's parody of Prodicus in the *Protagoras*.

28. *On Style*, tr. Fyfe. 12.

29. ibid., 68. Hiatus is the gap or absence of a consonant, when one word ends in a vowel and the next begins with one.

30. *Antidosis*, 46.

since. Cicero speaks of 'one man's astonishing eminence in oratory',[31] and though he finds some deficiency when he compares Demosthenes to his imagined ideal ('he does not always fill the measure my ear demands')[32] he finds in him 'all the subtlety of Lysias, the brilliance of Hypereides and the vivid vocabulary of Aeschines',[33] noting whole speeches that are marked by subtlety, others by weightiness like some of the *Philippics*, others by variety. Cicero follows well-known stories like that referred to in the introduction to Demosthenes (1) below, when he speaks of Demosthenes' stress on delivery,[34] and though he too avoided hiatus as harsh,[35] his is not the smoothness of Isocrates, but that of a practised and practising speaker. Pre-eminently this is what Demosthenes is, and even if there are passages in his work which are no more than practical and may even have dissatisfied Cicero, he can rise to oratorical heights, for instance in parts of *Olynthiac II* or in the *Philippic III*, which justify the language of the writer on *The Sublime*.

4. ORATORY AND POLITICS

Though oratory is an art particularly connected with politics, its rise in Greece coincides with a political decline. And this is no mere coincidence. The same factors at least contributed to both. To say this makes it necessary to attempt some assessment of the nature of this political decline and to justify the phrase, if we are to understand our orators themselves and to estimate them in the context to which they belong. We can therefore hardly avoid some brief historical summary. Here reference is made from time to time to the sectional introductions below, but inevitably there is some overlapping.

The Periclean age of the greatness of Greek, especially of Athenian, civilization ended with the outbreak of war between Athens and the Spartan alliance in 431 B.C. Pericles himself did not long survive. And, though there was an interval in the fighting, war continued till the collapse of Athens after the battle of Aegospotami in 405. This war, which in Gilbert

31. *Orator*, 6. 32. ibid., 104. 33. ibid., 110.
34. ibid., 56. 35. ibid., 150.

Murray's words 'destroyed the hope of Hellenism',[36] was fought to prevent the commercial expansion and imperialism of Athens from having full scope and leading to the enlargement of Athenian power. Ever since the Athenian assumption of the leading role after the defeat of Persia in 479 B.C. the power of Athens had shown this tendency to expand, when she changed a Confederacy of Aegean states, organized for defence against Persia, into an Empire geared to her own advancement – a gradual change which coincided with her development as a democratic and maritime community. During the war Athens' resources and Athenian popularity underwent serious vicissitudes, but she did not refrain from further imperialism, notably in the attack on Sicily between 415 and 413. This grandiose scheme ended in disaster, and the superstitious could look back on the sacrilege committed as it sailed (see the introduction to Andocides, p. 61). Signs of strain began to appear, when a *coup d'état* put the city for a time in the hands of an oligarchic *régime*, in which the orator, Antiphon, took a leading part. But Athens was not brought down till 404. By then Persia, almost forgotten for over forty years, had been invited back into Greek affairs by Sparta to combat the Athenian fleet. With her resources now at an end Athens had to submit to Sparta and to oligarchic control. There was a reign of terror under the so-called Thirty Tyrants (see the introduction to Lysias, p. 39), and though it was not long before Athens reverted to democratic ways, she did not regain her old wealth.

Then began the supremacy of Sparta, as the liberator of Greece from Athens. The Spartans inspired even deeper hatred than most liberators. The extraordinary Spartan community did not know how to govern except by rigid control. Within a few years Sparta was again at enmity with Persia and at war with an alliance in which Athens, now recovered, though not financially, was joined by Thebes, Corinth and Argos. Having brought Athens down less than twenty years before, Persia now helped her to a naval revival, and then, growing nervous, in 386 agreed to the much vilified 'King's Peace', whereby, with Spartan assistance, she dictated terms to the Greek states. After

36. *Journal of Hellenic Studies*, LXIV.

it Spartan exploitation continued, and resentment agai. Sparta increased. It was vain at this time for Isocrates to writ of unity (see the introduction to the *Panegyricus* of Isocrates, p. 99), to praise the greatness of Athens and urge her leadership, even in partnership with Sparta. It was just at this time, in 379, that Sparta caused the disruption of the rising confederacy of Olynthus, an act subversive of unity. However, dislike of Sparta did stimulate Athens, perhaps influenced by Isocrates, to form a new confederacy of her own, with altruistic intentions. Eventually in 371 a conference of the Greek states took place at Sparta, by which Athens and Sparta agreed to abandon empire in a pact of non-aggression. But Thebes, in the person of Epaminondas, claimed to sign on behalf of Boeotia. To this Sparta took exception and, in contravention of the treaty just made, attacked Thebes and, against the military genius of Epaminondas, suffered a severe defeat at Leuctra.

Now it was the turn of Thebes to liberate the world from Sparta. The process continued for nine years – just so long as Epaminondas remained alive to conduct it. It included attacks on the Peloponnese, the reconstitution of Messene, which was 'liberated', and, as a further counterpoise to Sparta, the foundation of Megalopolis as a new city in the heart of Arcadia. But Theban self-seeking and intransigence alienated Arcadia as well as other states, and brought Athens into the arms of Sparta. They were allies in the campaign of Mantinea (362), when they met the force of Thebes. Although successful in the battle, Epaminondas lost his own life; this was fatal for Thebes, and the Theban supremacy collapsed.

If we cannot quite talk of liberation from Thebes, whose dominance was less complete and more short-lived than Sparta's, yet she raised numerous opponents among the Greek states, two in particular at different times Athenian power had been regained in part, as has been seen, first in reaction to Sparta, when Persia allowed the repair of the fortifications (the Long Walls of Athens) and Conon revived her naval strength. Then, after the King's Peace, Athens returned to vigour in the Second Confederacy of 378, which started as a genuine attempt to avoid the exploitation of her fifth-century Empire. After this confederacy was directed against Theban power in alliance with Sparta. But Athens suffered from continual lack of funds, and could not long maintain power in the Aegean without resorting to some methods which did not live up to the aims of the Second Confederacy. The reappearance of cleruchies [37] and the exactions of the mercenary forces which fought for Athens, but subsisted on plunder, caused alarm and discontent. In 357 the important islands of Chios, Cos and Rhodes revolted under the influence of the ambitious tyrant of Caria, Mausolus (see introduction to Demosthenes (1), p. 170). Peace was made in 354, but by then Athens had lost several valued possessions to the rising power of Philip of Macedon.

The other, and later, opponent of Thebes was Phocis. Her rise in response to Theban attempts to use the weapon of the Amphictyonic League [38] against her, and the onset of the Sacred War, are referred to in the introduction to Isocrates' *Philip* (p. 138), and the rise of Philip of Macedon in that to Demosthenes (1) (p. 170). These need not be described in detail here. Peace between Philip and the Athenian alliance (excluding Phocis) was made in 346 and known as the Peace of Philocrates. For the last time Isocrates hoped to secure a leader and general support for his campaign for unity, and to induce Philip to assume this role. But the peace, which began with Philip's destruction of Phocis, only lasted as long as it suited him, and ended in 340, when the insistence of Demosthenes raised an alliance against him. In 338 Demosthenes' fears were realized, and Philip, himself making use of an Amphictyonic dispute, marched south through the pass of Thermopylae, and overwhelmed the Greek forces at Chaeronea. At last there had been a rally in support of the view Demosthenes had voiced since 351, but the Greeks could not match Philip's trained troops and superior tactics.

Philip turned on Thebes, but spared Athens. Not for the last time the past greatness of Athens saved her from destruction by a conqueror who appreciated it, and saw a chance to gain her assistance by leniency. By the terms of peace Athens was

37. See note on Isocrates, *Panegyricus*, 107, p. 120.
38. See note on Isocrates, *Philip*, 74, p. 152.

compelled to abandon her existing confederacy and join the new Pan-Hellenic union proposed by Philip. The hegemony of Greece now rested with Macedon, a monarchy outside the circle of the Greek states of the past. The first assembly of the new congress was summoned at Corinth, though it was not till a year later, 337, that Philip announced a new campaign against Persia, and the arrangements for it were organized. Isocrates wrote to Philip to express his delight that his aim had at last been accomplished. One enactment, however, the establishment of three Macedonian garrisons at strategic points in southern Greece to maintain control of it, might have made him wonder if he was right.

5. THE DECLINE OF GREECE

Having made our summary, we must return to the suggestion that in the fourth century in Greece the rise of oratory is connected with a political decline, and to the question of whether the orators could make any contribution to combat it. We may see this decline in several different ways; we may regard it as a political failure of the city state, the failure of the Greeks to achieve the unity which might have preserved their continued development in a political world to match their economic development. We may see it as a social failure of the middle class to maintain and extend democracy because it sought to remain exclusive; or as the cultural failure of a community which kept to slave labour instead of pursuing the curiosity which leads to fresh scientific developments.[39] Finally we may think of it as a psychological failure, a loss of confidence on the part of a world clinging to its own past. In any case it involves, as two interacting factors, a tendency to particularism in which narrower interests are preferred to broader ones, and a tendency to the static in which the enjoyment of what already exists takes the place of the pursuit of what is new. In a discussion of political oratory we shall be more concerned with the breakdown of the city state than with the other factors, though all are facets of a single situation.

39. See F. W. Walbank in *JHS*, LXIV.

GREEK POLITICAL ORATORY

This political disruption or particularization is due to individual or sectional self-seeking, which wished to establish its own desires at no matter what cost to the community. The grimmest chapters of Thucydides[40] describe the spread of this evil, which he calls by the name of '*stasis*', division in the state pursued with violence in quest of sectional ends, usually of a kind which we should call ideological. Thucydides specifies the symptoms in a horrifying analysis. This is the positive side of the disease, the virulent pursuit of private aims. The negative side is the reluctance to be active for public ones. This can be seen in lighter, but no less telling lines in the comedies of Aristophanes, in the *Ecclesiazusae*[41] (393 B.C.), or earlier in the *Acharnians* (425 B.C.), in the picture of an Assembly reluctantly giving itself to public business, or in the *Clouds* in that of the effect of Sophistic teaching in reversing traditional moral ideas.[42] Such changes of feeling, connected by common opinion, if that is what Aristophanes represents, with Sophistic teaching, were changes in the direction of individual self-seeking. And common opinion certainly took oratory, like Sophistic training, as detrimental in tendency to the sound outlook of conservatism. It is true at any rate that the practice of oratory arose in direct connexion with the Sophistic movement, and was obviously conducive to exploiting private advantage.

The Greeks themselves were not oblivious of the disease in its political aspect. Attempts were made to break new ground and achieve a new basis for the organization of society either by means of alliance on new terms or by actual federation. But the new was undermined or obliterated by the final efforts of the

40. III, 82, 83.
41. *Eccl.*, 205-207. (The title of the play might be modernized as 'Women in Parliament'.)
> It's your fault, people of Athens, who live
> On public money, but all you think about
> Is private gain, every man for himself.
42. *Acharnians*, opening lines; *Clouds, passim.* cf. Andocides, *Against Alcibiades*, 22: 'That (the encouragement given to unconcealed breaches of morals) is why the younger generation spend their time in the law courts instead of in the gymnasium, and while the old serve in the forces, the young orate, with the example of Alcibiades in front of them.'

26

old. The Olynthian or Chalcidic Confederacy, for instance, dates back to the fifth century. In 432 B.C. Olynthus, together with other states, seceded from the Athenian Empire, largely because the old Confederacy of Delos, as it was originally called, had been turned by Athenian exploitation into an empire over unwilling subjects. During the great struggle of the Peloponnesian War and after it the Chalcidic Confederacy began to rival Macedon as a fringe power of the Greek world. Macedon was largely disordered and inefficient between 400 and 359 B.C., when Philip rose to power, and the Chalcidic Confederacy seemed to promise better than others. One new feature of note appeared in it, a principle of dual citizenship, by which citizens of each member state were citizens also of the Confederacy as a whole, and all laws and rights were to be shared equally. Olynthus was the nominal head of the Confederacy, but assumed no privileges apart from the others. At first confined to a single promontory, the movement gathered adherents fast, but two cities which were unwilling to be brought in appealed to Sparta, who forcibly dissolved the League in 379 B.C. The new growth had proved inadequate to resist the old.

Two other instances show the contemporary tendency to try the confederate principle to secure ends which were out of reach of single cities. The Second Athenian Confederacy was conceived in a spirit of altruism and of unity against the detested power of Sparta. The confederate states were to have their own assembly distinct from that of Athens, and no measure affecting both was to be valid till passed by both. There were to be no cleruchies, no 'tribute', none of the hated features of the old Empire of the fifth century. Yet perhaps this was a negative approach with a limited aim. It failed eventually, as has been said, because Athens, perpetually short of funds, failed to avoid exploitation; cleruchies and the old abuses began to reappear, and in the Social War she was again involved against her allies. The Arcadian League, which was virtually created by Thebes after Leuctra to curb Spartan power, and involved the foundation of the new city of Megalopolis as a federal capital to replace villages in the neighbourhood, is a third instance, however specialized, of the attempt to supersede small units of organization in favour of larger ones.

These attempts to do what was necessary for Greek civilization by broadening its basis were altogether too weak for their purpose. They had not enough support to convince a world accustomed to warfare within itself. Thinkers and orators alike failed to see a solution, even if they envisaged a need for it. Plato, if he may represent the thinkers, exemplifies two opposed reactions to the problem, that of withdrawal and that of compulsion. To imagine a Utopia (as he did) is to make too little contact with the actual. This is a withdrawal into the spiritual realm different from, but comparable with the later withdrawal of Stoicism. But the *Republic* also suggests the way of compulsion with its arbitrary division of classes and its strong flavour of Spartan control. Compulsion is often enough used to end disagreement. The orators, too, had little to offer except to revert to the past and urge its virtues on the present. Isocrates alone had a sense of the needs of the time and an idea, however inadequate, of a remedy for them. In the letter to Archidamus he enlarges on the disorders of Greece as he does in the *Philip*,[43] and urges co-operation and unity. In the *Peace* he had urged the abandonment of empire and the making of a peace which should not merely rest on *ad hoc* principles to end the Social War, but should be permanent and embrace all the Greeks. Seventeen years later in the *Philip* he had decided, whether or not for the first time, that unity could only be achieved under the leadership of a single king or general. But throughout he saw the need of good will and some compelling principle of unity. When Pan-Hellenism came with Philip, and when the Stoic *homonoia* (concord) was prefigured by the ideas of Alexander, both father and son might have been conscious of a debt to Isocrates. Yet he failed for lack of a principle that was compelling enough. By the majority he went unheeded. It was easier to stimulate an unwilling community to energy than to concord. The stirring oratory of Demosthenes could animate a last stand for the aspirations of an earlier century, even if his hopes did not survive Chaeronea. By this achievement he

43. *Philip*, 96, 121, cf. *Panegyricus*, 167.

rendered Isocrates' hopes as vain as his own. After that any peace or agreement was one imposed on the Greek world, not generated by it, and any new deal would not arise from a settlement of differences, but from the enactment of a conqueror. So the splendid patriotism of Demosthenes reduced to ineffectiveness the ideals of Isocrates. It becomes vain to speculate whether either could ultimately have succeeded. We must probably agree that the Greek civilization which rose at last to the support of Demosthenes' efforts against Philip could never have risen to the pleas of Isocrates for concord and agreement with him.

TRANSLATOR'S NOTE

The introduction and the sectional introductions and notes are intended to cover ground necessary to the understanding of the speeches themselves. They do not take the place of a history of Greece, and matter not immediately relevant to the speeches is generally omitted. The text principally used has been the Oxford Classical Text for Thucydides, Lysias and Demosthenes, the Teubner text for the others. I have made considerable use of Mr D. M. Macdowell's edition of the *de Mysteriis* and of Prof. M. L. W. Laistner's of the *Philippus*. I am greatly indebted to Dr W. Hamilton for invaluable assistance with the translation, to Dr M. I. Finley for reading and criticising the Introduction, and to Dr T. T. B. Ryder for similar help with the sectional introductions and notes. The shortcomings which remain are, of course, mine and not theirs.

THUCYDIDES: PERICLES' FUNERAL SPEECH

INTRODUCTION

The funeral oration which Thucydides puts in the mouth of Pericles (Thuc. II, 35–46) is one of the acknowledged masterpieces of literature. It is stated to have been delivered during the winter of 431–430 B.C., on the occasion of the public funeral of the dead in battle. It is not to be supposed genuine in the sense of giving the ipsissima verba *of Pericles. There have been editors who have claimed to find in it an individuality distinct from other speeches in the work. But this is probably wishful thinking. The momentous, impressive style, and the tortuous sentences, are those of Thucydides. He must have known that Pericles made such a speech on this occasion, and he would probably have heard how he treated the subject, even if he was not himself there to hear it. It may have been Pericles who saw this as an occasion to praise the Athenian way of life. If so, it was Thucydides who later saw it as a subject admirably suited to a point in his* History *where that way of life was threatened by war, or even to a time after the war when it had been overthrown. On any assumption it may seem to go too far in idealizing a state which was soon to pay the penalty, as Thucydides himself unfailingly points out, for self-seeking and ruthless imperialism. But whether it is to be put down as history or oratory, it is, with the possible exception of the* Apology of Socrates, *by Plato, the best known speech in Greek, and it remains one of the great statements of human achievement in the spiritual field.*

THUCYDIDES: PERICLES' FUNERAL SPEECH

MOST of those who have spoken here before me have praised the enactment in the law that this speech should be made, since they think it appropriate that it should be spoken at the burial of the dead in battle. To me it would have seemed sufficient that men who were noble in action should by action have their honours displayed, as you see they are in the grave set here in public for them, and that the virtues of many should not be left to the hazard of one man's speaking, whether it be good or bad. For it is difficult for a speaker to give a fair estimate when even the appearance of truth can scarcely be assured. One who listens with remembrance and affection may think that in some respect his wishes and knowledge have been accorded less than justice, while another in ignorance may envy as excessive what sounds beyond his own ability. For the eulogy of others is acceptable only within the limits of a man's belief in his own power to achieve as much. What goes beyond this adds disbelief to envy. But I must follow what has met with approval in the past, and try my best to do justice to the wishes or the judgement of all.

I will begin with our ancestors, for at such a moment it is both just and appropriate that this tribute of memory be paid to them. This land was theirs, alone in perpetual succession, and by their valour they bequeathed it, in Freedom to this day. They deserve our praise, and still more do our own fathers. They gained possession of this empire beyond what they received, and, not without exertion, added it to our heritage. More of it we added ourselves, who are now of mature age, and equipped our city to meet all needs of war and peace alike. Their deeds in war, which won them each of these possessions, and all that we or our fathers did in whole-hearted defiance of the invader, Greek or non-Greek, all this you know, and since I do not wish to speak of it at length, I will omit it. But the way of life whose practice led to these achievements and the form of state and character which made them great, these I will

33

describe, and then proceed to praise the dead, since I believe that this is a time when it is not unseemly that such things should be said, and the whole throng of citizens and foreigners alike would profit from listening to them.

The constitution by which we live does not emulate the enactments of our neighbours. It is an example to others rather than an imitation of them. It is called democracy because power does not rest with the few, but with the many, and in law, as it touches individuals, all are equal, while in regard to the public estimation in which each man is held in any field, his advancement depends not on mere rotation, but rather on his true worth; nor does poverty dim his reputation or prevent him from assisting the state, if he has the capacity. Liberty marks both our public politics and the feelings which touch our daily life together. We do not resent a neighbour's pursuit of pleasure, nor cast on him the burden of ill will, which does no injury but gives pain to witness. Our private converse is untroubled, our life in the state free from illegality, owing mainly to respect for the authority of the magistrates of the day, and of the laws, especially laws laid down to help the wronged, and those unwritten laws whose neglect brings acknowledged discredit.

On the other hand we have devised and provided many forms of recreation from labour, and we make a custom of competitions and festivals throughout the year; and we have our own buildings of beauty, enjoyment of which drives away despondency. And because of the size of our city there come to us all the goods of every land, and it is our fortune to find our own native products no more familiar to us than are those of the rest of the world.

In the pursuit of warfare also we differ from our adversaries. We lay our city open to all, and at no time evict or keep the stranger away from the knowledge or sight of anything which it might help an enemy to see revealed. Our belief is not primarily in munitions and concealment, but in our own spirit in action. In forms of training, too, our adversaries strive for valour in laboured practice from their childhood up, while we live our lives unregimented, yet we go to meet danger as great as theirs. This is the proof; the Spartans do not invade our land alone, but with all their allies, and yet when we attack a neighbour's land, we do battle with men who are defending what is theirs, and often overcome them. Our full power together no enemy has ever encountered because of our naval activity as well as the frequent dispatch of troops to places within our territory. But if ever they do come into conflict with a portion of it, they boast of a partial success as a repulse for our whole force, a partial reverse as a defeat by the whole. Yet if we prefer relaxation to severe training, and face the risk of war with natural rather than forced courage, we are spared regrets for future ills before they come, and when they do, our daring is seen to be as high as that of lifelong toilers, while these achievements as well as others rightly earn our city admiration.

We are seekers of beauty, but avoid extravagance, of learning, but without unmanliness. For us wealth is an aim for its value in use and not as an empty boast, and the disgrace of poverty rests not in the admission of it, but more in the failure to avoid it in practice. It lies with all to superintend home life and state affairs alike, while despite our varied concerns[1] we keep an adequate acquaintance with politics. We alone regard the man who takes no part in it, not as unobtrusive, but as useless, and we all at least give much thought to an action, if we do not rightly originate it, supposing not that it is debate which is the undoing of action, but rather the lack of debate to warn us before it. For we are endowed with this marked quality: that in us great daring and the calculation of our aims are combined, while in others ignorance breeds rashness, while thought brings hesitation. And they can best be judged to think aright who have the clearest understanding of danger and of pleasure without wavering in the face of peril. Our idea of goodness, too, stands opposed to the majority. We do not win friendship from benefit received, but from service rendered. Lasting friendship comes rather from the doer of a benefit, who through good will towards the receiver keeps the debt in being; the debtor's gratitude is blurred by the knowledge that it is not free service he will repay, but a debt. And we alone do good less from calculation of advantage than from the trust that is born of freedom without thought of the future.

1. I accept the emendation, ἑτέροις ἕτερα.

35

In short I declare that our whole city is an education for Greece, and every individual in it would, I think, be capable in more respects than any other of fitting himself for many parts with grace and ease. That these are not the words of a moment's boasting so much as the actual truth is signalized by the power of our city which we have won by these methods. She alone, when she comes to the test, surpasses what is told of her, she alone causes an attacker no resentment at his suffering in defeat, and to a subject no complaint against the justice of his subjection. There are signal proofs and no lack of witness of the power we put forward, to cause the admiration of the present and of future generations. We have no further need of a Homer to praise us, or any other poet whose words give transient pleasure, but the real truth will discredit their account. We have put every land and sea within reach of adventure for us, and we have established at our coming an unfailing memory of both benefit and injury. Such is the city which in their gallantry these men thought should not be taken from the world, and died in battle for her, and for which every one of those who are left should rightly wish to strive.

Therefore I have dwelt at length on the subject of the city, to draw the lesson that the issue for us is not the same as for men who have no similar heritage, and to add to the subject of my present eulogy the distinction of clear example. The greater part has been told. The valour of these men and their like has brought honour to my song of praise for Athens, and there are few Greeks who could so balance such words with deeds. It seems to me that human virtue is given its first proof and its final confirmation by the passing of these men. For even when men are less deserving of praise in other respects, it is right that they should set bravery in war for their country high in the reckoning. They blotted out dishonour with honour, and did greater public good than private harm. None of them exalted the enjoyment of wealth and played the coward, nor in the poor man's hope of later riches put off the day of danger. More desirable to them than this was to match their enemies in battle; this they thought the noblest hazard of war, and sought to face it and avenge themselves, and so pursue their aims. Success was unsure, and they left it to hope. Upon deeds they relied for what lay before them, believing that salvation rested rather in action at whatever cost than in surrender. They fled from a name, the name of dishonour, enduring the reality of bodily action, and in one critical instant, at the height of glory, not of fear, they passed away.

They did what they did as Athenians should. Others that remain may pray to escape that day, yet demand that their spirit be no less dauntless in facing the enemy. They will contemplate not merely the words which may be spoken at length, well though you know the story of the great good which lies in fighting for your country, but rather set before them day by day the real power of Athens and fall to love of her. When you think her great, remember that by daring ? d right judgement, and in action by their sense of honour men secured that greatness. When they failed to gain their hopes, they did not therefore think they should deprive the city of their merit, but gave it freely as their finest offering to her banquet. As citizens they gave their lives for the good of all, but severally they gained unaging glory, and a memorial of matchless fame, not that in which they lie, but rather that which at every moment that presents itself for word or deed enshrines their undying renown. The whole earth is the tomb of famous men, and that fame is signified not only in their own country by words inscribed on stone. In lands that are not theirs their unwritten memorial lives on in the life of men, in the spirit rather than in material shape. You should now follow their lead, see happiness in freedom, freedom in courage, and not be anxious in your watch for the hazards of war. It is not men in misfortune, without new hope of success, who should most justly be unsparing of their lives, but men before whom, if they still live, there looms the opposite change and the greatest reverse in the case of failure. To a man of pride humiliation sprung of weakness brings greater misery than the reward which comes of strength with hope for the common good, and comes unnoticed, death.

So for their parents who are here I have not so much grief as comfort. They know that they were bred to varying chances. The greatest happiness is that honour should be accorded, to them in their death, to you in your sorrow, and that a life should be rounded in the happiness of its living and of its dying. I know it is hard to be persuasive in respect of those whom you will often remember in others' enjoyment of the happiness in which you once delighted; and sorrow is not felt at the loss of what has never been enjoyed, but at the deprivation of joys which long experience has made familiar. You must endure in the hope of other children, those of you who are still of an age to have them. In your private life the newcomers will make for forgetfulness of those who have gone, and for the state it will be a double gain, in making good the loss and adding to her security. For deliberations made in equality and justice are only possible between men who have an equal power to offer their children to the risk of danger. Those among you who are past the best of life should regard as gain your happiness in the greater part of it. Remember that what remains will be short, and be consoled by your lost ones' high renown. The quest for honour alone is unaging, and in the unproductive time of life it is not gain that brings pleasure, as some say, but honour. As for you, the children or the brothers of these who are dead, I see that, since all give praise to the dead, great will be your struggle to match them, and even if your merit be outstanding, it will not be judged equal, scarcely even within a little of theirs. The living feel envy against a rival, but where the challenge is there no more, honour is granted readily without opposition. If I must speak of the virtue of women to those who will now be widowed, I will express it all in one brief sentence of advice. It is high credit in a woman not to fall below her natural character, and to have least said of her among men either in praise or blame.

I have spoken according to the law what fitting words I had. In reality the dead have received their first distinction in this burial. The second is that their children will receive their sustenance from the city till they are grown men, and this is the city's crown of aid to them and to all who are left alive after such struggles. For where the greatest prizes of valour are set, there the best citizens are to be found.

Now, therefore, weep your last for your own, and so depart.

LYSIAS: AGAINST ERATOSTHENES

INTRODUCTION

Lysias was the younger son of Cephalus of Syracuse, well known as
a foreigner resident in Athens, a Metic, and mentioned by Plato in
the Republic. *The date of Lysias' birth is not certain, but it is*
known that after Cephalus' death he spent a considerable time
with his elder brother, Polemarchus, in the colony of Thurii in
Southern Italy, which had been founded in 443 B.C. *Whether or*
not he profited from the influence of Protagoras at Thurii, he is
stated to have learnt rhetoric from Teisias of Syracuse. When the
democratic party at Thurii was banished, the brothers returned to
Athens in 411, and lived probably in the Peiraeus, where they
carried on the manufacture of arms. In 405 they were prosperous
enough to be among the first chosen to be put to death by the Thirty
Tyrants who were put in power after the fall of Athens. Lysias
escaped (though Polemarchus did not), and strongly supported the
exiles under Thrasybulus. On his return to Athens he was awarded
full citizenship, and used it at once to impeach Eratosthenes, one
of the two among the Thirty who remained in Athens, in a speech
which he is said to have delivered himself and claims as his first.
It does not appear to have been successful. When the democracy was
fully restored, the right of full citizenship for aliens was disallowed,
and though he became a well-known and frequent pleader of private
suits, he could not repeat this first achievement. He was distin-
guished enough to be chosen to deliver the Funeral Speech at Athens,
probably in 392 B.C. *and a Panegyric Oration at Olympia in 388.*
He died at the age of over eighty in 378 B.C.

The speech is notable for its detailed account of a state under the
control of a violent minority, and its description of the so-called year
of Anarchy (404–403 B.C.*) suggests more recent periods of revolution.*
After the Athenian disaster at Aegospotami in June 405, the
Spartan victor, Lysander, laid siege to Athens; after holding out
against a state of starvation until the autumn, the city succumbed
to the influence of the oligarchic faction, which had been temporarily

in control fifteen years before. Now, as then, the most trusted of them, as a moderate of strong influence, was Theramenes. He was invited to negotiate with Sparta, but negotiations were prolonged and unsuccessful, and Athens survived only at the price of demolishing the 'Long Walls', surrendering all but twelve ships, and allowing the return of exiles. These last were largely oligarchic, and their return helped the change of constitution which was virtually demanded.

The change was initiated by the so-called clubs (see 43 below), who, using the Spartan title, appointed five Ephors to exercise control of the Ecclesia. Theramenes is not mentioned among them, though Critias and Eratosthenes are. But Theramenes was the leader in a meeting with Lysander, who claimed that Athens had forfeited the agreement by delay in pulling down the walls. This meeting inaugurated the government of the Thirty, who were nominated from circles favourable to the oligarchy, in accordance with terms drawn up by one of their number, Dracontides. They began with claims of a reformation, and proceeded against anti-oligarchic informers, but soon went on to eliminate all who opposed their views, using informers of their own. Their confidence was based on the presence of a Spartan garrison for which they had asked. The moderates among the Thirty disapproved of these methods, and Theramenes, supported, it was claimed, by Eratosthenes, opposed Critias and the extremists, both in their production of a 'Catalogue' of Three Thousand privileged people who were to be exempt from persecution, and in measures taken against the class of resident aliens, whose only crime was their wealth. The attack began on aliens and on any others who were thought ideologically unsound. There ensued a reign of terror whose nature is illustrated in Lysias' narrative. The death of Theramenes, which resulted from his opposition, freed the Thirty from all restraint.

In the winter of that year (404) Thrasybulus led from Thebes a small force of men who had been forced into exile by the violence of the Thirty, and held a strong point at Phyle, commanding the pass over Mt Parnes. The Thirty failed to dislodge him, and his force steadily grew. He later crossed the plain with over a thousand men, and made a night attack on the Peiraeus, occupying the high part called Munychia and fighting a successful engagement. Most *of the Thirty retired to a prearranged retreat at Eleusis. The Three Thousand deposed them, and appointed a new commission of ten, which included Eratosthenes and Pheidon, to treat with Thrasybulus. These, however, showed no spirit of compromise, and were soon besieged by the growing forces of democracy. When Lysander was superseded at Sparta, the uncompromising support for the oligarchy was abandoned and the garrison withdrawn. A new pact was made, affording an amnesty to everyone except the Tyrants themselves.*

LYSIAS: ERATOSTHENES

THERE is no difficulty in opening this prosecution, gentlemen. The difficulty will be to bring it to an end. The nature and the number of the charges are due to the character and the quantity of the facts. Invention could never exaggerate their heinousness, nor veracity reach the end of the list. The prosecutor would collapse, or the time run short. We seem likely to find in this case the reverse of the normal experience. Normally the prosecution needs to explain the grounds for hostility to the defendants. But in this case it is the defendants whose hostility to Athens needs explaining, and the ground for such outrageous conduct towards the state. I do not claim that I am free of personal reasons for animosity, but that everyone has abundant cause for it on private and public grounds alike. Personally, gentlemen, I have never before conducted a case for myself or for anyone else, but I have been forced by the circumstances to prosecute Eratosthenes. In fact I have been frequently troubled by the fear that inexperience may render inadequate and incompetent my presentation of the case for my brother and myself. I will try, however, to explain it from the beginning as best I can.

My father, Cephalus, was induced by Pericles to come to Athens, and lived here for thirty years, during which time neither he himself nor my brother nor I took any part in legal proceedings either as plaintiffs or as defendants. Under the democracy we lived without giving or receiving offence from anyone. When the Thirty began their government of wrong and intrigue, they declared that they must clear Athens of its worse elements, and set the rest on the path of right and virtue. They had not the courage to live up to their declarations, as I shall recall in regard to my own case and attempt to remind you in yours.

At a meeting of the Thirty, Theognis and Peison[1] made a

1. Two of the list of the Thirty given by Xenophon (*Hellenica*, II, 3, 2). They are not mentioned elsewhere.

statement that some of the Metics were disaffected, and they saw this as an excellent pretext for action which would be punitive in appearance, but lucrative in reality. In any case Athens was poverty-stricken, they said, and the Empire needed funds as well. They had no difficulty in persuading their fellows, to whom killing was nothing, while money was of great importance. They therefore decided to arrest ten people, including two of the poorer class, to enable them to claim that their object was not money, but the good of Athens, as in any other respectable enterprise. They divided up the Metics' houses between them, and visited them. I personally was giving a dinner party when they called. They turned out my guests and handed me over to Peison, while the rest went into the factory and took an inventory of the slaves. I asked Peison if he would let me go for a consideration. He said he would if it were a large one. I said I would give him a talent, and he agreed. I knew him to be a man without regard for right or reason, but in the circumstances it seemed absolutely necessary to exact an undertaking from him. He gave an oath involving himself and his children that he would get me off for a talent, so I went to my room and opened my chest. Peison saw what I was doing and came in. When he saw what was in it, he called two of his men and told them to take the contents. Instead of the amount agreed, gentlemen, it contained three talents of silver, four hundred Cyzikene staters, a hundred darics and four silver cups. So I asked for something for my journey, to which he replied that I ought to be thankful to get away with my life. I went out with Peison, and we were met by Melobius and Mnesitheides on their way from the factory. They met us actually at the doorway and asked where we were going. They were on the way to my brother's, Peison said, to have a look at things there as well. So they told him to go there, while I was to go with them to Damnippus' house. Peison came up to me and urged me to say nothing. It would be all right, he said, he would be along there. We ran into Theognis with some others in his charge, and they handed me over to him and went off. At this point it seemed to me that I was in great danger and my death warrant already sealed. So I called Damnippus and said, 'You are a friend of mine. I've been to your house. I've done nothing wrong, I'm simply being done to death for my money. That's what is happening, so please use what influence you have to protect me.' He said he would, but he thought it better to mention it to Theognis, who, he reckoned, would do anything for money. While he was talking to him, as I knew the house and realized that it had two doors, I thought I might try and escape that way. I reflected that if I were not caught, I should escape, and if I were, I should still get away if Damnippus persuaded Theognis to accept a bribe, and anyway nothing worse could happen than death. With this idea I made off. They had the front door guarded, but though there were three doors I had to pass, they were all open. I made my way to Archeneos, the shipowner, and induced him to go to the city and find out about my brother. He came back with the news that Eratosthenes had caught him in the street and put him in prison. After this news I went by sea next day to Megara. Polemarchus was given the usual sentence by the Thirty, the hemlock, without any indication of the reason for his execution, let alone any trial or defence. After his death, when he was taken from the prison, it was not permitted to use any of the three houses we possessed for his funeral. They hired a shed and used that for it. There were also plenty of clothes, but all requests were refused, and one of his friends lent a garment, another a pillow or anything else they could offer for his burial. They had seven hundred shields belonging to us, they had a mass of gold and silver, bronze, ornaments, furniture and women's clothing to an altogether unexpected extent, they had a hundred and twenty slaves, the best of which they appropriated, handing the rest to the public stock. Yet they made a demonstration of their self-seeking and dishonesty, and of their character. Polemarchus' wife happened to have some gold earrings, which she had had since she first came into the family. These Melobius removed from her ears. They showed us no mercy in respect of the smallest item of property. Because of our money they behaved to us as if they were filled with resentment for the most serious delinquencies, though in fact we had been entirely innocent of anything of the kind. We had carried out all our public obligations, we had made numerous contributions of money, we had been exemplary in our behaviour, we had performed every instruction we had been given. We had never made any enemies, but on the contrary had on several occasions provided ransom for Athenian citizens. This was the treatment they thought reasonable for people whose behaviour as aliens had been very different from theirs as citizens. They had frequently been guilty of driving Athenian citizens into enemy hands, of executions without burial, of deprivation of citizen rights and of prevention of intended marriages. They are now brazen enough to appear in defence of their case with the plea that they have done nothing wrong or objectionable. I wish this were true! It is a benefit which I should very largely share. As it is, it is not true of their conduct either towards the state or towards me. As I have said, my brother was done to death by Eratosthenes without any private provocation or any cause of public complaint against him. It was solely to satisfy his own lawless desires. But now, gentlemen of the jury, I propose to put him in the witness box and question him. Go into the box, please, and answer my questions.

LYSIAS Did you arrest Polemarchus or not?

ERATOSTHENES I carried out the government's commands because I was afraid.

LYSIAS Were you in the Council when our affairs were under discussion?

ERATOSTHENES I was.

LYSIAS Did you give your vote in favour of the execution or against?

ERATOSTHENES Against it.

LYSIAS In the opinion that we were not guilty?

ERATOSTHENES Yes.

LYSIAS In other words you were outrageous enough to vote for his release and then take part in his execution. When you had a majority in favour of release, you claim to have opposed the execution, but when Polemarchus' safety lay in your hands alone, you rushed him into prison. Do you suppose that the claim you say you made without success deserves to be called creditable, and yet that your actual violence should go unpunished despite my demand and the jury's?

Nor, indeed, if his statement of opposition is true, can one fairly credit his claim that he was obeying orders. Presumably

46

they were not exacting a guarantee from him in regard to the Metics. So who could have been less likely to be given the order than a man who had opposed the project and made his opinion clear? Who could have been a less promising agent than an opponent of their aims? To the majority of Athenians it seems an adequate account of what happened to attribute it to the Thirty. But if the Thirty attribute it to themselves, how can it be accepted as an account? If there existed a stronger power in Athens by which the order for homicide in defiance of right were given, one might see it as an extenuation. But in this case where can responsibility be placed if it is open to the Thirty to plead the orders of the Thirty? In addition the arrest was not carried out in my brother's house, but in the street, which means that Eratosthenes could have combined lenience with obedience to instructions. But he still seized and imprisoned Polemarchus. Everyone is enraged with people who enter their houses to demand possession of themselves or their relatives. Yet if the destruction of others for one's own safety deserves any consideration at all, such marauders deserve it more than Eratosthenes. It was dangerous for them not to fulfil their mission, or to deny it when they had found someone. Eratosthenes could have denied meeting or seeing his victim. There was no form of proof or examination which could have convicted him if his opponents had wanted to. Had you been a man of high character, Eratosthenes, you should have given information to likely victims of injustice rather than collaborate in their arrest. Actually your attitude is manifest from your actions. It is not that of antagonism, but of satisfaction at these proceedings, and the jury should base their decision on your actions, not on your words, and use known facts to judge what statements were made at the time, where eye-witnesses are not obtainable. It was impossible for us to be on the spot, or even in our own homes, so that they were in a position to do all the harm they could to the public interest while they attributed all the good to themselves. However, your denial is something I will not contest but acquiesce in, if you so desire. I only wonder what you would have done as a supporter of the Thirty, when as a so-called opponent you did Polemarchus to death.

Tell me this, gentlemen. Suppose you had been Polemarchus' brothers or sons. Would you have acquitted him? You see, gentlemen of the jury, that Eratosthenes is committed to one of two statements, either that he did not arrest Polemarchus or that he was right to do so. He has admitted to having wrongfully arrested him, so he has made the choice of verdict easy for you. And in fact numbers of Athenians and aliens alike have come here to learn your view. Either they will come to the conclusion that misdeeds will get punished, or else this: that if they achieve their aims they will have absolute power, while if they fail, they will be on an equality with everyone else. Aliens in Athens will know whether they are justified in proclaiming the banishment of the Thirty from their cities or not. If the sufferers themselves are going to let them go when they have them in their power, the aliens will certainly regard it as superfluous to trouble about them. Surely it must be thought outrageous that the victorious generals at Arginusae should have incurred the death penalty for refusing to pick up the casualties at sea,[2] on the score that retribution should be exacted for the death of patriots, and not men like this, who as private individuals did all in their power to cause a defeat on that occasion, and on accession to power admit to having deliberately caused the death of numerous Athenians. Should not they and theirs be subjected to the extreme penalty at the hands of this court?

I regarded the charges as sufficient at this stage. I consider that a limit can be set at the point at which it appears that the defendant merits the death penalty, this being the severest penalty that can be exacted. I am therefore uncertain of the relevance of repeated accusations in the case of men who, even if it could be doubly inflicted, would not be adequately punished for their actions. It is not legitimate for a man like this to adopt the frequent practice of abandoning any defence to the charges, and pursuing irrelevant personal topics. Such men are sometimes successful in deception by describing their military valour, the ships they have captured at sea or the towns they have brought into friendly relations. Make Eratosthenes tell you when they have brought about the death of as many enemies as

2. In 406 B.C.

they have of their own fellow-countrymen, when they have captured as many ships as they have surrendered, when they have secured the friendship of any city to compare with our own which they have enslaved. Let us hear of the enemy arms seized that will match what were taken from Athenians, of the fortifications destroyed to equal the wreck of their own city's. They even pulled down the armed posts round Attica, and proved that even the Peiraeus was not dismantled at the instance of Sparta, but because they thought this would strengthen their own régime.

I have often felt astonished at the audacity of any defence of such people, till I reflect that to stick at nothing oneself is of a piece with upholding men like this. This is not the first time the defendant has acted in opposition to the Athenian people. At the time of the Four Hundred he took part in the oligarchical revolution in the fleet, after which he abandoned his ship when in command of it and fled from the Hellespont with Iatrocles and others, whose names I need not give. On his arrival in Athens he was engaged in opposition to the democratic party. I now put forward evidence of this.

(*Evidence of witnesses*)

To omit the intervening period, when disaster came to Athens at Aegospotami, during the existence of the democracy from which the *coup d'état* emerged, a body of five Ephors was appointed by their fellow-members of the so-called Clubs,[3] to assemble the people and to lead the conspiracy in action against the democracy. Eratosthenes and Critias were among their number. They nominated leaders for the Tribes, gave instructions on proposals for decision and persons to hold office, and

3. The political clubs were associations developed in the 5th century mainly for the propagation of oligarchic ideas. We hear of them particularly in Thucydides' account of faction as a feature of the politics of the latter part of the century, and again in connexion with the oligarchic movement in Athens (Thucydides, iii, 82 and viii, 54). They are idealized by Isocrates in the *Panegyricus* (79), though elsewhere he joins the majority view in Athens by condemning them. The Aristotelian *Constitution of Athens* (34) dissociates Theramenes from them, but this is probably because it is largely concerned to voice Theramenes' views.

assumed authority for any other measures they chose. There thus came into being a conspiracy against the state not merely on the part of the enemy, but also among these Athenian citizens, to prevent good decisions and secure widespread want. They were well aware that the only condition of their survival was calamity in Athens. They supposed that in your anxiety to be rid of immediate disasters you would not give a thought to the future. That Eratosthenes was one of these Ephors I will provide evidence, not from his associates, which would be impossible, but from his own hearers. Had these been wise, their evidence would have been used for his condemnation, and they would have taken severe measures against the authors of their present troubles. Had they been wise, they would not have held to their oaths when the result was injury to individual Athenians, and yet lightly discarded them when the state might have been the gainer. That concludes what I have to say on this subject. Call the witnesses to the platform, please.

(Evidence of witnesses)

You have heard the evidence. Now, finally, after attaining to office Eratosthenes has nothing good to his name, but plenty that is the opposite. Had he been a man of integrity, his duty would have required him to avoid illegal proceedings, and to make representations to the Council about the falsity of all the indictments, about the untrue statements of Batrachus and Aeschylides,[4] which were mere figments concocted by the Thirty for the detriment of Athenian citizens. Indeed, gentlemen, the antagonists of democracy did not suffer by holding their tongues. There were plenty of other tongues and hands to achieve the greatest conceivable disasters for Athens. But good will towards her could surely have been made fully clear by good sense and opposition to wrong.

Perhaps he could maintain that he was frightened, and some of you will find that adequate. But he must not let his plea prove him in open opposition to the Thirty. If he does, it will be clear that he agreed to their proceedings and had enough power to avoid being victimized for any opposition. But he

4. Informers used by the Thirty.

should maintain that it was the general interest he was concerned for, not that of Theramenes, who did much to injure
Athens. But Eratosthenes regarded Athens as his enemy and
her enemies as his friends. I have plenty of proof to establish
this, also that the differences which arose among the Thirty
did not concern the interests of Athens, but their own, and the
decision which party should carry out this plan of action and
control the state. Had the dispute been to secure the interest of
Athens, what finer moment for a man in power to display his
patriotism than at the seizure of Phyle by Thrasybulus? Yet
instead of making any declaration or taking action in support of
the group at Phyle, he joined his colleagues in a journey to
Salamis and Eleusis, where they threw three hundred Athenian
citizens into prison and sentenced them to death in a body.

When the scene changed to the Peiraeus and the disturbances
there, and discussions began about a settlement, each side had
high hopes of its success, as both showed. The Peiraeus party
had won the day and allowed the others to leave. They then
retired to the city and expelled the Thirty with the exception
of Pheidon and Eratosthenes, and chose a government of their
bitterest opponents, taking the view that it would be reasonable
for opponents of the Thirty to be supporters of the Peiraeus
party. This body included Pheidon, Hippocles, Epicharis of
Lamptra and others thought to be most opposed to Charicles,
Critias and their club. As soon as they assumed power themselves, they gave rise to still more violent dissension in Athens,
against the Peiraeus. This clearly proved that their violence
had not been directed to the support of the Peiraeus party or
that of the victims of injustice, and that it was not feeling for
the dead or for probable victims that stirred them, but the
existence of greater power than theirs, or a quicker way to
wealth. On assuming control of the government and the city,
they made common cause against the Thirty who had been the
cause, and the people's party who had been the victims of all
the trouble. But it was made universally clear that if the expulsion of the Thirty was just, yours was unjust, and if yours was
right, that of the Thirty was wrong. The course of events which
led to their accusation and expulsion was in no way different

from these. So there is cause for deep resentment that Pheidon, who was elected to secure a reconciliation and the recall of Athenian citizens, should have pursued the same course as Eratosthenes, adopting the same point of view, and should have been prepared to use the popular party to attack their own superiors among the Thirty, while they refused to hand over the control of Athens to the party who had been deprived of it unwarrantably. Instead Pheidon went to Sparta and tried to engineer an attack on Athens on the pretext that the city would fall into Boeotian hands, with other statements designed as inducements.[5] As this failed, either owing to religious opposition or Spartan antagonism, he borrowed a hundred talents to secure a mercenary force and petitioned for Lysander to act as commander. Lysander was strongly in favour of the oligarchy and against a free Athens, and most strongly of all against the Peiraeus party. They hired all kinds of people in an attempt to destroy Athens, they brought whole cities into action, eventually including Sparta and any of her allies they could, and made their preparations, not for reconciliation, but destruction – had it not been for certain true patriots, to whom you must make it clear by punishing their enemies that you intend to show your gratitude. All this you already know, and I am not sure there is any need to provide evidence. However I will provide it. I need a rest myself, and some of you prefer to hear the same thing repeated.

(Evidence of witnesses)

Well, now I propose to tell the story of Theramenes, as shortly as I can. And I must beg for your indulgence for the city's benefit as well as for my own. I hope it will not appear to anyone that in a case against Eratosthenes accusation of Theramenes is out of court; because I gather that Eratosthenes intends to make use of the claim that he was an associate of Theramenes and a partner in his actions. He would have had a strong claim to have partnered Themistocles in building the walls, one may

5. Many exiled democrats had been given asylum in Boeotia, and it was rumoured that Thebes had assisted Thrasybulus. This prediction was calculated to induce Sparta to act.

suppose, if he claims to have assisted Theramenes in pulling them down! But I hardly think the case is parallel. Themistocles built them in defiance of Sparta, Theramenes pulled them down by a fraud upon Athens. The result to Athens is the opposite of what might have been expected. If the friends of Theramenes had perished with him, unless they had adopted the opposite course to his, it would have been no more than they deserved. Instead of this we find a defence made of him, and attempts by his associates to take credit as the authors of numerous benefits instead of untold detriment. In the first place, he was the prime cause of the first oligarchy, when his influence caused the election of the Four Hundred. His father was one of the Commissioners, and furthered the same movement, while he himself was held to be one of its firmest supporters, which led to his own election as Strategus. So long as his stock w as high he maintained good faith with Athens. But when he found that Peisander, Callaeschrus[6] and others were gaining ground on him, while the citizen body were no longer in their favour, he yielded to his jealousy of them and his fears of the populace, and joined the faction of Aristocrates. He wanted to appear to be in with the popular party still, so he accused and secured the death of his great friends, Antiphon[7] and Archeptolemus. His dastardly conduct allowed him to sacrifice both the freedom of Athens for his adherence to the oligarchs, and the life of his friends for his adherence to the populace of Athens.

But when he was in a position of the highest honour and estimation,[8] he announced his intention to save Athens, and then promptly caused its destruction, on the specious claim that he had devised a scheme of great importance and enormous value. He promised to secure peace without the surrender of

6. Peisander played a considerable part in the oligarchic revolution of the Four Hundred (see Thucydides, viii, 54, 3 and 67, 3). Of Callaeschrus it is only known that he was one of the Four Hundred on that occasion, while Aristocriates is mentioned by Lysias, but not by Thucydides, as a leader of the moderates among them.

7. See General Introduction p. 10, 11 above.

8. There is an abrupt change here, and we pass from the account of Theramenes in the revolution of 411 B.C., to refer now to his conduct after the battle of Aegospotami.

hostages, the destruction of the walls or the forfeiture of the navy. He refused to reveal his scheme, urging that he should be trusted. The Council of the Areopagus[9] was in charge of measures for the protection of Athens, and there was much opposition to Theramenes. They knew that normally secrets are preserved in dealing with an enemy, whereas Theramenes in the presence of his own people refused to reveal what he intended to tell the enemy. And yet the people trusted him with the safety of their wives and children and themselves. He broke all his promises. So obsessed was he with the need to make Athens small and weak that he led her to a proceeding as far removed from the proposals of the enemy as from the expectation of Athens. He was under no compulsion from Sparta. It was he himself who put forward the proposal to pull down the walls of the Peiraeus and abolish the existing constitution. This was because he fully realized that unless every hope Athens had was speedily removed, instant retaliation would be taken upon himself. Finally, gentlemen of the jury, he did not allow a meeting of the Assembly until the moment laid down by Sparta had been faithfully observed by him, and he had summoned Lysander's fleet and the enemy force had taken up its position in the country. Then, with this position established, with Lysander, Philochares and Miltiades on the spot, they held an assembly, to forestall opposition or threats from any speaker, and to prevent a right choice by Athenian citizens, who were compelled to vote for the measures they had decided on. Theramenes now rose and ordered the city to be put into the hands of thirty individuals, and the constitution in preparation by Dracontides to be adopted. Even as things were, there was a violent outburst in refusal. It was realized that the issue of the meeting was slavery or freedom. Theramenes, as members of the jury can themselves testify, declared that he cared nothing for this outburst, as he knew that a large number of Athenians were in favour of the same measures as himself, and he was voicing the decisions approved by Sparta and Lysander. After him Lysander spoke,

9. The Areopagus had been deprived of political functions in 462 B.C. It is not known whether any enactment gave it a general power of supervision at this time of trouble.

and among other statements pronounced that he held Athens under penalty for failing to carry out the terms of the truce, and that the question would not be one of her constitution, but of her continued existence, if Theramenes' orders were disobeyed. True and loyal members of the Assembly realized the degree to which the position had been prepared and compulsion laid on them, and either stood still in silence or left, with their conscience clear at any rate of having voted the ruin of Athens. A few despicable characters whose deliberate intentions were traitorous held up their hands to vote as they were told. Instructions had been given to elect ten men secretly nominated by Theramenes, ten laid down by the established Ephors, and ten from the company present. They saw the weakness of the Athenian position and their own strength so well that they realized beforehand what would happen in the Assembly. You need not take this from me, but from Theramenes. All I have said he himself included in his Defence in the Council,[10] with his reproach to the exiles that they owed their return to him while Sparta had never thought of them, and to his associates in power that everything that happened, as I have described, had been due to him, and this was his reward for it – when in fact he had given every sort of pledge and exacted oaths of fidelity from them. All this and more, great and small, late and soon, stands to his name in defiance of morality and right. And yet people are brazen enough to call themselves his friends, though it was not for the welfare of Athens that he met his death, but for his own outrageous conduct. It was a penalty that would have been as just under the oligarchy he had dissolved as under democracy. He had twice enslaved Athens in his contempt for her existing régime and his desire for revolution. He made constant claim to the finest of titles, when he had instigated the foulest treason.

10. In the Council, i.e. in Theramenes' defence against the attack made on him by the party of Critias, to which he owed his death.

Lysias' account of Theramenes is understandably coloured by strong feeling against a champion of oligarchy, but even nowadays it is hard to assess Theramenes. (See for the earlier period Thucydides, viii, 68 and 90–94, for the later Xenophon, *Hellenica* II and III.)

On Theramenes the indictment is now complete. You have
realized the need to exclude sympathy and pity from your view,
and exact from Eratosthenes and his associates in power the
punishment they deserve. You have worsted your enemies in
the field. You must not submit to your opponents in this court.
You must not let gratitude for their professed intentions outweigh your indignation at their actual conduct. You must not
conspire against them in their absence, and then, when you
have them, let them go. When fortune has surrendered them to
Athens, you must not fall short of her lead.

This completes the indictment of Eratosthenes and the friends
to whom he will refer in his defence, as they were his assistants
in malpractice. But his position is not a true parallel with that
of Athens. He dealt with his victims as accuser and judge in
one; we resort to accusation and defence. His party put the
innocent to death without trial; you insist on fair trial for men
who were the ruin of Athens, whose penalty, however illegal,
could never match their misdeeds. What treatment could bring
upon them fair retribution for their actions? Could their own
death and their children's atone for fathers, sons and brothers
put to death untried? Could the confiscation of their property
compensate for their many depredations from the city, or for
individual citizens whose houses they sacked? Since, then, no
action of any kind could match their deserts, it must be held unjustifiable to omit any penalty that could be inflicted upon them.

But it seems to me that a man who can appear before a jury
not of neutrals, but of the very people he has victimized, to
put up a defence before the very witnesses of his evil actions,
has set no limits either to his contempt of this court or to his
confidence in outside support. Both these factors deserve
considering in the realization that the defendants' past conduct
would have been impossible without assistance, and their
present appearance could not have been made without the
prospect of support from the same quarter, from people who,
without intending to aid the Thirty, yet hope to secure immunity themselves for past and future actions alike, if you acquit
the ultimate engineers of wickedness when you have them in
your hands. One may also feel surprise at any intention to plead

for them. Will such a plea be made in the guise of respectable
citizens who expect their own merits to outweigh the defendants'
guilt? I wish they had shown as much concern for the welfare
of Athens as these did for her destruction. Or will they adopt
the defence of sophistry and claim special indulgence for the
acts of the Thirty? Remember that for the rights of Athens
they never set out to claim even bare justice.

It is also worth observing the witnesses whose testimony for
the Thirty is their own condemnation. They must think very
poorly of your memory and intelligence, if they expect a free
acquittal for the Thirty at the hands of Athenian citizens, when
Eratosthenes and his associates made it dangerous for them even
to conduct a funeral. Yet the defendants, by their release, could
regain the power to bring Athens down. Their victims by their
death have passed beyond retribution on their enemies. And it
is a scandal that men who were unjustly done to death should
have had none who lived to show their friendship, while the
absolute destroyers of Athens should have crowds to attend
their funeral, to judge by the hundreds preparing to defend
them. But I regard it as easier to stand alone in defence of your
sufferings than to defend the actions of the Thirty. Yet it is
claimed that of the Thirty the least harm of all was done by
Eratosthenes, and they make this a reason to defend him. But
it was greater than was inflicted by all the rest of Greece. Is
this not to be made a reason to condemn him? You must show
your clear opinion. A verdict of guilty for Eratosthenes will
make clear your indignation at his actions. An acquittal will
prove that you desire a repetition of them. Nor will you be in
a position to say that you acted on the instructions of the Thirty.
There is no one now to make you repudiate your opinion. I
urge you therefore not to condemn yourselves by acquitting
him. Nor must you imagine that your vote will be secret.[11] You
will make your own decision manifest to Athens.

11. The ballot in Athenian legal cases was kept secret, as the final guarantee
of good faith, by the practice of having two voting discs for each juryman,
one marked for acquittal, the other for condemnation, and two boxes, one
for operative, the other for rejected votes. It was then impossible for anyone
to see which disc was put into which box. Lysias' point, of course, is that the
total vote will show the general attitude of the jury.

There are a few points which, before I close, I want to bring before the parties both of the city and of the Peiraeus, so that you can keep the disasters they brought on Athens in your mind when you give your vote. First I address members from the city. Remember that your domination at the hands of the Thirty was so absolute that you were compelled to fight a war against your own brothers and sons and your own fellow-citizens, a war in which defeat has set you on an equality with the successful, but victory would have meant slavery at the hands of the Thirty. As to private houses, the Thirty would have extended theirs owing to their position, while civil war has reduced yours. They did not reckon to share their benefits with you, but they compelled you to share in their ill name, and adopted an attitude so overbearing that they were not prepared to be generous to gain your loyalty, but expected you to take on their unpopularity and keep your good will to them. Since, then, you are now in the position of security, it is for you to do your utmost on your own behalf and that of the Peiraeus party in exacting retribution. Reflect first that you were once in the power of the most reprehensible elements in Athens, then that you now stand among the highest of her citizens, that you fight her enemies and deliberate on her problems. Remember too the foreign soldiers then established on the Acropolis to preserve their domination and your slavery.

There is much more I could say to you, but this must suffice. I now turn to the party of the Peiraeus. First I urge you to recall the matter of your arms. You fought many engagements on foreign soil, yet you were never disarmed by an enemy, but only by the Thirty, and in time of peace.[12] Remember, then, that you were proclaimed exiles from Athens, the heritage of your fathers, and even in exile your extradition was demanded. Let this rouse in you the indignation you felt at your expulsion, and remind you as well of the other barbarity inflicted on you, of men seized from the market and the temple and done to death, of men dragged away from children, from parents and wives and forced to suicide, and not even allowed the burial which

12. After the formation of the catalogue of Three Thousand the rest of the citizens were deprived of their arms by a trick on the part of the Thirty.

custom sanctions, because there were others who thought their own power stronger than the retribution which heaven lays upon the wicked. Those of you who escaped death were subject to dangers in many lands to which you wandered, invariably proclaimed as exiles, starved of the needs of life, some with children left behind in the hostile country which had been your own, some elsewhere abroad. Yet against all opposition you returned to the Peiraeus. Many and great were your perils, but you behaved as men should, and set your people free or brought them back to their country. Had misfortune caused you to fail, you would have fled in fear of the same fate as before: that the cruelty of the Thirty would have denied their victims any of the rights of religion or sanctuary which served to protect even the perpetrators of it, that your children in Athens would have been left to their barbarity, while those abroad would now be in slavery for default on small loans, and there would be none to preserve them.

However, I do not intend to talk of what might have been when it is beyond me to describe the truth of what was perpetrated, which would be beyond the scope of any number of accusers. But there has been no slackening in my eager regard for our temples, which they sold or desecrated, for our city, which they brought low, for our shipyards, which they destroyed, or for the dead, whom they failed to protect in their life and whom you must avenge after their death. I believe these dead are listening to what we say, and will know that you are making your vote, and feel that every vote of not guilty will be a vote for their own condemnation, every vote of guilty one of retribution on their behalf.

I will bring the charge to a close. You who have heard and seen and suffered, yours is the power. Cast your vote.

ANDOCIDES: ON THE MYSTERIES

INTRODUCTION

Andocides is best known for his connexion with the mysterious incidents which occurred in Athens in the summer of 415 B.C., *just before the great expedition to Sicily set sail. The fleet was on the point of departure, when it was learned that during the night the images of Hermes in the streets had been defaced.[1] A further report said that a party of people, including one of the leaders of the expedition, Alcibiades, had conducted parody performances of the Mysteries, the sacred rituals of Demeter and Persephone at Eleusis, whose secrecy was protected by oaths of the greatest possible solemnity. This profanation may have been a sophisticated rebellion against convention, but by the account given in this speech it seems to have been carried out with surprising recklessness, in the presence of uninitiated slaves. As regards the mutilation of the Hermae, it has been suggested that it may have been done either in an attempt to postpone the expedition by the deliberate creation of a bad omen, or as a first step towards an oligarchic conspiracy which would create the need to limit the control of the state to a select few. It is not clear how it would have served these ends, and even if we allow for Athenian superstition, the incidents remain hard to understand. But the news caused widespread consternation at such acts of horrifying sacrilege, and led to an immediate attack on Alcibiades. However, he was allowed to sail on the expedition, since his enemies felt that if the case were brought up at once, his great popularity would save him. When he had gone, they recalled him to stand his trial, but he thought it prudent to leave Athens for Sparta.*

Andocides, a member of an old, distinguished and wealthy family, with political, perhaps oligarchic, interests, was among a

1. See glossary, p. 266. Thucydides' account of the incident, of the charge that Alcibiades was involved in it, of his demand to be tried before sailing on the expedition, and of his final escape to Thurii in S. Italy are in Book VI, 27–29, 53, 61.

*number denounced as implicated in these affairs. He is said to have
escaped conviction and punishment by admitting his own guilt and
incriminating others. In his speech he denies this. But soon afterwards the so-called decree of Isotimides forbade all who were guilty
of sacrilege and had admitted it, to enter the temples or the Agora
again. This may have been directly aimed at Andocides. In any
case he went into exile in Cyprus. He also visited other parts of the
Greek world, and acquired some considerable wealth. He made
several attempts to return to Athens, but without success, until the
general amnesty after the expulsion of the Thirty in 403 B.C.
allowed him to do so. He now took part in public life, and held
some minor offices. But in 400 B.C. he was accused by Cephisius,
prompted by the rich and cultured Callias, of violating the decree
of Isotimides by attending the celebration of the Mysteries. His
defence on this charge involves him in two main questions, (i)
whether he was in fact guilty on the charges covered by Isotimides'
decree in 415 B.C., and (ii) whether it is not itself invalid since the
amnesty of 403 B.C. Whatever may be thought of the legal issues,
Andocides won his case, and continued in Athens as a politician,
being sent on an embassy to Sparta in 392 B.C., which led to his
speech,* On the Peace. *But with the rest of the embassy he was
prosecuted for bribery, among other charges, and to avoid trial he
returned once more to exile.*

ANDOCIDES: ON THE MYSTERIES

THE preparation my opponents undertook and the eagerness they showed to injure me in every respect, right or wrong, from the first moment I arrived in this city, is something you realize for the most part, and I need go to no length about it.[1] What I shall ask of you, gentlemen, is my rights, which are as easy for you to grant as they are valuable for me to receive. And the first thing I want you to keep in mind is that I am here under no compulsion either in the form of bail or of physical force. I trusted in justice and in your integrity to determine rightly and not allow me to be wrongfully done to death by my antagonists, but to preserve me in accordance with justice, with Athenian law, and with the oaths you swore before embarking on the vote you are going to make. It would be reasonable for you to hold the same view about people who voluntarily submit to the risk of the courts, as they hold themselves. Any who were unwilling to abide by the court's decision and are self-condemned wrong-doers[2] may reasonably be accorded the same decision as they have themselves implied. But those who are confident of their innocence and have stood by it may also reasonably expect from you the same opinion as their own, and not be condemned out of hand. I am myself a case in point. I received news from several sources that my enemies were saying that I would not stand firm, but would be off and away. 'Why would Andocides want to face a suit of such a vital nature? If he left, he would have all he needs. He has only to sail to Cyprus, where he came from, and there will be plenty of land and a present of money all ready for him. Do you suppose a man in his position is going to stand trial for his life? What would be the idea? He must realize the attitude of Athens towards him.' Personally, gentlemen, I hold the opposite view. To live elsewhere in perfect comfort and be deprived of my country is something I would

1. Parts of the early chapters are derived from rhetorical stock-in-trade and also appear in Lysias.
2. i.e. by their failure to appear.

never accept, and even if Athens is in the condition my opponents declare, I would far rather be her citizen than belong to any of the other states, prosperous though they may be at the present time. This being my view, I left it to you to decide on my life. I therefore beg you, gentlemen, to show greater good will to me in my defence than to the prosecution. You must realize that, however fair you may be, it is the defendant who is the worst off. The plaintiffs have thought the whole case through at length and made their accusation without any danger to themselves. I have fears and dangers and adverse prejudice to contend with in making my defence. So it is reasonable that you should be more favourable to me than to my accusers. You should bear in mind also the number of instances there are of accusations which have been shown up at once as such manifest lies that it would be much more welcome to you to punish the accusers than the accused. Others again, after telling lies which have brought people to undeserved execution, have been convicted of perjury too late to benefit their victims. After numerous instances of this kind you may reasonably disbelieve the statements of the prosecution. Whether their accusations are serious or not the prosecutor's statement will show. Whether they are true or false will only become clear after you have heard my defence.

I therefore wonder, gentlemen, at what point to begin my defence. Should I start with the most recent item, the illegality of the information laid against me, or with the decree of Isotimides,[3] which is obsolete, or with the laws and the sworn agreements made, or should I begin my account at the very beginning? I will tell you what gives me the greatest difficulty. It is that you do not all feel equally strongly about all the charges, but each has his own particular point which he would like replied to first. But to mention them all at once is impossible; so it seems to me best to tell the whole story from the beginning without omitting anything. If you hear a correct version of the facts, you will easily grasp what lies my opponents have told against me. I think you personally are prepared to make a just

3. For this decree see introduction to the speech. It may even have been passed to force Andocides himself out of the city, despite his acquittal.

decision (which is what induced me to stand my ground), in the realization that in private and public affairs alike your first concern is to give your vote in accordance with the oaths you have sworn. And this is the saving of the state, despite certain opponents of this view. Here is my request to you; show a good understanding in listening to my case, do not be adverse to me nor suspicious of what I say, nor seize on individual words, but hear my defence right through before giving your vote, as seems to you most equitable or most in accordance with the oaths you have sworn. As I said before, I will make my defence from the beginning, first of all on the actual charge that gave rise to the information laid against me, which is the reason for my submitting to this case: namely on the subject of the mysteries; on this I shall plead Not Guilty, either of impiety, or of informing, or of any admission, and shall disclaim knowledge of the truth or falsehood of the information brought before you. This is the first point I shall establish.

An Assembly was held for the generals for the Sicilian expedition, Nicias, Lamachus and Alcibiades. Lamachus' flagship had already set sail, when Pythonicus rose and made this announcement to the people: 'Athenians, you are sending out a force on a large scale, and are prepared to take this risk while one of the generals, Alcibiades, has been holding a private performance of the mysteries in his house with certain others. If you will grant immunity to the man I name, a servant of one of the men involved, who has not been initiated, he will recite the mysteries to you. In any case you can do what you like to me, if this is untrue.' Alcibiades made strong expostulations of denial, and the prytaneis[4] decided to order the uninitiated to withdraw, while they themselves went in search of the young man Pythonicus named. They came back with Polemarchus' servant, whose name was Andromachus. They passed a vote of immunity; he then said that mysteries were being celebrated at Pulytion's house, and Alcibiades, Niciades and Meletus[5] were the actual

4. See glossary.
5. There were several persons called Meletus. This one is not to be confused with the accuser of Socrates. Phaedrus, however, whose name appears among those denounced by Teucros, is the friend of Socrates.

celebrants. He was among the people there, and saw it. There
were slaves there too, himself and his brother and Hicesius, the
flute player, and Meletus' servant. He was the first to give this
information, and provided the following names. Of these
Polystratus was arrested and put to death, while the rest went
off over the border and were officially condemned to death.
Take the list, please, and read the names.

(*The list is read*.) Denounced by Andromachus: Alcibiades, Niciades,
Meletus, Archebiades, Archippus, Diogenes, Polystratus, Aristo-
menes, Oionias, Panaitius.

This was the first information, gentlemen, given by Andromachus against the men cited. Now call Diognetus.

(*Diognetus replies to Andocides' questions*.)
Were you Commissioner of Inquiries, Diognetus, when Pythonicus
reported Alcibiades in the Assembly?
I was.
Are you aware of the information laid by Andromachus of events at
the house of Pulytion?
Yes.
Are these, then, the names of the men against whom the informa-
tion was laid?
That is so.

Now came a second lot of information. Teucros was an alien
in Athens who had gone secretly to Megara, and from there
gave notice to the Council that, if he were given immunity; he
would lay information about the mysteries in which he had
taken part, and give the names of his associates in it, and report
what he knew of the mutilation of the Hermae. The Council
(which had full powers) passed a vote and sent for him from
Megara. When he arrived, he was given immunity, and gave
the names of his associates. These fled from Athens on Teucros'
information. Now read the list of their names, please.

(*The list is read*.) Denounced by Teucros: Phaedrus, Gniphonides,
Isonomus, Hephaestodorus, Cephisodorus, himself, Diognetus,
Smindurides, Philocrates, Antiphon, Tisarchus, Pantocles.

Remember, gentlemen, that all this is agreed by you too.
Then there was a third lot of information. The wife of Alc-

maeonides, who had previously been the wife of Damon – her name was Agariste – gave information that at the house of Charmides near the Temple of Zeus, mysteries were conducted by Alcibiades, Axiochus and Adeimantus. These also fled on this information.

There was one further source of information. Lydus, the slave of Pherecles of Themacus, gave information of mysteries conducted at the house of his master, Pherecles, at Themacus. Among others whom he denounced was my father, who he said had been there, but was asleep with his cloak over his head. Speusippus, who was a member of the Council, passed the names on to the court. Then my father provided sureties, and prosecuted Speusippus for illegality. The case came before a jury of six thousand,[6] and Speusippus only got two hundred votes. The person who persuaded and begged my father to stay was myself, together with the rest of the family. Now call Callias[7] and Stephanus, and also Philippus and Alexippus, who are relations of Acumenus and Autocrator, who were exiled after the information of Lydus. The first is a nephew of Autocrator, and the second uncle to Acumenus. They must be presumed to have had no liking for the man who caused the exile of their relatives, and they must have known who this was.

Please face the jury and give your evidence as to whether my statements are true.

(*Evidence given*)

You have heard the facts, gentleman, and they have been attested. Now recall what my accusers have had the audacity

6. 6000 was the total number of jury empanelled at one time (see glossary), and it appears that this is the only known instance of the whole body sitting as a single court. This must be taken as indicating the degree of feeling caused by the affair.

7. Callias is here probably the son of Telocles and brother-in-law to Andocides (see 42 below). He must be distinguished from Callias, the son of Hipponicus, Andocides' opponent in the case, who is referred to in the latter part of this speech, and who is also the Callias of Plato's *Protagoras*. It was his grandfather, also Callias the son of Hipponicus, whose name was given to the Peace between Athens and Persia in 448 B.C. Yet another Callias appears in the decree (77 below), Callias of Angele.

to say. This is the right procedure: to listen to the prosecution
and refute it. They stated that I gave information about the
mysteries, denounced my own father as having been there, and
was in fact an informer against him, which is a horrifying and
outrageous statement. The informer against him was Lydus,
the slave of Pherecles, while it was I who urged him, indeed
went on my knees and begged him to stand his ground and not
run away abroad. What could have been the object of my
giving information against my father, as they claim, and then
begging him to stay and be victimized by my action? Did I
persuade him to face a trial in which he was bound to undergo
one of two appalling results? Because, if so, either I would be
thought to have given true information against him, in which
case I should be the cause of his death, or he would survive
and cause mine. As the law stood, a true information earned
immunity, a false one was punished by death. But you know
that my father and I both survived, which was impossible on
the assumption that I informed against him. One or other of us
must have been executed. Well, then, even if my father had
wanted to stand firm, do you suppose his friends would have
allowed him to stay or gone bail for him, instead of begging
and beseeching him to go somewhere where he could expect to
survive without causing my death? But in fact even when he
was bringing a suit for illegality against Speusippus, he continued to make this declaration: that he never went to Pherecles'
house at Themacus. He demanded the torture of his own
slaves, without any question of passing over owners who offered
it, and compelling the unwilling.[8] When my father said this,
what was there left for Speusippus to say, if this story is true,
except, 'Leogoras, what is the point of talking about slaves?

8. To us the practice of torturing slaves seems both barbarous and useless.
But it is often mentioned by Greek authors, usually in instances which imply
that the master invited or allowed the torture of slaves, because this would
elicit the truth and so improve his case (cf. Aristophanes, *Frogs*, 619–20, where
a list of 'all the regular tortures' is added with comic intent). The implication
also follows that torture was not carried out except with the permission of the
master. This case of the Hermae, however, seems to have been thought so
important as to justify special instructions for the use of torture in some cases
without such permission.

Has not your own son given information against you to the
effect that you were at Themacus? Cross-examine your father,
Andocides, or else your immunity is forfeit.' Is this what
Speusippus would have said, or not? I should say it is. So if I
did go into court, or if there was a story about me, or any
information against me or any declaration, not by me against
anyone else, but by someone else against me, I invite anyone to
stand up here and refute me. But in fact I have never heard
of a more outrageous or misleading argument. All they thought
necessary was to have the nerve to make an accusation. Whether
it would be proved false, they couldn't care less. If their charges
against me had been true, you would have been enraged and
thought no penalty bad enough for me. Accordingly ⁑ claim
that you should conclude that they are liars, and regard them
as abominable, and take it as proved by the fact that, if the worst
of their accusations are shown to be manifest lies, it is quite
certain that it will be perfectly easy to prove it of the others,
which are far less serious.

These, then, are the sets of information that were laid about
the mysteries: four of them. The names of the men who were
exiled after each of them have been read out in my defence, and
duly vouched for. But I will add a further proof, to make
assurance doubly sure. Of the men who were exiled over the
case of the mysteries some died in exile, while others have
returned, and are here in court at my request. I therefore invite
anyone to use my time allowance⁹ to raise an objection and claim
that I was responsible for the exile of any of them, or that I laid
information against them, and that their exile was not due to
the information I have mentioned. If I am proved wrong, I
accept any penalty. I now pause and make way for anyone who
wishes to say anything.

Well, then, gentlemen, what happened next? After all this
information had been laid, a question arose about the reward.
This had been fixed at 1000 *drachmae* by the decree of Cleonymus, and at 10,000 by that of Peisander, and there was a dispute
between the informers and Pythonicus, who claimed to have

9. The maximum length of speeches made in a law-suit was laid down, and
they were timed with a water-clock.

been the first to bring an indictment, while Androcles put in a
claim on behalf of the Council[10] itself. It was therefore decided
in the court of the Thesmothetae, that judgement should be
given by the initiated, when they had heard the information
given by each claimant. They voted the rewards first to Andromachus, secondly to Teucros; and they received them at the
Panathenaic Festival, Andromachus 10,000 *drachmae* and
Teucros 1000. Please call the witnesses to this.

(*Evidence given*)

As regards the mysteries, gentlemen, about which the information was laid, and about which you who are initiates have come
into court, it has been proved that I committed no sacrilege,
laid no information against anyone, and made no admission
about it, nor was there any single misdemeanour, large or small,
on my part against the two goddesses. And this is what it is
most important to me to convince you of. The statement of my
accusers, who let loose all these frightful outcries and made
tirades about how others in the past had done acts of sacrilege,
and what punishments had been inflicted on them – what has
all this to do with me? I am all the more inclined to make these
accusations against *them*, and take this as my reason for claiming
that they deserve death for their impiety, while I deserve
acquittal for having committed none. It would be unconscion-
able if I were to be pilloried for other people's offences, while
in the knowledge that these lies were uttered against me by my
enemies, you regarded them as more convincing than the truth.
It is obvious that for such offences as this there exists no such
defence as mere denial. A stringent test is needed, when people
know the facts. In my case the investigation is pleasant enough,
because I do not need to beg and beseech you for mercy to save
myself on a charge of this sort. All I need do is to cross-examine
the prosecution and remind you of the facts. You will give your

10. i.e. for distribution of the reward to the Council as being responsible
for getting the information. The reward seems to have been 1000 drachmae
in the first place, with the larger figure added when the other seemed
inadequate. Cleonymus and Peisander are both made the target of Aristophanes' wit in several places (e.g. *Clouds*, 673 seqq., *Cleonymus*).

vote under stringent oaths. You invoked tremendous imprecations on yourselves and your offspring, and swore to vote justly on my case, and besides you have been initiated, you have witnessed the ritual of the two goddesses, which will make you punish impiety and preserve the innocent. You must regard it as just as sacrilegious to condemn the innocent for sacrilege as to fail to punish the guilty. So with much greater force than my accusers I lay on you the charge, in the name of the two goddesses and for the honour of the rites you have witnessed, and of all the Greeks who come here for the festival, that if I have committed any sacrilege, or if I have made any admissions, or laid information against any human being, or if anyone else has done so about me, you put me to death, and I make no defence. On the other hand, if I have committed no fault, and prove it to you with certainty, I request you to make it clear to all the Greeks that I was unjustifiably brought to trial. If my accuser, Cephisius, fails to gain a fifth of the votes and is disfranchised, he will not be allowed to enter the precinct of the two goddesses on pain of death. So if you think my defence adequate on these charges, please indicate it, to encourage me in continuing it.

As regards the mutilation of the Hermae and the information laid about it, I will fulfil my promise to you, and recount all that happened from the beginning. On Teucros' arrival from Megara and the grant of immunity to him he told what he knew about the mysteries and also about the mutilation of the Hermae, and denounced eighteen people. Some of those denounced fled the country, while others were arrested and put to death on Teucros' information. Please read me the names.

(*The list is read.*) Denounced by Teucros in the case of the Hermae: Euctemon, Glaucippus, Eurymachus, Polyeuctus, Plato,[11] Antidorus, Charippus, Theodorus, Alcisthenes, Menestratus, Eryximachus, Euphiletus, Eurydamas, Pherecles, Meletus, Timanthes, Archidamus, Telenicus.

Some of these have returned to Athens and are here now, and there are also a number of relatives of those who were executed; I invite any of them to stand up in my time allowance and

11. Plato here is not the philosopher. Meletus is the same as in note 5.

charge me with responsibility for the banishment or death of
anyone named here.

After this Peisander and Charicles, who were among the
Commissioners of Inquiry, but seemed most inclined at that
time to favour the popular party, declared that what had been
done was the work of a number of people, and was a plot to
overthrow the democracy,[12] which should be investigated without remission. Popular feeling was such that the moment the
proclamation was made for the Council to assemble in their
Hall, and the signal was down, the two events were simultaneous,
the arrival of the Council and a flight from the Agora in a general
dread of arrest. This public disaster induced Diocleides to lay
information to the Council to the effect that he knew the men
responsible for the mutilation of the Hermae, who were about
three hundred altogether, and to state that he had witnessed
the affair and how he had come across it.

Now gentlemen, I ask you to give this your attention and
recall whether my statement is true, and discuss the matter.
He said he had a slave at Laurium and had to take his earnings
to him. He got up and started early, because he had mistaken
the time owing to the full moon. When he got to the entrance
of the Theatre of Dionysus, he saw the figures of a lot of men
going down from the Odeum[13] into the Orchestra. He was
frightened at this, so he sat down in the shadow between the
pillar and the slab on which stands the bronze statue of the
Strategus. The men he saw were about three hundred in
number, standing in a circle in groups of fifteen or twenty. He
saw their faces in the moonlight and recognized most of them.
His first idea, gentlemen, and an outrageous one, in my view,

12. It is not easy to understand why this should have been supposed, why
such alarm should have been roused, or why Peisander, who took part four
years later in the oligarchic revolution of 411 B.C., should have thought it
called for a witch hunt of this kind. The parody of the mysteries may have
had no political basis, the mutilation of the Hermae was perhaps designed as
an omen to prevent the sailing of the expedition to Sicily and to discredit
Alcibiades, but there is little to connect anything that happened with any
serious attempt to overthrow the constitution.

The nature of the 'signal' referred to is unknown.

13. The Odeum was next to the Theatre. There were bronze statues of
Mitiades and Themistocles in the Theatre. It is not clear which is meant.

was that he was in a position to say that any Athenian he chose
was among their number, and to deny the presence of anyone
he chose. After seeing this sight he went to Laurium; next day
he heard of the mutilation of the Hermae, and at once realized
that this was what these people had been doing. When he got
back to town, he found Commissioners already appointed, and
the informer's fee set at 100 *minae*. Then he saw Euphemus (the
son of Callias, son of Telocles) sitting at the blacksmith's, and
took him over to the temple of Hephaestus, and told him what
I have told you, how he had seen us that night. He said he'd
just as soon take money from us as from the state, so as to keep
on terms with us. Euphemus said it was decent of him, and
told him to come with him to Leogoras' house, 'so as to meet
Andocides there with him, and some others concerned'. So he
came next day and knocked at the door, when as it happened
my father was just going out, and said to him, 'Are you the person they are waiting for? Well, a friend like you is not to be
lightly dismissed.' With that my father went off. This was the
way he tried to get at my father with the claim that he was in
the plot.[14] What we said, according to him, was that we had
decided to give him two talents of silver instead of the official
100 *minae*, and if we succeeded in our plot, he should be in on
it, and we gave all due guarantees. To this he said his reply was
that he would think it over, and that we then told him to come
to the house of Callias, son of Telocles, so as to have him there
too. This was his way of trying to incriminate my brother-in-
law. Then, he said, he went to Callias', where he reached agreement with us and swore an oath on the Acropolis, while we
agreed to give him the money the following month, but we let
him down and didn't produce it. So he came forward with his
information.

These were the circumstances of his indictment, gentlemen,
and the men denounced were those he said he knew, forty-two
in number. The first he specified were Mantitheus and Apsephion, who were members of the Council in session, and the

14. Leogoras' remark might have implied the knowledge either that the
club were about to offer Diocleides money, or that Diocleides could divulge
the plot. Either implication could suggest that Leogoras was involved.

rest followed. Peisander then rose and proposed the repeal of
the statute passed under Scamandrius, so as to subject the men
to torture and not let a night pass without the discovery of all
the names. This was received with applause. At this Mantitheus
and Apsephion took refuge at the altar, begging to be spared
the rack and to stand for trial on bail. This they were reluctantly
granted, but the moment bail was laid down, they jumped on
their horses and deserted to the enemy, leaving their guarantors
high and dry, and faced with the same punishment as the
friends they had gone bail for. The Council took steps in secret
and arrested us and put us in the stocks. They called out the
Strategi and instructed them to give orders for Athenians living
in Athens to arm and go to the Agora, for the guard on the Long
Walls to go to the Theseum, and residents in Peiraeus to the
market place of Hippodamus, and for the trumpet to sound for
the Knights to go to the Anakeion.[15] The Council were to go
to the Acropolis and sleep there, the prytaneis in the Tholos.
Meanwhile Thebes got wind of the business, and mounted
guard on the frontier. But the cause of all the trouble, Diocleides, was hailed as the saviour of the country, and led crowned
in a chariot, to the Prytaneum, where he was given a dinner.

This is the first thing I want you to recall, those of you who
were there, and to pass on to the rest. Next please call the
prytaneis who were then on duty, Philocrates and the others.

(Evidence is given)

Very well, now I will read you the names of those who were
denounced, to show you the number of my relations he tried
to incriminate, first my father, then my brother-in-law. My
father he put down as being in the plot, my brother-in-law as
providing the house where the meeting was held. You shall
hear the rest of the names. Read them, please.

(The names are read while Andocides comments)
　　Charmides, son of Aristoteles.　(This is a cousin of mine. My
father and his mother were brother and sister.)

15. The mobilization must have been ordered in fear of a Peloponnesian
attack which might accompany the supposed conspiracy. For Anakeion, see
glossary.

Taureas.   (A cousin of my father's.)
Nisaeus.   (Taureas' son.)
Callias, son of Alcmaeon.   (My father's cousin.)
Euphemus.   (The brother of Callias, son of Telocles.)
Phrynichus, the ex-dancer.   (Another cousin.)
Eucrates, brother of Nicias.   (Callias' brother-in-law.)
Critias.[16]   (Yet another cousin of my father's – their two mothers
were sisters.)

These were all among the forty-two denounced.

We were imprisoned all together. Night fell, the prison was
locked up, and relatives had arrived, a mother or sister or a
wife and children, and there was a miserable noise of weeping
and wailing at the situation. Charmides, who was my cousin
and my own age, and had been brought up with me in the same
house from childhood, said to me, 'Andocides, you see what a
terrible situation this is. I've never had occasion in the past to
say anything to worry you. But in the present state of things I
must. The people you've gone about with and been friends
with outside the family, they're the ones who have been charged
with the things people are using to incriminate us, and they
have been executed for it or else fled the country self-condemned.
So if you have heard anything about this business, say so, and
you'll first of all save yourself, then your father, who may be
supposed to be your first consideration, and your brother-in-
law, husband of your only sister, and all the rest of your relations
and friends, myself included. I've never really done you any
harm in my life, and I've been your enthusiastic supporter at
all times of need.' When Charmides said this, and every one
of them begged and prayed me in the same terms, I thought to
myself, 'I am really in the most terrible situation possible. Am
I to see my own relations ruined unjustly and done to death,
and their property confiscated, and allow them to be recorded
publicly as guilty of unspeakable sacrilege, when they are
completely innocent, to let three hundred other Athenians be
unjustifiably victimized, and disastrous mutual suspicion spread
all over the country – or tell Athens what I heard from Euphiletus, the real culprit?' There was this further consideration in

16. This is the Critias of the Thirty.

my mind, that I reckoned that the wrong-doers who were really responsible had some of them been executed on Teucros' information, while others had fled and been condemned to death, and there were only four left who had not had information laid against them by Teucros for their offences – Panaetius, Chaeredemus, Diocritus and Lysistratus, who were the most likely of all Diocleides' victims to be thought guilty, as they were friends of some who had lost their lives already. These four could ill rely on survival in any case, while my relations had certain death before them, unless someone told the government the truth. I therefore thought it better to cause four men the loss of their rights with good reason (and they are still alive now and back here in possession of their property) than to allow the others to perish without justification. So if any of you gentlemen, or any other citizens, imagined previously that I gave information against my own friends to procure their destruction and my own safety, which was the libellous tale my enemies told against me, I ask you to judge the matter in the light of the facts. For at present I have got to render a truthful account of my actions in the presence of the very men who were guilty and fled the country for being so, and have the clearest knowledge of the truth or falsehood of my statements. Indeed, it is open to them to refute me in my own time. I give my permission. You, meanwhile, have to discover the truth. The most important thing for me in this case is to be acquitted and clear my reputation, and that first of all you yourselves, and then everyone else, should understand that there was nothing vicious or cowardly in anything I have done. It all came of a misfortune to the country and to us, and when I said what I was told by Euphiletus, I was thinking as much for the country as for my family and friends, and for good reasons, not for any reprehensible ones, in my opinion. And if that is so, I claim acquittal and exoneration. Now I ask you, gentlemen, because you ought to take a human approach in your reckonings, as though you were actually involved in this trouble – what would you have done? If you had a direct choice between a noble death and ignoble survival, one or the other, you might justifiably take a low view of what I did, though a good many people would have chosen as I did and preferred life to a noble death. But when the exact opposite was true, silence would have meant my dying a disgraceful death myself, when I hadn't committed sacrilege at all, and letting my father go to his death, and my brother-in-law and all those relations and cousins, whose only danger was my refusal to reveal that others were to blame. Diocleides perjured himself to imprison them, and they had no chance of escape unless the whole truth were made public. I was on the way to becoming their murderer, if I hadn't told you what I heard, and I'd have brought three hundred Athenians to their death, and it would have been utterly calamitous to the city. That would have been the result of not speaking. But as I did speak, I was in a position to survive myself and rescue my father and my family, and save the city a lot of anxiety and trouble. Four men were due for banishment on my account, and they were guilty. Of the others previously denounced by Teucros those who were executed didn't owe their death to me, nor the others their exile. With all this in mind I came to the conclusion that the least of the necessary evils was to tell the truth at once, convict Diocleides of perjury, and secure our own safety and his punishment for an unjustifiable attempt to ruin us and deceive the authorities – and gain the reputation of a benefactor and make money into the bargain. I therefore informed the Council that I knew who the culprits were, and made known the facts, namely that the suggestion had been made at a party by Euphiletus, but I had opposed it, and that on that occasion it was due to me that it did not take place. Later I went up to Cynosarges after a pony of mine, had a fall and broke my collar-bone, and was carried home on a stretcher. Euphiletus saw the state I was in; he told the others I had been persuaded to come in on the scheme, and had agreed to take part and to deface the Hermes at the shrine of Phorbas. This statement was untrue, and that is the reason why the Hermes by our family house, which was erected by the Aegeis tribe, was the only one in Athens not to be damaged, on the ground, according to Euphiletus, that I intended to deface it. When they discovered this, there was an outcry that I had knowledge of the affair, but had not kept my promise. Meletus and Euphiletus came to me next day, and said, 'We've done this job, Andocides, and if you see fit to keep quiet, we'll be friends as before. Otherwise you'll get more trouble from us than any good you get on our account from others.' I told them the affair made me think Euphiletus a crook, but the danger to them wasn't the fact that I knew of it, but what they had actually done. In proof of this I provided my slave's evidence under torture that I was ill and unable to get up, and the Prytaneis seized the servants of the house which had been the starting-place for their actions. The commissioners and the Council investigating the affair and finding my account substantiated and universally admitted to be true, next called for Diocleides. Not much questioning was needed before he admitted he was lying and begged for mercy, giving the names of the men who had urged him to tell the tale, namely Alcibiades of Phegus[17] and Amiantus of Aegina. These two took fright and fled the country. On hearing this you put Diocleides in court and condemned him to death, and on my account released my relations, who had been imprisoned and were in danger of death, took back the two exiles, and returned home yourselves and disarmed, well rid of your troubles and dangers. In all this I deserve pity all round for what I went through, but in regard to my responsibility for what happened I should be accorded the highest possible credit. When Euphiletus suggested that I should put my trust in a pledge which could not have been more treacherous, I opposed him and refused, and gave him the abuse he deserved; though after they had committed the wrong, I joined in concealing it, and it was on the information of Teucros that they were put to death or exiled, before we were imprisoned by Diocleides and were in danger of our lives. Then I denounced the four, Panaetius, Diocritus, Lysistratus and Chaeredemus. They owed their exile to me, I admit. But my father, my brother-in-law, three cousins and seven other relations were saved unjustified execution.[18] That they are all still in the light of day is due to me, as they

17. Not the famous Alcibiades, but a cousin. The 'exiles' mentioned below must be Mantitheus and Apsephion.

18. The numbers do not tally with the names given in Andocides' list of relatives above. There are various possible remedies.

admit, while the disturber of the whole city and the cause of extreme danger to it, was convicted, and you escaped considerable risk and mutual suspicion. Again, I want you to recall the truth of this, gentlemen, or to enlighten any who don't know it. Now, please, call the men who were released by my action. They know the facts and will have the most certain evidence to give the jury. This is the truth, gentlemen, and they will go on the platform and tell you so for as long as you want them to. After which I will continue with the rest of my defence.

(Evidence given)[19]

Well, in regard to what happened on that occasion you have heard the whole story, and my defence has been complete, I am convinced. But if there *is* anyone who wants to ask anything or thinks it inadequate or that I've left anything out, let him stand up and say so, and I will add to my defence accordingly.

I will now proceed to the legal aspect. Cephisius here informed against me according to the law now in force, but his accusation belonged to an earlier law proposed by Isotimides, which does not concern me. His proposal was that those who were guilty of sacrilege and admitted it should be excluded from religious rites. But I was guilty of neither. I committed no sacrilege and made no admission. Also the decree is obsolete and not valid, as I will demonstrate. However, I will put up a defence on the point, in which, if I fail to convince you, it will be my own loss, while if I succeed, I shall provide a defence for my opponents.[20] The truth shall be told. After the destruction of the fleet and the siege of Athens you debated the subject of unity, and decided to restore the franchise to those who had lost it, and the proposal was made by Patrocleides. Who *were* the disfranchised, and what were the circumstances in each case? I will tell you. First, people who owed money to the treasury: who had held offices, but not had their accounts passed, or were in debt for wrongful possession of property, or

19. This rubric is omitted in the text, but must be assumed.
20. If he proves the decree of Isotimides invalid for events before 403 B.C., he will be giving his opponents a defence for their own offences committed before that date.

in consequence of the failure of public suits or fines imposed
by a court, or failure to make good the rent for a public lease
or sureties to the state. All these were permitted to pay at or
before the ninth prytany, and in case of non-payment they
were to be fined double and their possessions sold for the
benefit of the state. And there were examples of conviction for
embezzlement or bribery, whose offspring shared their deprivation.[21] This was one kind of deprivation of rights, but there was
another kind, where the person was deprived, but the property
retained and held in possession. These were cases of desertion
or of avoiding military service or keeping a ship out of action
or of abandoning arms, or of wrongful summons on three occasions, or of injury to parents; these were all punished by loss
of personal rights, but not of property. Others retained rights
with some limitations, being not wholly deprived, but in part,
like the army; who for remaining in the city under the tyrants[22]
retained their rights in other respects, but were not permitted
to speak in the Assembly or be members of the Council. Of
these rights they were deprived, and this was the limitation
imposed on them. Others were restrained from bringing actions
or from laying information, others from sailing to the Hellespont
or to Ionia, others from entering the Agora. Well, you voted
to erase all such decrees in their official form and in all copies,
and to give a general pledge of unity on the Acropolis. Please
read the decree of Patrocleides dealing with these events.

Decree Proposed by Patrocleides: Inasmuch as the people of Athens
decreed an indemnity in respect of the disfranchised and of debtors,
in order to make it possible to move measures and discuss them, the
People shall pass the same decree passed at the time of the Persian
war, which proved in the interest of the People. In regard to those
registered as debtors with the Collectors or with the Treasurers of
the Goddess Athena and the other Gods, or with the Basileus, or to
any whose name has not been included in the list up to the last

21. I follow D. M. Macdowell's text, which makes a necessary alteration in
the list of debtors to the state. The 'ninth prytany' means the ninth of the
ten divisions of the year.
22. The 'tyrants' meant are apparently the oligarchy of the four hundred
in 411 B.C.

Council in the archonship of Callias, those who were deprived of citizenship or were debtors, and all those who have had accounts condemned in the Auditors' office, by the Auditors or their assessors, or in whose case a prosecution on the audit had not been taken, or who have had imposed on them limitations or the fulfilment of guarantees up to the relevant time, or any of the Four Hundred whose names are still registered or any in respect of whom enactment of the oligarchy remains on the books, except such names as are officially recorded as not having remained in Athens, or who have been condemned either by the Areopagus or the Ephetae or the Prytaneum or the Delphinium or the Basileus, or have been exiled for murder or sentenced to death either as homicides or as tyrants; all others shall be obliterated by the Collectors and the Council in all instances,[23] and all existing duplicate copies shall be handed in by the Thesmothetae and other magistrates, the operation to be completed within three days on the decision of the People. Such copies as have been ordered to be obliterated must not be privately retained, nor used for retrospective complaints. Any breach of this enactment shall render liability to the same penalties as those convicted or charged before the Areopagus, to ensure the highest trust among Athenians in the present and in the future.

This was the decree which restored the disfranchised to their rights. But the return of the exiles was not proposed by Patrocleides nor decreed by you. After the peace with Sparta, the destruction of the Long Walls, the return of the exiles and the establishment of the Thirty, and then afterwards with the holding of Phyle and the capture of Munychia, and all the miseries which I do not care to remember or to recall to you,[24] when, in fact, you returned from the Peiraeus, you were in a position to impose penalties, but you decided to let bygones be bygones, and preferred the preservation of Athens to private revenges, resolving to wipe the slate clean all round. On this decision you elected a board of twenty to administer the city till legislation could be passed. Meanwhile the code of Solon and the enactments of Draco were to hold. But after drawing lots for a Council and electing a legislative committee you found that a good many of Solon's and Draco's enactments left a

23. Deleting the unintelligible ἐν τῷ δημοσίῳ. See Macdowell.
24. See introduction to Lysias, *Against Eratosthenes*, p. 40.

number of citizens liable to penalties for former activities. At an assembly on the point you passed a measure to make an examination of all the laws and inscribe in the Stoa such as were approved. Now read the decree.

Decree. It is enacted by the People on the proposal of Teisamenus that the city conduct its affairs according to the ordinance anciently established, follow the laws of Solon and his weights and measures, follow also the enactments of Draco as observed in time past: that any further legislation which may be needed this committee elected by the Council shall inscribe upon boards and exhibit before the Eponymi[25] for public inspection, and set them before the magistrates within one month. Laws so set before them shall first be examined by the Council and also the legislative committee of 500 chosen by the *demes* under oath. It shall be permitted to any private citizen who so desires to enter the Council and make recommendation for any improvement in the laws. When the laws are laid down, the Council of the Areopagus shall be charged with superintendence of the laws, and their maintenance by the magistrates. Laws ratified shall be posted on the wall where they were previously inscribed for public inspection.

The laws were therefore examined in accordance with this decree, and those ratified were posted in the Stoa. This being done, we passed a law by which you all act. Read the law, please.

Law. No unwritten law[26] shall be put into operation on any subject whatever.

Is there anything omitted here which could occasion a magistrate bringing a case or any of you taking any action except in accordance with the written laws? Where therefore the invocation of an unwritten law is forbidden, it must be impossible to invoke an unwritten decree.[27] Since, then, we realized that a lot of

25. The heroes after whom Cleisthenes named the ten tribes. Their statues stood in the Agora. For the complicated provisions of the decrees of Teisamenus see Macdowell, pp. 195 seqq. In particular there is doubt about the clause committing the guardianship of the laws to the Areopagus, and how this privilege is related to that removed from the Areopagus in 462 B.C.

26. 'Unwritten laws' in this passage are those not officially inscribed: the phrase is not used in our familiar sense of practices accepted by convention.

27. A decree is a more temporary measure than a law.

Athenian citizens were in positions of misfortune as the effect
of laws or decrees previously passed, we laid down the code I
have referred to for the precise circumstances which now hold,
to prevent anything of this kind happening, or the possibility
of vexatious prosecution of anyone. Read the laws in question.

Laws. No unwritten law shall be put in operation on any subject
whatever. No decree either of the Council or of the People shall have
superior validity to that of a law. And no law shall be laid down to
apply to a single individual, unless it applies also to the whole
People of Athens, if it is not decided by six thousand voters by
secret ballot.

What remains? This law. Read it please.

Law. The judgements and arbitrations made in Athens under the
democracy shall be valid. And the laws shall be in force as from the
Archonship of Eucleides.[28]

You enacted that the judgements and arbitrations made in
Athens under the democracy should be valid to prevent the
cancellation of debts or the repetition of suits, and to maintain
the validity of private agreements. But in the case of public
offences which admit of public prosecutions or indictments or
information or summary processes, for these purposes you
decreed that the laws dating from the Archonship of Eucleides
should hold good. When it was decided to examine the laws,
and after examination to post them, and that no unwritten law
should be brought into operation about anything, that no decree
either of the Council or the People should have superior validity
to a law, that no law should be passed to apply to a single
individual, if it did not apply to all Athenian citizens, and that
the laws passed in the Archonship of Eucleides should be valid,
then is there any possibility that any of the decrees made before
the Archonship of Eucleides can have any validity at all? I
think not. But consider for yourselves.

Well, then, what about your oaths? The one which holds
good for the whole city, and which you have all sworn since the
general reconciliation, is this: 'And I will bear no ill will against

28. To the Archonship of Eucleides in 403 B.C. belongs the revision of the
laws which followed the expulsion of the Thirty.

any citizen except the Thirty and the Eleven, and not even against one of these if he is willing to render account of his conduct of office.' Where, then, you have sworn an oath not to bear ill will even to the Thirty (who were responsible for the greatest miseries of all), if they rendered account of their office, you could scarcely have thought fit to do so against any other citizens. Again, what is the oath of the Council in power at any time? 'I will not accept any information or summary process in respect of previous events except against the exiles.'[29] Finally what is your own oath, before you became members of this court? 'And I will bear no ill will nor induce another to do so, but I will give my vote in accordance with the existing laws.' And you must consider whether I seem right in claiming to speak on your own behalf and that of the laws.

Now, gentlemen, consider both the laws and the accusers in court, and ask yourselves what basis there is which justifies them in making accusation. Cephisius here leased a tax[30] from the treasury, collected the profits from farmers on the land to the tune of 90 *minae*, but instead of paying it in absconded. Had he appeared, he would have been put in the stocks. The law provided that the Council should have the power, in the case of non-payment of dues, to put the delinquent in the stocks. So in view of the enactment in favour of the laws passed under Eucleides Cephisius claims not to repay what he appropriated, and the outlaw has now recovered his citizenship, and the disfranchised citizen has turned informer because you are operating the laws at present in vogue. Meletus again, as you all know,[31] arrested Leon under the Thirty, which resulted in Leon's death without trial. Yet this law was previously in force, and has been retained in operation as desirable: that the instigator of an action is liable to the same punishment as the actual perpetrator of it. Now Meletus is out of danger of a prosecution for homicide from Leon's heirs, because the laws to be enforced

29. The oligarchs who fled to Eleusis in 403. See introduction to Lysias, *Eratosthenes*, above.
30. See notes 34 and 42 below.
31. On the celebrated occasion when Socrates, ordered by the Thirty to accompany Meletus on this assignment, refused.

are those in operation under Eucleides. That he arrested Leon,
he himself cannot deny. Epichares is another instance. A man
of the lowest character and intentionally so, who directs his ill
will against himself, he was in the Council under the Thirty,
but what is the wording of the law inscribed over the Council
chamber? 'Anyone who served on the Council after the dissolution of the democracy, may be put to death with impunity,
and his killer is without stain on his character, and can take the
property of the dead man.' In that case, Epichares, is not anyone
who kills you regarded as being without a stain according to
Solon's law? Read me the law on the stone.

Law. Decreed by the Council and People. Prytanis, the tribe
Aeantis: Secretary, Cleigenes: Chairman, Boethus: drafted by
Demophantus. The commencement of this decree is to date from
the year of the Council of five hundred appointed by lot for which
Cleigenes was the first secretary.

   If any man overthrow the democracy at Athens, or if any man
hold office after the democracy is overthrown, he shall be an enemy
of the Athenians and be killed without penalty to his killer, and his
property shall be confiscated to the state, and a tenth part of it
given to the Goddess. And whoever shall kill such a man or shall
take counsel for his killing, shall be without stain and without
guilt. And all Athenians shall swear upon unblemished victims,
tribe by tribe and *deme* by *deme*, to kill any man who has done so.
And the oath shall be this: 'I will kill by word and by deed and with
my vote and with my hand, if I am able, whosoever shall overthrow
the democracy in Athens or whosoever shall hold any office after
the democracy has been overthrown, or whosoever shall set himself
up to be a tyrant, or take part in setting up a tyrant. And if any
other man kill such a one, I will hold him sinless before gods and
spirits for that he killed an enemy of the Athenians, and I will sell
all the property of the man so killed, and will give one half of it to
the killer, and I will not hold back any of his share. And if any man
in killing such a one or in seeking to do so be himself killed, I will
do good for him and his offspring just as for Harmodius and
Aristogeiton and their descendants. And all oaths that are sworn in
Athens or in the camp or anywhere else which are adverse to the
People of Athens, I cancel and renounce.' These things all Athenians
shall swear upon unblemished victims as the customary oath before
the Dionysia, and they shall call down many blessings on all such

as keep this oath, but upon him that shall break it destruction for him and his offspring.

I ask you, as a practitioner of deceit and misrepresentation, is this law valid or not valid? The reason why it has suddenly become invalid, I suppose, is that the laws in force have to be those of the time of Eucleides. As for you, though you carry on your existence and go about Athens, you are not entitled to. Under the democracy you lived by informing, and under the oligarchy you avoided being made to disgorge the profits of your informing[32] by bootlicking the Thirty. And you talk to me about 'association' and taking people's characters away? It wasn't a single individual you 'associated' with – it's a pity it wasn't – you got a little from anyone who cared to, as everyone here knows, and lived a life of immoral practices, despite your squalid appearance. Yet he had the temerity to accuse other people, when by the laws of Athens he cannot even make a case for himself. As a matter of fact, gentlemen, sitting as defendant during his prosecution of me I felt, as I looked at him, exactly as I would after arrest by the Thirty. If I had been pleading my case then, who would have been my accuser? He would have been ready for the job, if I didn't offer him his price. So it is now. Who would have been my interrogator but Charicles, with his question, 'Tell me, Andocides, did you go to Decelea[33] and fortify it against your country?' 'No, I didn't.' 'Well, did you raid Athenian territory and carry off property, either on land or sea, at the expense of your fellow-citizens?' 'No.' 'You didn't fight against your country at sea either, or help in pulling down the walls, or in abolishing the democracy, or force your way back to Athens?' 'No, I didn't do any of these things.' 'Do you expect to get away with it, then, and not die like so many others?' Do you imagine, gentlemen, that I should have

32. On informers under the Thirty see introduction to Lysias, p. 40. Greek orators not infrequently resorted to abuse, even when it was irrelevant, if they thought it likely to produce an effect on the jury.

Charicles here appears as a member of the Thirty associated with Critias, and is imagined as a presiding magistrate opening a prosecution and accusing Andocides of failure to take part in the disloyal proceedings of the oligarchs.

33. Decelea in North Attica was fortified by the Spartans, as a base for attacks on Athens, in 413 B.C., and many oligarchs fled there.

met any other fate on your account, if I had been caught by
the Thirty? And don't you think it appalling that, considering
that I would have been done to death by them for doing no
harm to Athens, as happened to others, I should not be acquitted now that I am on trial before you, whom I have never
harmed? If any human being can be acquitted, I must be. As a
matter of fact the information against me was given in accordance with established law, [34] but the accusation rests on the
decree made previously about others. So if you propose to
condemn me, have a care that it may not be my special
business to give an account of what happened in the past, and
a good many other people's business even more, either opponents in the fighting with whom you have had a reconciliation,
or exiles you have allowed back, or disfranchised citizens you
have restored. For their benefit you have published proclama-
tions or cancelled laws or deleted decrees, and they now remain
in Athens and trust you. If they realize that you are accepting
the accusations of the accusers of the past, what do you think
they will suppose in their own cases? Which of them do you
imagine will want to enter a suit on the events of the past?
Rows of enemies and malicious prosecutors will appear who
will be eager to contend with them. Both classes are here now
to listen, but not with the same point of view. One lot will want
to know whether they can trust existing laws and the sworn
agreements between you, and the other to test your attitude
and see whether they are going to be free to make false accusations and indictments with impunity, and to inform against
people and even get them imprisoned. This is the position,
gentlemen. My life is on trial in this business, and your vote
will give public demonstration whether your enactments are to
be trusted, or whether one needs either to square the informers
or to run away from them and leave Athens with all possible
speed.

But to show that your proceedings in aid of union are not a
failure, but that what you have done is indeed to your credit
and your advantage, I want to say just a little about this.

34. That of Isotimides. If this is regarded as still valid, then so are other
measures under which Andocides' accusers are guilty of other offences.

During the time of great disasters to Athens, when the tyrants[35] held the city and the popular party were in exile, your ancestors defeated the tyrants in battle at Pallenium under the command of Leogoras, my great-grandfather, and Charias, whose daughter my grandfather married, and killed or condemned the tyrants to exile or else let them stay, but not as citizens. Later, when Persia invaded Greece, your ancestors realized the extent of the threatened disasters and the size of the Persian armament, and they decided to accept their exiles back and restore their citizen rights, and let the success and the danger be the same for all. After this they made mutual undertakings under the most solemn oaths, and claimed the right to take the front line of the Greek force and meet the enemy at Marathon, on the assumption that their own valour would be found sufficient to battle with the great numbers of the enemy. They fought and conquered, and set Greece free and saved their country. After so tremendous an achievement they did not think it right to harbour ill will. This was the reason why, when they found their city devastated, their sacred places burnt and their walls and houses fallen to the ground, their unity of spirit enabled them to acquire the sovereignty of Greece and hand down a city as great and splendid as ours. Later on, in a time of no less disaster than that, you yourselves with the noble spirit of a noble race displayed the generosity that was in you, when you thought it proper to receive the exiles home, and restore their rights to the disfranchised. What remains in you of their nobility? The refusal to harbour ill will, in the remembrance that our city rose from a small beginning in time past to greatness and success. Such it could still be, if we, its citizens, could keep good sense and unity together.

But these people even accused me on the score of the olive branch which they said I deposited in the Eleusinium,[36] when the traditional law said that to offer supplication at the mysteries

35. This refers to the tyranny of Peisistratus and his sons. The battle to which Andocides refers is hard to identify, but perhaps belongs to the time of the expulsion of Hippias with the aid of Cleomenes in 510 B.C.

36. A sign of supplication forbidden on religious grounds during the celebration of the mysteries.

was punishable with death. They are brazen enough, in an arrangement they themselves concerted, to be dissatisfied with failing to succeed, and they raise an accusation against me as the person guilty. When we returned from Eleusis, and the information had been laid, the Basileus appeared, to report on the performance at the festival at Eleusis in accordance with custom. The Prytaneis said they would take him to the Council, and ordered him to notify me and Cephisius to attend at the Eleusinium, because the Council intended to hold its session there according to Solon's law, which lays down a session in the Eleusinium the day following the mysteries. So we appeared in accordance with instructions. When the Council were all present, Callias, son of Hipponicus, in his official garb, stated that there was a suppliant branch on the altar, and displayed it. The Herald then proclaimed the question, who laid it there, and there was no answer. But we were there and Cephisius saw me. As no one answered, and Eucles here, after making the inquiry, had gone in again – but call him, please. First of all, Eucles, witness to the truth of this statement of mine.

(Evidence of witness)

As to the truth of my statement, evidence has now been given. But it seems to me very different from what my accusers said. They said, if you remember, that the two goddesses themselves misled me into depositing the branch in ignorance of the law, so as to get me punished. But my contention, gentlemen, even if my accusers' statement is as true as you like, is that I was saved by the goddesses. If I deposited the branch, but failed to answer, wasn't I working on my own destruction in placing it, and owed my survival to the chance of failing to answer, which was obviously due to the goddesses? Had they wished to destroy me, I'd have been bound to say I'd deposited the branch, even if I hadn't. But in fact I didn't answer because I didn't deposit it. When Eucles declared in the Council that no one had answered, Callias stood up again and declared that there was an ancient law that anyone depositing a branch in the Eleusinium should be put to death without trial, and that Hipponicus, his father, had once expounded this to the

Athenians, and he heard that I had laid the branch there. At this point up jumped our friend, Cephalus, and said, 'Callias, you are the most unprincipled crook in existence. First of all you give explanations when you're one of the Heralds and are not allowed to, and secondly you call it an ancient law when the tablet you're sitting by orders a fine of a thousand *drachmae* for placing a branch in the Eleusinium. Then again, who told you Andocides placed it there? Call him, if you like, and we can hear too.' Then when the inscription was read, Callias himself couldn't say where he got the information, and it was obvious to the Council that he'd put it there himself.

Well, now, gentlemen, – perhaps this is what you'd like to know yourselves – what was Callias' idea in placing the branch there? I'll tell you the point of this plot against me. Epilycus, son of Teisander, was my uncle, my mother's brother. He died in Sicily without sons, but he left two daughters who came to the charge of Leagros and myself. At home his position was none too good. The property he left was worth less than two talents, and the debts were more than five. However, I called on Leagros, and said in front of our family that the right thing to do in the circumstances was to honour our relationship.[37] 'In our position,' I said, 'it's not right to put other money affairs or personal considerations in front of Epilycus' daughters. If he had lived, or had died worth a lot of money, we should have expected, as the nearest relations, to take his daughters. In that case it would have been our regard for Epilycus or for his money. Now it'll be our regard for what is right. So you put in a claim for one, and I'll have the other.' He agreed, and we took them, as we'd agreed to do. Now it so happened that the one I claimed as my bride took ill and died. Her sister's still alive, and Callias induced Leagros, with the promise of a

37. If a man died intestate and left a daughter, but no male heir, his property and his daughter passed to the next of kin, who could claim to marry the daughter, or else provide a dowry for her to marry someone else. In the case of the poorest class, to which Epilycus may have belonged, he was obliged to do one or the other. The complication of this incident is due to the fact that Epilycus was also related to Callias, but not so closely as to Andocides and his cousin, Leogoras. The only way in which Callias could forestall Andocides' claim, therefore, was by causing him to leave the country.

present, to let him have her. When I got word of this, I at once
paid the deposit and brought a suit, first against Leagros, saying
in effect, 'If you want to put in a claim for her, good luck to it,
but otherwise I will.' Hearing this Callias entered an action for
his own son to marry the heiress, on the tenth of the month,
to prevent me making my claim. On the twentieth – this was
the time of the mysteries – he paid Cephisius a thousand
drachmae, and informed against me and entered this suit.
Seeing that I was holding my ground, he placed the branch with
the object of securing my death without trial, or getting rid of
me and offering an inducement to Leagros, so as to live with
Epilycus' daughter himself. But as he saw that even so he
couldn't get his own way without a fight, he then approached
Lysistratus, Hegemon and Epichares, who he realized were
friends of mine and went about with me, and was so lacking in
respect for law or decency as to say to them that if I were at last
prepared to give up Epilycus' daughter, he was prepared
to stop molesting me and to take Cephisius off and give me
compensation, according to my friends' estimate, for what had
been done to me. I told him he could go on accusing and
framing me, and if I could get an acquittal, and Athens
got to know the truth about my case, I thought he in his turn
would be in danger of his life. And I'll be as good as my word,
if you gentlemen will agree. Call the evidence to the truth of
my statement.

(Evidence of witnesses)

After all, think of the son for whom he wanted to make a match
with Epilycus' daughter. Consider how he was born, and how
Callias acknowledged him. It is another point you ought to
know of. He married the daughter of Ischomachus, and he
hadn't been living with her a year before he took up with her
mother and started living with her – mother and daughter at
once, of all unspeakable things for a priest of the Mother and
Daughter to do,[38] keeping them both in the house. He had no
shame or scruple in regard to the goddesses. Ischomachus'
daughter felt that death was better than going on as she was,

38. i.e. Demeter and Persephone.

and tried to hang herself, but was found before she succeeded. When she recovered, she ran away, so the mother drove the daughter out. But she did no better, because as soon as he was tired of her he threw her out too, though she said she was pregnant by him. So when she gave birth to a son, he denied that it was his. The wife's relations took the baby and came to the altar at the Apaturia with a victim, and told Callias to begin the ceremony. He asked who the father was, and they said, 'Callias, the son of Hipponicus.' 'That's me!' 'Yes, it's your son.' He put his hand on the altar, and solemnly swore that he had no son except Hipponicus, whose mother was the daughter of Glaucon. He called down complete destruction on himself and his whole family, if this was not so. And so it will indeed be. Later he fell in love with the old war-horse[39] again, took her home and brought the boy, who was by now quite big, to the Keryces, and declared that he *was* his son. Callicles spoke against accepting him, but the Keryces voted according to their rules, that when the father swore on oath that it was his own son he was introducing, he should introduce him. Then he touched the altar and again solemnly swore that it was his own son, the true-born child of Chrysilla, whom he had previously disowned. Now please call witnesses of all this.

(*Evidence of witnesses*)

Now just consider, gentlemen, whether such a thing has ever happened in the Greek world before, that a man married a wife, then married her mother to follow the daughter, and the mother drove the daughter out. Now, while he is living with her, he wants to get Epilycus' daughter, so that grand-daughter can drive out grandmother, though what name we are to give to the son, I can't think. I defy anyone, however ingenious, to work out a name for him. As there are three women his father will have lived with, he is the reputed son of one of them, the brother of another and the uncle of a third. Who would he be himself? Oedipus or Aegisthus, or what?

But there is still a small matter connected with Callias which I want to remind you of. Cast your minds back to the time

39. 'Battle-axe'; Macdowell.

when Athens was supreme in Greece and at the height of her prosperity, and Hipponicus was the wealthiest man in Greece. Then was the time, you well know, when there was a saying among the women and small children which ran through the whole city, that Hipponicus was bringing up an evil genius who upset the balance of his affairs.[40] You remember that, gentlemen. Well, how do you think the story of that period came out? Hipponicus thought he was producing a son, but it was his evil genius, who turned his estate upside down, and his good sense, and his whole existence. That is the conclusion we must come to about him, that he was Hipponicus' evil genius.

But, gentlemen, why was it that people who are assisting Callias in this attack on me, and helping to rig this action against me and contributing money for it, did not think me guilty of sacrilege in the three years since I came back from Cyprus, though I initiated A**[41] from Delphi and other friends from abroad, when I entered the Eleusinium and did sacrifice, as I think myself entitled to do. On the contrary, they kept nominating me for public services, first as Gymnasiarch at the festival of Hephaestus, then to lead the Athenian representatives at the Isthmian and Olympic games, and then I was to be a controller of the sacred treasury on the Acropolis. But now apparently it is impious and wrong of me that I appear at religious ceremonies. I will tell you why these people take this line. Our distinguished friend, Agyrrhius, became chief collector of the two-per-cent for two years,[42] and bought the tax for thirty talents, with the assistance of these associates who met by the poplar, and you are aware of their character. It seems to me that they held this gathering there for two reasons, to receive money for not bidding higher, and to get shares in the business at a cheap rate. They made three talents, and then, realizing the sort of business it

40. I owe to Mr Macdowell this rendering of a pun in the Greek.

41. A name is lost from the text here (unless it is concealed in the words μεν ἀδελφον).

42. This was a tax on exports and imports. Athens, like Rome later, made use of tax farmers for purposes of collection. In this instance they worked in syndicate, and Agyrrhius and his friends bought the contract twice in succession for a lower rate than was necessary, making a profit which Andocides prevented on the next occasion.

was, and how valuable, they all clubbed together and shared it
out to the rest, and then offered thirty talents again the next
year. As no one was offering more, I came forward and put a
higher bid to the Council, till I got the contract for thirty-six.
I thus got rid of them, arranged guarantors for myself, collected
the money and paid it over to the treasury. Nor did I lose by it.
Our company made a small profit. And I prevented the other
lot from appropriating six talents. They realized this and had a
little discussion, 'This chap isn't going to get anything out of
the public funds, or let us do so either. He's setting up to
mount guard against any profit-making there. And besides,
any of us he sees departing from the straight and narrow he'll
have in court, and it'll be the end of us. We'd better put him
out of the way by hook or by crook.' This was the job they had
before them, while yours was the opposite. Because I'd like you
to have as many like me as possible, then for choice people like
them could be eliminated, but failing that there should be a force
to prevent their activities, consisting of men of good, honest
character in dealings with the people as a whole. Then, if they
want to, they will be able to be of service to you. I promise you
either to put a stop to such practices, and make them mend their
ways, or bring the culprits to court and punish them.

They also accused me in connexion with my sea-going
commercial undertakings, as if the reason why the gods saved
me from danger was, apparently, to come here and be done to
death by Cephisius. But I don't believe the gods could hold
such a view as not to punish me when they had me in such
terrible danger, if they thought I had done them wrong. What
greater danger could a man undergo than going on voyages in
the winter? When they had me physically exposed to this, and
were in control of my life and property, did they let me off in
spite of it? Couldn't they have gone further and had my body
deprived of burial? Or again there was a war on, there were
warships constantly at sea, and pirates, and many were captured
by them and lost all their property and ended their lives in
slavery; there was alien territory, and many were stranded
there and subjected to the most terrible hardship, and died of
personal, physical injury – and then are we to suppose the gods

preserved me from all this, only to put their vengeance in the
hands of the most unprincipled man in Athens, who claims to
be an Athenian citizen when he is not, a man no one among you
in the jury, who know his character, would trust with any of
your personal affairs? No, I think we ought to regard this sort
of risk as under the control of men, and those at sea as the
province of the gods. Then, if one can be permitted to make a
guess about the nature of the gods, I think they would be filled
with anger and resentment if they saw people they had preserved being done to death by human beings.

There is a further consideration worth keeping in mind,
gentlemen, that you now have the reputation throughout Greece
of outstanding good character and wisdom by not turning to
retaliation for the past, but towards the preservation of our city
and unity among its citizens. Many others have suffered disasters
as great as ours. But the settlement of existing differences in
happy reconciliation is rightly thought a sign of goodness and
wisdom. So, since it is universally admitted that you have this
character towards friend and foe alike, do not change your
minds, or agree to the loss of this distinction, or to a vote on
your own part which appears based on chance rather than on
thought.

So I ask you all to hold the same opinion of me as of my
forerunners, so that I may be enabled to follow their lead.
Recall that they have resembled the city's greatest and most
extensive benefactors for numerous reasons, but principally out
of good will towards you, and the desire that, should they or
any of their descendants be in danger or trouble, they might be
preserved by the fellow-feeling you would have for them. And
you would have good reason to remember them. The whole city
experienced the value of the character of previous generations
in Athens. When the fleet was destroyed, and there were plenty
who wanted to plunge Athens into irreparable disaster, it was
the Spartans who, enemies as they were, then determined to
preserve the city because of the valour of the men who were
the founders of freedom for all Greece. Since, then, the city as
a whole owed its preservation to the valour of your ancestors,
I claim that the qualities of my ancestors may be the cause of

my own preservation. To the deeds which then led to the safety of Athens, my ancestors made no small contribution. It is therefore just that I should share at your hands in the preservation you yourselves were accorded by the Greeks.

Consider too the character you will find in me, if you acquit me. First of all, after possession of an income of which you know, I was brought, through no fault of mine, but through the misfortunes of Athens, to the depth of want and poverty. After that I made a fresh livelihood for myself by honourable means, by my own wits and my own hands. I knew what it was to be a citizen of such a city, and what it was to be an alien resident in a foreign country, and I understood the nature of sound and wise thinking, and the nature of error and adversity. I had experience of many people and many different circumstances, which have brought me hospitality and friendship with kings and cities, and private friends as well, who will be yours too, if you acquit me, and you will be able to make use of them whenever occasion offers. In fact, gentlemen, this is how it stands with *you*. If you put an end to me, there is no one left of my family, which is destroyed root and branch. Yet you have incurred no disgrace from the house of Andocides and Leogoras, since it has been ours. There was much more to be ashamed of when I was in exile, and Cleophon,[43] the lyremaker, lived in it. There has never been a time when any of you passed this house of ours with the memory of any ill treatment at our hands. My family held countless commands and can show numerous trophies won from the enemy by land and by sea, held endless other offices, handled your finances without ever failing in the examination of accounts, and without any offence committed on either side. It was a house of great antiquity and great liberality to anyone in need. Nor was there a single occasion when any of them was involved in a suit and asked any return for these services. Do not, because they are dead, forget what they achieved. Remember their deeds, and believe that you see their figures before you begging you for my acquittal. Whom can I bring before you to plead for me?

43. From the revolution of 411 B.C. till the end of the war Cleophon was the leader of the democratic party in Athens.

My father? He is dead. Brothers? I have none. Children? They are not yet born. You must take the place of father, brothers and children. In you is my one refuge, and to you my prayers and supplications are addressed. Beg for me from yourselves, and spare me. Do not consent to create citizens from Thessaly and Andros because of your shortage of manpower,[44] and at the same time destroy men who are true citizens, and who have a duty, and the desire, and the power, to be good ones. Do not, I beg you. And I ask this, too. I have done well by you. Honour me for it in return. Then if you grant my wish, you will not be deprived of the further good I have it in my power to do. But if you accede to my enemies, then, if you later regret it, you will not be able to do anything. So do not deprive yourselves of your hopes in me, nor me of mine in you. And I ask these friends, who have always given proof of nobility towards the people of Athens, to stand here and give you testimony of their opinion of me. Come forward, Anytus,[45] Cephalus, and my fellow-tribesmen who have been chosen to act as my advocates.

44. A number of measures were taken between 406 and 401 B.C. to increase the citizen body by enfranchising various classes of men.

45. Anytus had been a leading politician since being associated with Alcibiades and later Thrasybulus. Still later he appears as the prosecutor of Socrates.

ISOCRATES: PANEGYRICUS

INTRODUCTION

Isocrates was born in 435 B.C., *and died at the age of ninety-eight.
He was well educated, and early in his life came under the influence
of the leading intellectuals of the period of the early Sophists,
in particular of Gorgias, and he is mentioned in the* Phaedrus
*of Plato (279a) as a follower of Socrates and a young man
of very great promise. Financial difficulties during the Peloponnesian
War made it necessary for him to earn his living, and after a
period of writing speeches for use by litigants in the courts,
he turned to teaching, first in Chios, but after about 390* B.C., *in
Athens. He was extremely successful, and after the publication of
the* Panegyricus *extended his clientèle outside Athens through the
Greek world. His aims and methods are referred to in the General
Introduction (see p. 13 seqq.). He published a number of works which
were oratorical in form, but were not intended to be delivered, but
to be read. He describes in the* Philip *(81) his reasons for giving up
practical oratory and preferring to affect the course of the political
world partly by his teaching and partly by such essays as these.
Two of them appear in this book, the* Panegyricus, *in form an
oration for a Pan-Hellenic gathering, and the* Philip, *a letter
addressed to Philip of Macedon when Isocrates was already ninety
years old.*

The Panegyricus, *published in or after 380* B.C., *was ostensibly
devoted to one of Isocrates' main themes, the unification of the
Greek world. For this he looks to a reconciliation of Athens and
Sparta. But much of the treatise concerns the fitness of Athens for
the leadership of Greece, and its general praise of Athens affords
some interesting comparisons with the Funeral Oration of Pericles
(p. 33 seqq.). It is the more remarkable because Athens, though in
part recovered from her collapse in 404* B.C., *was still far from her old
wealth and greatness in a world dominated by Sparta, whose
disastrous policy is much emphasized. The* Panegyricus *thus refers
for the most part to events after the Peloponnesian War and*

*before the rise of Thebes at the battle of Leuctra in 371 B.C. It deals
in particular with the methods and unpopularity of Sparta (117)
during the period, with the career of Conon and with the King's
Peace.*

*Left supreme over Greece after 404 B.C. Sparta earned universal
hatred for the rigid control she exerted. Democratic constitutions
were thrown aside and a garrison installed in each city under a
Spartan governor called a harmost (117) and a board of ten
(decarchy) to govern. Even when the decarchies proved so unpopular
that they were discarded, their place was taken by oligarchies,
while tribute was levied by former Athenian dependencies to maintain a fleet.*

*But in spite of unpopularity Sparta maintained her hegemony,
and after the rebellion of Cyrus began to make attacks upon Persia
for the recapture of Greek states in Asia, even though faced with
difficulties at home and a confederacy of opponents in the so-called
Corinthian War. One of the heroes of these events was the Athenian
admiral, Conon, who, having escaped from Aegospotami burning
with hatred of Sparta, made his way to Evagoras, the pro-Athenian
ruler of Salamis in Cyprus. Together they reinvigorated the naval
power of Persia, and it was Conon who brought about the defeat of
Sparta at Cnidus in 394 B.C. This was the main event of what
Isocrates calls the Rhodian war (142) because the main battle was
not far from Rhodes, whose revolt from Sparta Conon had secured.
This battle, with its military counterpart at Coronea just afterwards, so reduced Spartan power as to compel an accommodation
with Persia. Sparta succeeded in turning the Persian King against
his Greek allies, and in 387–386 B.C. imposed on the Greek world
the King's Peace, devised by Sparta and approved and dictated by the
King. The only recalcitrant was Evagoras, who despite the fact
that the Peace assumed Persian control of Cyprus, stood against
Persia until forced to sue for peace in 381. It was in this period that
Ionian forces were used against him by Persia (124 and 134).*

*Events between the fall of the Thirty in Athens (see Lysias,
Eratosthenes) and the publication of the* Panegyricus *are covered
by Xenophon's* Hellenica *(tr. Rex Warner in Penguin Classics as*
A History of My Times), *Books III, IV, V.*

ISOCRATES: PANEGYRICUS

THE institution of festivals[1] which include athletic competitions
has often led me to feel surprise at the large rewards offered for
mere physical successes, while the unselfish endeavour of men
who have set their whole being to work for the benefit of others
receives no recognition, though they merit the greater consideration. Athletic physique might be doubled without any benefit to
others, while the public spirit of a single individual may bring
profit to all who care to participate in it. Nonetheless I have
not been discouraged or reduced to inactivity. In the aꞌurance
that the repute my words will win me is sufficient reward I
come here to advocate a policy of war outside the bounds of
Greece, and unity within. I am aware that many who claim to
be men of intelligence have come forward to deal with this subject. But I make a double claim to it, first in the hope of establishing such a distinction from them that mine will be thought the
first word on the subject, and secondly in the initial belief that
the best oratory is that which deals with the greatest themes
and combines a display of the speaker's powers with the interests of his audience, as this does. In addition, favourable
circumstances still hold, so that the subject has not yet become
obsolete. A theme should be brought to a close when the circumstances which gave rise to it are over and with them the need
to consider it, or when the discussion can be seen to have
reached its conclusion and nothing further is left for others to
add. When the position remains unaltered and the ideas offered
are inadequate, there is surely need to consider in a philosophical
spirit a view whose successful presentation will rid us of the
present internecine war and dissension with its unequalled evils.
Again, if there were but a single way in which to present the
same material, the reply might be made that it is a waste of time
to weary an audience by repeating it. But as the nature of the
theme is such as to allow numerous variations of treatment, to

1. The *Panegyricus* was written as though for a Pan-Hellenic festival,
though it was never delivered at one.

make it possible to increase or diminish the prominence of different aspects, to use a novel approach to early instances or see the new in the light of the old, there is no cause to avoid ground already explored, but rather to attempt to improve on previous approaches to it. Past history is indeed a common legacy. But to make appropriate use of it, to take a right attitude to its details and document it fully requires real soundness of thought. And this, I think, is where the greatest advance can be made in any art, not least in the culture which comes through oratory. It demands that we shall value and give credit, not to the first in the field, but to the best performance, not to an original choice of subject, but to the ability to outdistance all rivals.

There is some tendency to criticize speeches which are too highly elaborated for the ordinary man. Such critics make the great mistake of viewing a very elaborate discourse in the same light as a speech in a private suit, as though both should have the same character. They do not realize that one kind aims at accuracy, the other at display, that their own eye is on simplicity, but that the power to command perfection in oratory would be incompatible with a simple style. There is no difficulty in seeing that they give their approval within their own familiar understanding. I am not concerned with them so much as with the view that will reject any looseness of expression and will irritably demand qualities in my work which will not appear in any other. To this I will speak a bold word in self-defence before embarking on my theme. In general, opening passages are designed to mollify the audience and make excuse for the discourse which is to follow, by claiming either hasty preparation or the difficulty of finding words to match the greatness of the subject. I take the opposite approach, and declare that, if I fail to do justice to my subject, to my reputation and to the length, not only of the time now occupied by it, but of my whole life, I ask for no sympathy, but ridicule and contempt. I deserve it in the fullest measure, if I have no more than ordinary qualifications for so lofty an undertaking.

So much, then, by way of preamble on personal grounds. If I now turn to public concerns, the claims made at the outset, that we should sink our own enmities and divert them outside

Greece, and the lengthy accounts of the disasters of war between Greek states and the benefits of an expedition against Persia, are true enough. But they do not begin at the best point to secure their ends. The Greek states are divided between Athenian and Spartan spheres of influence, the division being in most cases ideological. Any idea, therefore, of doing common service to Greek states without reconciling the leaders is naïve and unrealistic. Any attempt to go further than demonstrations and achieve something practical requires arguments to persuade these two states to divide the leadership on a basis of equality, and to turn the selfish demands which they now make on Greek states into expectation of gain from Persia. It is easy to lead Athens to this view, but Sparta is still hard to influence, having taken upon herself the false idea of supremacy as her heritage. But a demonstration that this priority is ours of right rather than theirs may induce them to pursue the general advantage instead of standing on precise legal claims.

This should have been the starting point for the other speakers, who should not have introduced discussion of points of agreement before dealing with controversial issues. At any rate there are two aims which justify me in devoting considerable time to this subject. I hope, preferably, to effect something of value, to see an exchange of internal disputes for external war. Failing this, it is my purpose to demonstrate which are the states which stand in the way of the best interests of Greece, and to show that, while our previous maritime supremacy was just, our present claim to leadership is no less so. In the first place, if in every field experience and influence are to be the qualification for honour, we have an indisputable claim to recover the supremacy which was once ours. It is impossible to point to a state which can boast as overwhelming a superiority in land warfare as is ours at sea. Secondly, if the justice of this criterion is denied, and stress is laid on the frequency of political change and the ephemeral character of political power, if it is urged that leadership, like any other distinction, should go where either priority of possession or service to Greece afford a claim, then it is my unaltered opinion that that claim is ours. A full historical scrutiny of both qualifications will only serve to show our superiority

over our rivals. Our claim to be the most ancient, the greatest
and the most universally famed of all cities is admitted. But
distinguished as is the basis which underlies it, there is closely
connected with it an even clearer ground for honour. Our title
to possession is not based upon the eviction of others or the
acquisition of an untenanted wilderness, nor on forming a mixed
collection of races.[2] The distinction and purity of our line has
enabled us to remain in unaltered possession of the land of our
birth. We sprang from its soil, and can use the same names for
it as for our own blood. We are the only Greek state which can
properly call our land by the names of nurse, fatherland and
mother. Any justifiable pride, any reasonable claim to leadership, any memories of ancestral greatness, must show some
such racial origins to support it.

Such, then, is the extent of our original gifts which were
bestowed on us by fortune. The total of the benefits we have
conferred on others can most properly be reckoned by a systematic account of the history of Athens from the beginning.
To her, it will be found, the debt is almost entirely due, not only
for the uncertainties of war, but for all the organization which
forms the *milieu* of daily existence, the basis of political activity,
and the means of life itself. But we are bound to set in the forefront, not those benefits whose insignificance makes them forgotten and neglected, but those others whose great importance
in the past, as now, sets them everywhere high in the memory
and in the records of all mankind.

First, then, it was by means of our country that the first need
of man's nature was provided. Even though the story may be
legendary, it is still right that it should be recounted here.[3]
When Demeter arrived in this district in her wanderings after
the rape of Persephone, she showed favour to our forbears for
benefits received which can only be mentioned to the initiated,
and conferred two gifts which surpass all others, the cultivation

2. This seems to refer to the semi-legendary 'synoecism of Attica', a
voluntary merger of small sovereignties in Attica which in historical times
was celebrated by the feast of the Synoikia. The inhabitants of Attica were
commonly supposed to have been autochthonous.

3. See note 7 below.

of crops, which brought a higher form of life than that of the animals, and the mysteries, which gave their initiates more enviable hopes both for the conclusion of this life and for all eternity. It has come about that this city of ours was endowed not merely with the love of the gods, but with love for mankind, and consequently, having such wonderful things in her control, did not grudge them to others, but allowed all to participate in them. We still perform these mysteries annually, and the state gave instruction about the practices conveyed to man and their development and value. These are facts which, with a little information added, no one could call in question.

First of all, the very reason which might be given for disregard of these stories, namely their antiquity, provides a valid argument for belief in their truth. Their frequent repetition and universal currency are good cause for regarding them as reliable, though not recent. Secondly, we need not merely resort to the claim that the story and the tradition of it come from a remote period. We can bring stronger evidence. Most of the cities retain a memorial of the original benefit conferred on them in the form of first fruits sent annually to ourselves, and those which omit the practice have frequently been enjoined by the Pythian oracle to bring the amount due and perform the ritual hereditary in our community. Indeed there is nothing which more clearly commands belief than words of divine enactment and wide agreement among Greek peoples, which claim the witness of ancient myth and present practice alike, and are subscribed to by current custom as well as by past records. In addition, if we set all this aside and begin our investigation from the beginning, we shall find that the first inhabitants of the earth did not at once come upon a form of life like the present, but gradually joined together to bring it into being. So there is no one who could be thought to have a better claim to have been divinely provided with it, or else to have searched and found it themselves, than men who are universally admitted to have been the first inhabitants, the most talented craftsmen and the greatest devotees of religion. To dilate on the degree of honour due to men who brought such benefits is time wasted. No one could devise a reward to equal such achievements as theirs.

So much is to be said about this greatest and first and most universal of benefactions to mankind. About the same period[4] it was Athens who observed that most of the world was in the hands of non-Greek people, while the Greek states were confined to a small territory, and led by shortage of living space into conspiracy and internal strife, and decimated by starvation or war. She refused to acquiesce in these circumstances, and despatched leaders into the Greek cities, who took over the most poverty-stricken, established themselves in command of them, fought and defeated the non-Greek inhabitants and founded communities on all the islands, securing the preservation of their followers and the remaining population alike. They left these with enough room for survival, and afforded the colonists more than they had before, since they took in all the territory which, as Greek states, we now own. Thus they also rendered easy later attempts at colonization on Athenian lines, by making it unnecessary to face the risks of acquiring territory for it, when colonists could go and live within the limits we had laid down. It is impossible to point to any title to leadership more our own than that which was established before most Greek communities were first colonized, or more suitable than that which dispossessed non-Greek people and brought such prosperity to the Greeks.

But the part she played in these great achievements did not make Athens neglect the rest of her duty. This was the beginning of her services to others, the provision of sustenance to the needy, which is a necessity for men who intend to order the rest of their lives well. But taking the view that a life that depended solely on this did not offer enough motive for the desire to live, she gave enough care to the rest to ensure that the good things of human existence which are not the gift of providence, but the result of our own thought, should in no case be outside the provision of this city, and in most instances be due to it. When she took charge of the Greeks, they lived a lawless life in scattered communities under the violent control of arbitrary power, or at the mercy of anarchy. She freed them of these distresses by means

4. Already in Herodotus' time the ancients spoke of a migration to Ionia led by Athenians, and perhaps caused by the pressure of the Dorians into north-western Greece and the Peloponnese (see Herodotus, I, 147).

either of her own government or of her example, by being the
first state to establish law and organize a constitution. This is
proved by the fact that in the earliest cases of homicide, plaintiffs who desired to decide the issue by the use of reason instead
of force brought their suits under Athenian law.[5] Indeed it is
true of the crafts as well, that those which concern the necessities
of life, and those directed to its well-being, were discovered or
approved by Athens, and so passed on to other people for their use.

The general organization of Athens was contrived in a spirit
of such universal friendliness and consideration as to be suited
both to impecunious communities and to wealthy ones with
rising prosperity, to be of value alike to the successful and the
unsuccessful in their home affairs. Both classes derive benefit
from us, and gain either pleasant association or a refuge of the
utmost security. Again, as states in this region do not enjoy
individual self-sufficiency, but production is inadequate or excessive in different respects, and conditions are such that it is
very difficult to secure markets, in some cases for exports, in
others for imports, Athens brought assistance in these difficulties
as well, by establishing in the Piraeus a central market of overwhelming value, in which commodities which others found it
hard to secure piecemeal elsewhere, could all be obtained.

The institution of festivals, then, has earned proper commendation for numerous reasons: it promotes among the Greek
states the custom of a general truce,[6] at which ingrained differences are settled and there is a meeting together, and then after
the performance together of religious ceremonies the relationship of blood which exists between us is recalled, and improved
relations maintained with each other, renewing old associations
and making new ones. In these festivals the time is not wasted
either for private individuals or for outstanding leaders. They
allow a general gathering of the Greeks, and there is an opportunity for the latter to demonstrate their successes, and for the
former to watch the competition of the great. Neither group

5. Traditionally the first court for homicide was the Areopagus, whose
foundation derived from the trial of Orestes by Athena, which is the subject
of Aeschylus' *Eumenides*.
6. The so-called 'sacred month' at Olympia.

need feel discontented, but both have some ground for pride, either as they see the endeavours of the athletes for their gratification, or as they reflect that everyone has come to enjoy watching them. Such are the benefits which arise from these festivals, and here too Athens has not failed to shine. She has provided numerous displays of the highest quality, outstanding for their lavish expenditure or artistic excellence or both, while the vast number of our visitors has ensured that any benefit derived from association together is also included in her bounty. A further gift of Athens is the chance to encounter the most sure of friendships, the most varied of associations, and to witness contests not only in the field of speed and strength, but of word and wit, and of all sorts of other activities, for which high prizes are awarded. In addition to the prizes Athens actually offers she incites others elsewhere, because awards made by Athens are held in such esteem as to be the object of universal admiration. Finally, festivals elsewhere are periodic gatherings which soon disperse, while the city of Athens is a standing festival for its visitors which will last to the end of time.

Philosophy took a part in the discovery and development of all these, and gave us education in the field of affairs and civilized relations with each other, drawing the distinction between misfortunes due to ignorance and others due to necessity, and teaching us to guard against the former and bear the latter bravely. Our city showed the way to it, and also gave honour to skill in words, which is the desire and the envy of all. She realized that this alone is the particular and natural possession of man, and that its development has led to all other superiorities as well. She saw that other activities showed such confusion in practice that wisdom was often the way to failure in them, and folly to success, while good and skilled powers of speech were outside the scope of the ordinary people, but were the province of the well-ordered mind: and that in this respect wisdom and ignorance are furthest apart, and the birthright of a liberal education is marked not by courage, wealth and similar distinctions, but most clearly of all by speech, the sign which presents the most reliable proof of education, so that a fine use of words gives not merely ability at home, but honour abroad. Athens has so far outrun the rest of mankind in thought and speech that her disciples are the masters of the rest, and it is due to her that the word 'Greek' is not so much a term of birth as of mentality, and is applied to a common culture rather than a common descent.

But I do not wish to dwell on the parts when I have undertaken to deal with the whole, nor do I make these the grounds for my eulogy of Athens for lack of the ability to turn to the battlefield for it. This must suffice, therefore, for the claim to honour in these fields. I think our ancestors deserve no less glory for the dangers they have faced than for their other benefactions. The struggles they endured were not slight, nor few, nor undistinguished. They were many, they were severe and they were tremendous. They fought sometimes for their country, sometimes for the freedom of the world; for they continued always to make their city the common possession of the Greeks and the defender of the victims of oppression. This leads to some accusations of wrong policy, because of our habit of support for the weaker, as though such ideas were not consistent with the desire to eulogize us. It was not failure to realize how much safer large alliances are that led us to this policy, but, despite a much keener realization of the consequence than others show, we still preferred to support the weaker even against our advantage rather than join the aggression of the stronger to secure it.

An indication of the character and power of Athens can be seen in some of the appeals that have been made to her. I omit recent or trivial instances, but long before the Trojan wars, which must provide evidence in a dispute about ancestral custom, we were visited by the children of Heracles, and a little earlier by Adrastus, son of Talaus, king of Argos.[7] Adrastus

---

7. Throughout these treatises of Isocrates, as elsewhere in ancient prose, the modern reader may feel surprise at the naïveté of reference to stories to which we now deny historicity. Sometimes, as in the case of the Heraclidae, we may rationalize them on a basis of greater knowledge. What are called the Dorian invasions, tribal movements in a southerly direction into the Greek peninsula, were seen as the return of the children of Heracles (Heraclidae), who were driven out by his great persecutor, Eurystheus, and at one time

came after the disastrous expedition against Thebes because he found himself unable to recover the dead at the Cadmeia, and asked Athens to assist him in a calamity which affected everyone, and to refuse to see the dead in battle left unburied, or ancient custom and established law set aside. The children of Heracles, in flight from the malice of Eurystheus, turned their face away from other cities as unable to help them in their plight, and assumed that ours alone was capable of gratitude for the benefits their father had conferred on all mankind.

This gives a clear indication that even at that time Athens showed the quality of leadership. No one would deign to ask aid from an inferior or a subject state to the exclusion of the more powerful, especially in an issue which was not private, but common to all, and which was unlikely to find any champion except the aspiring leaders of Greece. Secondly, they were not deluded of the hopes which had led them to seek their refuge with our ancestors, who took up arms against Thebes on behalf of the dead in battle and against the power of Eurystheus on behalf of the children of Heracles. In the first case they mounted an expedition and compelled the surrender of the dead to their relations, in the second they made a counter-attack against the Peloponnesian troops which had invaded our territory with Eurystheus, and defeated him and halted his aggression. They had earned admiration for other actions, but these exploits added to their high repute. These were no narrow successes, but made so great a change in the fortunes of each of the suppliants that Adrastus went home rewarded for his mission to us by the complete success of his request, despite his enemies, while Eurystheus, who had expected to force his demands, found himself a prisoner and compelled to make supplication in his turn. His adversary had been more than human, born of the blood of Zeus, a mortal, though with divine strength, and Eurystheus had subjected him to servitude and hardship without a pause. But when he treated Athens wrongly, his pride was reversed,

---

given refuge in Athens (see Bury, *History of Greece*, p. 80). Adrastus, defeated in the attack of the Seven against Thebes, is said to have fled to Athens and been given refuge and support.

and he was made subject to his victim's children and brought to a contemptible death.

There are many benefits to Sparta which stand to our credit, but that of the Heraclidae is the only one which it has occurred to me to mention. My point is this; after the opening of relations with them by our rescue of them, the ancestors of the present kings of Sparta, that is the successors of Heracles, descended on the Peloponnese, captured Argos, Lacedaemon and Messene and were the founders of Sparta, and so initiated all their present prosperity. This should have remained in their minds, and they ought never to have invaded a country which showed them the way to such high fortune. They ought not to have brought danger to a city which had itself risked danger for the sons of Heracles, or to have first offered a kingship to his descendants and then tried to bring slavery upon the state which preserved them. But if we set aside questions of gratitude and fair dealing, and return to the original thesis in the accurate pursuit of truth, it is not the tradition of Greek states that leadership should go to the invader against the native, to the recipient against the giver of benefits, or to suppliants against their preservers.

There is an even briefer proof. Of the Greek cities, apart from our own, the greatest were, as they are still, Argos, Thebes and Sparta. But it is clear that our ancestors so far surpassed them all, that it was we who, when Argos was worsted, gave orders to Thebes at the height of her pride, and who in aid of the Heraclidae defeated Argos and the other Peloponnesians, and brought safety to the founders and leaders of Lacedaemon, when they were in danger from Eurystheus. Thus, as far as concerns the premier power in Greece I do not know what clearer proof could be given.

I think I should also say something of Athenian action outside Greece, especially as the thesis I have set myself concerns the leadership against non-Greek peoples. A complete account of all these emergencies would take too long, but I will try to describe the greatest of them in the same fashion as just now. Of all these races the highest capacity for rule and the strongest power is in the hands of Scythia, Thrace and Persia; all these have actually harboured designs against Athens, and she has been in conflict with them all. In fact what argument remains valid for any opposing view, if it is proved that every Greek state which could not secure her rights turned to us for aid, and every non-Greek state which sought to enslave Greeks made her first attack on us?

The most famous of these wars was that with Persia, but in a dispute about ancestral precedence equally valuable evidence can be derived from ancient times. When Greece was still inconspicuous, Athenian territory was invaded by Thracians under Eumolpus, the son of Poseidon, and by Scythians together with the Amazons,[8] the daughters of Ares, not simultaneously but during the time when both peoples were trying to gain power over Europe. They hated the whole Greek race, but they made particular complaints against Athens, and thought that by this means conflict with a single state would lead them to the control of all. They did not succeed, but though our ancestors were their only opponents, they suffered defeat on a scale that might have suggested a war against the whole of mankind. Evidence of the extent of the disaster they incurred is to be seen in the length of time through which its story endured, which would not be true of any but a most outstanding calamity. In the case of the Amazons it is recorded that not one of the invading force returned, and the remainder were driven from their country as a result of their defeat here. In the case of the Thracians, though they had previously been neighbours of Athens, the distance between them was greatly increased by the battle in question, which allowed the establishment of numerous races, tribes of all lands, and large cities in the intervening space.

These were splendid feats, exploits fitting for claimants to leadership. Akin to these which I have described, and credible in their descendants, were the great achievements of the wars against Darius and Xerxes. They were the greatest of wars, and brought more perils than ever occurred at any one time. The enemy supposed themselves invincible from their numbers, and our allies thought their own courage incomparable, yet the Athenians surpassed them, in each case, in their appropriate respect, showed their superiority in the face of every danger, and

8. These mythical wars appear in Greek authors of the great period, as the prototype of wars between Athens and Eastern peoples.

on the field were awarded the palm of honour, soon afterwards to
assume the sovereignty of the sea by the gift of the other Greeks
without dispute from the states which now wish to seize it from us.⁹

Let no one suppose me ignorant of the many services performed by Sparta for the Greek cause in those great days. But
this is a reason to give still greater praise to Athens: that with
such rivals to emulate she yet outdid them. But I desire to speak
at somewhat greater length of these two cities, and not pass them
too quickly by, so that we may have a memorial of both, of the
courage of their ancestors and their hostility to the enemies of
Greece. Yet I do not forget how hard it is for one who comes
late in time to speak of subjects which an earlier generation has
made its own in words spoken by the leaders of the state on days
of public funeral.¹⁰ It cannot but be that the greatest of these
themes have been used before, and only those of lesser note
remain. However, since it is of value to my discourse, I must not
hesitate to recall some of what is left.

The most numerous of good services and the highest praise
belong, I think, to the men who risked their lives for Greece.
Nonetheless, the generations which held power in the two cities
before that cannot properly be forgotten. It was they who gave
their successors their first training, who first urged the people to
the pursuit of courage, and made them fierce antagonists of the
invader. They did not neglect the common good, nor exploit
their own gain in it to the disregard of others. They made it
their care, because it was theirs, but rightly kept their hands
from what was not. They did not reckon value by monetary

9. Isocrates refers several times to this general acknowledgement which
accorded to Athens the meed of valour in the Persian wars, but it does not
appear in Herodotus. The 'Thalassocracy' or sovereignty of the seas, which
before 487 B.C. was held to belong to Aegina (and previously to other states)
went to Athens as the result of war with Aegina in 487 in which Themistocles
is credited with persuading the Athenians to build ships, thus leading to her
supremacy at sea. At Salamis Aegina was given the first prize for bravery,
but after this the superior force of Athens and the desire of Sparta to confine
herself to the defence of her own land territory gave Athens a natural
supremacy.

10. Notable occasions of this sort, besides the Funeral Oration of Pericles
translated above, had included one such speech by Gorgias and one attributed to Lysias on the dead in the Corinthian war in 394 B.C.

gain, but believed the safest wealth, and the most honourable, to lie in a life conducive to present honour and to the glory of generations to come. They did not compete with each other in daring, nor promote rash conduct of set purpose, but they were more afraid to be dishonoured by fellow-citizens than to die nobly for their city, more ashamed at public wrong than now we are at personal misconduct.

The reason for this was their concern for the precision and right intent of the laws, not so much those of private commerce as those of common practice in the life of every day. They knew that for men of high breeding there is no need of many written words, since agreement in a few principles will bring accord in private and in public alike. So deep-set in their thought was the community, that even their dissensions arose, not in dispute as to which party should destroy the other and control the state, but which should be first to bring benefit to the whole. Their clubs were associated, not for individual advantage, but for the good of the nation.[11] The same interest governed their approach to the affairs of other states. They treated the Greeks with courtesy, not insolence, laid claim to command, not despotism over them, and desired to be called their leaders, not their masters, for their protection, not their injury, winning their cities to friendship by good treatment, not subduing them by force. They made their word more sure than an oath is in our time, and expected to abide by an agreement as binding beyond avoidance. They did not take pride in power so much as credit for restraint, demanding in themselves the same attitude towards inferiors as they received from superiors, since they thought of their individual towns as their own abode, but of Greece as the fatherland of all.

It was by adopting ideas such as this, and by training the young in these habits of thought, that they raised so fine a generation in those who fought against the invaders from Asia, that neither thinker nor poet could reach the height of what they accomplished. And this may well be pardoned. It is as hard to praise men of outstanding merit as men of none. If these last have no actions worthy of praise, the first can engender no fitting

11. On the political clubs see Lysias, *Eratosthenes*, 43, p. 49, and note.

praise to match their actions. What praise could be of equal
measure with the stature of men who far surpassed the warriors
at Troy, in so much as while the latter took ten years over a
single city, these in a short time beat down the whole strength
of Asia and not merely gave safety to their own countries, but
freedom to the whole of Greece? How should they shirk any
effort, any toil, any danger, to gain fame in life, when for the
glory they were to acquire at its ending they were so prepared
to die? Indeed, I think the war itself was divinely inspired in
admiration of their high courage, to ensure that such character
should not go unobserved or come to death without renown,
but should be accorded the same honour as the sons of the gods,
who are called demi-gods. For while their bodies bowed to the
necessity of their mortal nature, heaven made immortal the
memorial of their virtue.

Continuously, then, our ancestors and those of Sparta were in
contention with each other, but at that time it was contention
for the prize of honour, and they held themselves not in enmity
but rivalry. They did not seek the enslavement of Greece, to
court the outside world, but about the safety of all they were of
one mind, and contention arose only for the decision which
should further it.

They made the first display of their courage in facing the force
sent by Darius. When the Persians made their descent on Attica,
the Athenians did not wait for their allies, but made their own
a war which was universal, and met an army which had dis-
dained the whole force of Greece with their own force alone.
That little army met their tens of thousands as though the
danger belonged to other lives than theirs. The Spartans, without a moment's delay after the report of the war in Attica let all
else go and came to our aid, with all the eager haste which
would greet the ravaging of their own country. And here is
proof of their speed in matching us. It is said of our ancestors
that within one day after they heard of the Persian landing they
were there to resist on the boundaries of their soil, and won the
battle and set up their trophy in token of victory, while the
Spartans within three days and nights covered twelve hundred
stades with their army on the march. Such great haste there was,

in the one army to take their part in meeting danger, in the other to meet it before assistance reached them. Later comes another example, when the second expedition[12] came, under the leadership of Xerxes, who left his royal domain and ventured to make himself a general, collecting the whole of Asia in his army. About him everyone has used extravagant language, only to find it came short of the truth. He showed such overbearing arrogance as to think it a slight thing to subdue the land of Greece, and to desire to leave a memorial higher than human pride can reach. He did not give way until he had planned and helped to force into being a design which is the common talk of the world, how with his army he sailed over the mainland and marched on foot across the sea, when he bridged the Hellespont and drove a canal through Athos.

Against the pride and the achievements of Xerxes and the host of which he was master, the Greeks marched out. They divided the responsibility, and the Spartans moved to Thermopylae against the land army with a thousand picked men and a few of their allies, to hold the pass and prevent further advance there. Our own people went to Artemisium, with a citizen force of sixty triremes to meet the whole enemy fleet. Their courage was not inspired by contempt of the enemy so much as by desperate rivalry among themselves. Sparta envied Athens the victory at Marathon, and hoped to set themselves on equal terms, in the fear that twice successively our city might be the saviour of Greece. For Athens, the main desire was to preserve the glory she had won, and to make it universally clear that courage, and not chance, had won that victory, while her second aim was to induce the Greeks to fight at sea, to demonstrate that in battle at sea as well as on land courage is more than numbers.

But equal though their daring was, their fortunes were unequal. The Spartans were destroyed, and for victory in spirit they laid down their lives. It would be wicked to say that they suffered defeat, when not one of them deigned to seek escape. Our navy defeated the Persian advance guard, but

12. i.e. the Second Persian War of 480 B.C., as distinct from the campaign of Marathon in 490.

hearing that the enemy held the pass, they sailed back, and employed such strategy thereafter, that, great as had been their achievements before, in the later fighting they were still more outstanding. The allies were one and all in despondency. The states of the Peloponnese were engaged in fortifying the Isthmus and looking to their personal safety. The others were under the subjection of the Persians, and co-operating with them, except such small cities as had been left out of consideration. Twelve hundred Persian ships were on the sea, and numberless land forces threatened Athens. Without a glimpse of safety, her allies lost to her and every hope dispelled, she might not only have escaped the dangers that faced her, but accepted the signal honours which the king held out to her in the hope that, if he could join the Athenian fleet to his, he would at once subdue the Peloponnese as well. Yet they refused his gift, and would not let anger at their betrayal by the Greeks rush them willingly into compromise with Persia. They prepared to fight for their own survival, yet they pardoned the rest who had preferred slavery. They held that humbler states should seek their safety as they might, but the claim to the leadership of Greece was not consistent with escape from danger. A man of nobility, they felt, preferred a glorious death to a life of dishonour; and in the same way, for a state that stood among the greatest it was more profitable to be blotted out of the sight of men than to be seen in slavery. It is obvious that this was their belief, since, being unable to match themselves against both forces at once, they took with them their whole people and sailed to the neighbouring island,[13] to make it possible to encounter each in turn. Indeed, it would be impossible to point to any greater lovers of their country or of the Greek people than men who, to avoid bringing slavery on the rest, could endure to see their city desolate and their land devastated, their sacred places pillaged and their temples set on fire, and the whole war centred on their own country. Even this was not enough for them: against twelve hundred warships their intention was to sail alone. They were not left to carry it out. The Peloponnesians

13. Most, according to Herodotus, moved to Troezen on the mainland, but some to Aegina and Salamis.

were filled with shame at such courage, and reflected that, if our force were first destroyed they would never survive, and if we succeeded, their cities would be dishonoured. They were thus compelled to take their share of the danger. The uproar which took place in the action, the shouting and cheering which are general in sea battles, I do not think it worth taking time to describe. I am concerned with what is particular and relevant to leadership and in accord with my previous argument. So outstanding was Athens, with her force unimpaired, that after the city was sacked she contributed more ships to combat the perils of Greece than all the others who fought at Salamis, and there is not a man so much at enmity with us as not to agree that it was due to this battle at sea that we were successful in the war, and that it was a victory which should be put down to Athens.

Indeed, when a campaign is intended against Persia, who ought to be given the leadership of it? Surely it should go to the winners of the greatest distinction in the previous encounter, who have many times stood alone in the forefront, and in the ranks of the allied force have been given the highest award of valour. Surely it should go to the country which abandoned its own land for the safety of the rest, which in ancient times founded most other states, and later rescued them from the most signal disasters. It would be outrageous treatment if, after shouldering the greatest burden of hardship, we were expected to receive less than our share of honour, if, after standing in the front line, we were compelled to follow in the rear of other states.

Up to this point I am sure that it would be universally agreed that the credit of Athens for benefactions to the Greek state stood the highest of all, and the leadership would rightly be accorded to her. Afterwards, however, we are already faced by the accusation that after assuming the naval supremacy, we have been guilty of a great deal of harm to Greece, including the enslavement of Melos and the destruction of Scione.[14] My

14. Scione and Melos, both reduced by Athens and the population massacred or enslaved, were not parallel cases. Scione had been a full member of the Athenian Confederacy, but had revolted and asked aid of the Spartan

own view is, first, that it is no proof of bad rule that some opposing states are shown to have been severely dealt with. It is a much more certain proof of good administration of our allies' affairs that none of the states under our control was involved in such troubles. Secondly, had any other states dealt more leniently with the same situation, they might have reason for criticizing us. On the other hand, if this is not true and if in fact it is impossible to control so large a number of states without punishing offenders, we are surely to be commended for successfully maintaining our empire for the longest possible period with the fewest instances of harsh treatment.

I suppose there would be general agreement that the best leaders to represent the Greek world are the people under whom their subjects are happiest. Under Athenian supremacy we shall find that individual households progressed most rapidly towards happiness, and cities increased in size. This is because with us there was no envy of advancement, no artificial creation of disturbance by promoting dissident parties so that both should court Athenian influence. Our belief was that amity between allies meant the success of the empire as a whole, and we organized all states on the same legal system. We thought of them not on the basis of despotism, but of alliance, in which we maintained control of the whole, but allowed freedom to individual members; though we lent assistance to democracy and opposed autocratic powers, because we held it to be unjustifiable that the majority should be subject to the minority, that a class suffering from economic, but no other inferiority should be ousted from political control, that in a country which belongs to all there should be a distinction between the constitutionally privileged and unprivileged, or that when nature has made men fellow-citizens, law should disfranchise them.

Such among others were the objections to oligarchy which led us to establish for other states the same constitution as our own, and I hardly think it needs justifying at greater length, especially

---

Brasidas and his army which had marched to Northern Greece. Melos had never joined Athens at any time, but was attacked for her obduracy in refusing. Both incidents, however, were held reprehensible, and Isocrates is clearly in some difficulty to make a defence.

when it can be done in brief. Athenians lived with it for seventy years[15] untouched by tyranny, free from external domination, untroubled by civil disaster and at peace with all the world.

Good sense demands gratitude for this far more than obloquy for the cleruchies,[16] which we sent to depopulated states for local protection, not out of self-interest. As evidence of this I point out that we held very little territory in relation to our numbers, but a large empire; that our warships were twice as many as all the rest together, and fit to contend with twice as many again; that Euboea, lying close to Attica, was naturally well sited to assist our naval empire, while her other assets made her superior to any of the other islands, and we could control her better than our own territory. I add further that we knew from the experience of Greek and non-Greek alike that the greatest prestige went to states which by devastation of their neighbours secured for themselves a life of idleness and plenty; yet nonetheless none of these facts could induce us to maltreat the people of Euboea. We were alone among the great powers to tolerate a lower standard of living than people who were accused of subservience to us. Indeed, had we pursued our own interest we should presumably not have conceived a desire for Scione, which, as is common knowledge, we handed over to our refugees from Plataea, leaving untouched the large territory of Euboea, which would greatly have increased the prosperity of us all.

Such has been our character, and such the proofs we have given of our freedom from rapacity. Yet we are unjustifiably accused by participants in the decarchies,[17] who did violence to their own countries, made the atrocities of their predecessors look trivial and left no room for further extremes in the history of wickedness – men who on the pretext of Spartan principles pursued exactly the opposite practices, who lamented the

15. A rough estimate of the period between the Persian wars and the fall of Athens.

16. The 'cleruchies' were a device whereby Athens allotted land in conquered Greek territory to Athenian citizens, who became the owners. These settlements formed a major grievance against the Athenian Empire in the Peloponnesian War.

17. On the decarchies and harmosts see 117 and sectional introduction.

miseries of Melos but inflicted irreparable injury on their own people. There is nothing in the realms of wrong and cruelty which they have left unexplored. They set their trust in defiance of law, they cultivated treachery as right conduct, they chose subjection to one of their own Helots[18] in order to outrage their own countries, they did more honour to murderers who shed the blood of their people than to their own fathers, and reduced us all to such inhumanity that, while in the previous happy period even small misfortunes found numerous sympathizers, the multitude of personal distresses in the time of the decarchies made us give up all pity for each other. No one had time for sympathy with others. There was no limit to their cruelty, no one was remote enough from politics not to be forced into contact with the suffering to which men of that character drove us. Can they be unashamed, when they treated their own cities without regard to law, and accused ours without thought of justice, can they, in addition, dare to criticize the public and private cases we conducted, when they put more to death without trial in three months than were ever brought to trial under the Athenian empire? As to banishment, civil strife, disruption of law, denial of rights, violence against children, indecency against women, seizure of property, there is no end to the list. I have this to add of the whole subject, that the wrong-doing of which we were guilty could easily have been ended by a single decree, but the murders and the lawlessness of that period would be beyond any remedy.

And indeed the present peace and the autonomy, which does not exist in Greek states, though it appears in the terms of peace, are neither of them to be preferred to Athenian rule. It would hardly be possible to be enthusiastic about a state of affairs in which the sea is commanded by pirates and the cities taken over by fighting men; when instead of war taking place between cities about territorial claims it is carried on inside the walls between fellow-citizens; when more cities are reduced to subjection than before peace was made; and when the frequency of revolution makes the inhabitants of cities more despairing than the victims of exile, because they live in dread

18. Lysander was born of a Helot (i.e. serf) mother.

of the future, while the others always expect to return. So far are the people removed from freedom or autonomy that in fact they are either under tyrannies, or under the power of the harmosts, or in some cases depopulated or subject to Persian despotism. Yet, when the Persians had the daring and the unjustifiable insolence to cross into Europe, we dealt with them to the extent of not merely ending their invasion but forcing them to undergo the devastation of their territory, and submitting the fleet of twelve hundred ships to the humiliation of being prevented from launching a single warship west of the Phaselis.[19] They were compelled to keep the peace and wait for events instead of feeling confidence in their existing force. That this situation was due to the great qualities of our ancestors is clearly proved by the disasters of Athens. The decline of our empire coincided with the beginning of troubles for the Greek states. After the defeat at the Hellespont,[20] when the leadership of Greece passed to others, Persia gained a naval victory and secured the control of the sea, won the supremacy over most of the islands, made a descent on Laconia, stormed Cythera and sailed round the Peloponnese, raiding the country.

The clearest complete view of the transformation is given by a parallel reading of the terms of peace in our time and now.[21] It will be clear that then it was we who laid down the boundaries of Persian territory, and in some cases stated tribute to be paid, and barred her from access to the sea. Now it is the King who directs the affairs of the Greek world, gives orders for individual states, and almost establishes a governor in each city. There is little else lacking. It was he who took control of the war and presided over the peace, and he who remains as a supervisor of the present political situation.

19. The reference is to the mysterious Treaty of Callias in 448 B.C. which concluded hostilities between Greece and Persia.

20. The defeat at the Hellespont is the battle of Aegospotami, and the naval victory over the Greeks is that of Cnidus in 394 B.C. under the Athenian Conon, once a commander at Aegospotami, who later joined Persia to serve against Sparta.

21. The treaty referred to is the King's Peace or Treaty of Antalcidas, in which Persian terms were imposed on Greece by Sparta. See sectional introduction.

He is a despot to whose court we sail to accuse each other. We call him the Great King, as though we were subject prisoners of war, and if we engage in war with each other, it is on him that our hopes are set, though he would destroy both sides without compunction.

We should be ready to reflect on this, to resent the present position, and to desire to regain our place as leaders. We should cast blame on Sparta for beginning the war with the aim of liberating the Greeks and in the end reducing so many of them to subjection, for causing the revolt of the Ionian states from Athens – which had been the source of their foundation and, so often, their salvation – and putting them at the mercy of Persia, the enemy of their very existence and their unceasing opponent in war. At that time they were incensed at our perfectly legal claim to control some of the cities, but now that these have been reduced to such slavery they feel no more concern for them. For these unfortunate cities it is not enough that they should be subject to tribute and see their strong places in the grip of their enemies; their communal troubles are intensified by personal suffering greater than under the tax collectors of Athens. No Athenian inflicts such cruelty on his slaves as the Persian punishment of free men. But the greatest misery of their subjects is the compulsion to join in the fight for slavery against the cause of freedom,[22] and to endure the prospect of defeat which will cause their instant destruction or a success which will plunge them further into slavery in the future.

At whose doors but Sparta's can we lay the blame for this? Despite their great power they stand aside and watch the pitiable plight of people once their allies, and the construction of a Persian empire out of the strength of Greece. In the past their habit was to expel tyrants and to give their support to the people, but now they have so changed as to make war on free states and throw in their lot with despotism. The city of Mantinea, at any rate, is an instance. After peace had been made, the Spartans razed it to the ground. They captured the Cadmeia

22. On the war between Artaxerxes and Evagoras see 134, 141 below, and sectional introductions p. 100.

at Thebes. They have now laid siege to Olynthus[23] and Phlius, and they are giving assistance to Amyntas, king of Macedon, Dionysius, tyrant of Syracuse and the Persian power in Asia, to help them to supremacy. Indeed, it is surely a paradox that the leading power in Greece should make one man master of such countless numbers, and not allow the greatest of cities to be autonomous, but drive it to an alternative of slavery or utter disaster. The final degradation is to see the claimants to the leadership of Greece at war day after day with Greek states and in permanent alliance with a non-Greek people.

Let it not be supposed to be due to ill will that I make a somewhat brusque reference to these subjects after a prelude promising reconciliation. My intention in speaking in this way is not to defame Sparta in the eyes of others so much as to put a check on her, in so far as my discourse is able, and to put an end to her present attitude. It is impossible to prevent wrong aims or inspire better without strong denunciation of the old ones. But one should put down damaging attacks as accusation, but beneficent criticism as admonition. The same words should be taken in different ways according to the intention. A further criticism could be made of the Spartans, that they reduce their neighbours to serfdom for the benefit of their own country, but they refuse to do the same in dealing with the common interests of the allied states, when they could settle differences with us and make the whole non-Greek world subsidiary to the Greek. Yet for men whose pride springs from nature rather than circumstances this is much more the right pursuit than collecting tribute from islanders who deserve our pity, when we see them farming the rocky hills for lack of good soil, while the mainland[24] is so productive that most of the land can be left idle and great wealth comes from the only part which is cultivated.

It seems to me that an outside observer of the present political situation would condemn it as utter insanity on both sides that

23. Olynthus capitulated to Sparta in 379 B.C. (see general introduction to Demosthenes (1)). Phlius in the Peloponnese was also reduced by Sparta in 379. On Dionysius see note 35 below.
24. i.e. inhabitants of Asia Minor under Persian power as a result of the Peace.

we risk disaster on such slender grounds, when we might enrich
ourselves in a moment: we tear our own land to pieces and
neglect the harvest we could reap in Asia. Nothing is more
profitable for Persia than to ensure our continuing to fight each
other for ever. But we never think of interference with Persian
affairs or of raising insurrection. When chance disturbances do
arise, we help to allay them. Now that there are two armies
engaged in Cyprus[25] we allow Persia to make use of one, and
besiege the other, though both are Greek. The rebels are
friendly to Athens and subordinate to Sparta, while in the case
of Tiribazus' force, the most valuable section of his infantry
comes from Greek districts, and the greater part of his naval
force was commissioned in Ionia and would be much readier
to share in a raid on Asia than to fight against each other for
little profit. We never give any thought to this. We enter into
disputes about the Cyclades[26] when there are these important
cities which we have gratuitously presented to Persia, and
which she holds, or will hold, or on which she has designs, and
while she shows justifiable contempt for all the Greek states.
The King has indeed achieved something which is beyond the
achievements of all his ancestors. He has secured the admission
from both Athens and Sparta that Asia belongs to him, and has
assumed such authoritative control of the Greek cities there as
either to raze them to the ground, or build fortifications in
them. And all this is due to our folly, not to his power.

Yet there exists a sense of the impressiveness of Persian
dominion, and an idea of it as invincible because of the great
impression it has made on Greek history. My own opinion is that
this is no deterrent, but an incentive to the proposed expedition. If we have achieved agreement while Persia is in difficulties,
and yet are still going to find it hard to face her, there must surely
be a great deal to fear, should there come a time when Persian
affairs are secure and Persian opinions united, while we are in
our present condition of mutual hostility. Nonetheless, even if
such critics do agree with my contentions, they still do not give
a correct view of the power of Persia. If they could show that
the King has in the past proved superior to the two principal

25. See note 22 above.   26. Islands in the south Aegean.

cities together, they might justifiably try to rouse some alarm. But as this is not the case, as Sparta and Athens were in opposition when he simply added his weight to one side and caused its prestige to rise, this is no evidence of his power. In such circumstances as this it often happens that a comparatively small power may turn the scale. I could use this argument in the case of Chios, and say that whichever party it joins becomes the leading naval power. But it is not a sound criterion of the power of Persia to ask what have been the results of her accession to one side or the other. What have they been from her own unaided engagements? First of all, after the revolt of Egypt, what steps have been taken against its inhabitants? The King sent his most distinguished generals, Abrocomas, Tithraustes and Pharnabazus, to the scene.[27] They waited three years, during which they did more harm than good, and concluded with so dismal a failure that the rebels, not content with freedom, are now trying to secure control over their neighbours. Next there is the operation against Evagoras. He holds a single city, which, however, is surrendered to Persia by the terms of the peace. His kingdom is an island and he has had an initial setback at sea, and can only muster three thousand light infantry for the defence of his land. Yet this modest force is beyond the power of the King of Persia to overcome. He has already wasted six years, and if the past is evidence for the future there is more probability of a new revolt than of the suppression of this one by the siege; such are the delays which are endemic in the King's affairs. In the Rhodian War[28] he had the good will of Sparta's allies because of the severity of the conditions imposed on them, while he made use of Athenian crews and enjoyed the leadership of Conon, who was both outstanding as a general and unequalled in Greek opinion for reliability and experience of the hazards of war. Yet despite the assistance of so redoubtable an ally the King allowed the power which stood for the defence of Asia to remain under siege by a hundred ships, during which time he kept his men short of pay for fifteen months. So as far as the King was concerned the force would have been disbanded

27. This occasion is not known except from this passage.
28. On the Rhodian War, see sectional introduction.

two or three times, though owing to its commander and the
alliance made with Corinth they continued till at last they
won a victory. This is the truly royal and impressive aspect of
his proceedings which is so unceasingly emphasized by the
advertisers of the King of Persia's greatness.

Thus it cannot be claimed that the examples I quote are not
apt, nor that I pursue the trivial at the expense of the important.
It is to avoid such a charge that I have made the greatest events
in Persian history my subject, without forgetting other items,
such as Dercyllidas'[29] success against Aeolis with a thousand
men, or Dracon's capture of Atarneus and his devastation of
the Mysian lowlands with three thousand light troops, or
Thimbron's action in crossing and ravaging the whole of Lydia
with only a few more, or Agesilaus' conquest with the army of
Cyrus of virtually the whole district beyond the Halys.

The army which wanders about with the King gives no more
ground for anxiety than Persian bravery. The former were
given clear proof by the army which marched in with Cyrus[30]
that they were no better than the coastal forces. I omit their
earlier defeats, assuming them to have been divided in their
views and unwilling to contend whole-heartedly against the
King's brother. But in circumstances such as after the death of
Cyrus, when all the people of Asia were united, their conduct
was so inglorious as to leave no room for the customary eulogies
of Persian courage. They faced six thousand Greeks,[31] not

29. Dercyllidas was Spartan commander in 399 B.C., having succeeded
Thimbron. Draco was a harmost appointed by Dercyllidas. The campaign of
Agesilaus is that of 395 B.C. (see Xen., *Hellenica III*, 4 seqq.)

30. The rebellion of Cyrus is referred to here for its indication of weakness in Persia and for Cyrus' instigation to the Greeks in Asia to revolt.
This is Cyrus II, not Cyrus the Great. He made an attempt against his
elder brother, Artaxerxes II, to secure the Persian throne in 401 B.C., marching
on Babylon with an army of mercenaries, many of them Greek, including
10,000 hoplites, among them the writer, Xenophon. At the battle of Cunaxa
close to Babylon Cyrus was killed owing to his own impetuosity. The
Greek leaders were betrayed and put to death by the Persians, and the
remainder marched back to Trapezus (Trebizond) on the Black Sea, and so
home. (See Xenophon's *The Persian Expedition*, tr. Rex Warner – Penguin
Classics. See also Isoc., *Philip*, 89 2077, p. 155 below.)

31. Xenophon says 8600.

picked for their quality, but whose poor circumstances made it impossible for them to make a living at home, who were ignorant of the country, devoid of allies, betrayed by their associates in the march and deprived of the leader they had followed. Yet the Persians proved so inferior to them that the King was in despair at the position and, having no opinion of his own forces, resorted to seizure of the mercenary leaders, despite the truce, in the hope that this illegality would throw their army into chaos, preferring sacrilege to open fighting with them. His plot failed, because the army did not dissolve, but nobly weathered the storm. As they departed, the King sent Tissaphernes and the cavalry with them. The Greeks were the victims of their machinations throughout this march, but still carried it through as though they were under escort, despite their fear of un- inhabited districts and the feeling that their best hope was contact with the enemy in strength. To conclude the subject, this force had not been conducting a raid to take booty or sack a town, but had been in direct warfare against the King; yet they returned to the coast in greater safety than his representa- tives in a mission of friendship. It thus seems to me that the Persians gave a clear demonstration of their own lack of spirit. They have been defeated frequently in the coastal region, and when they crossed into Europe they met with retribution in either a miserable death or a dishonourable escape till eventually they made themselves ridiculous at the very doors of the Royal domain.[32]

None of this is extraordinary; it is entirely natural. It is impossible for people with an upbringing and political habits of this kind either to know what courage is in general, or to record victories over their enemies. There could never arise either an outstanding general or a good soldier in a régime like this, where the bulk of the population is utterly incapable of sustain- ing discipline or facing danger, and lacks the toughness needed for war after an upbringing more suited to servility than that of servants with us. Men of the highest distinction there live a life

32. This appears to refer merely to the battle of Cunaxa, when after the death of Cyrus the victorious Greeks waited a long time close to the King's palace, and then could not be kept from marching home.

which exists on a single level, not one of shared outlook or free institutions. They spend their time showing arrogance towards one class and subservience towards another, in the fashion most calculated to demoralize humanity. Physically their wealth has made them over self-indulgent, while psychologically their monarchical constitution makes them degraded and cringing, since they are subject to constant regimentation at the palace itself, falling to the ground and practising all sorts of self-humiliation, and prostrating themselves in adoration of a man whom they address as a god, while it is gods rather than men whom they treat with disdain. Hence the so-called satraps, who go down to the coast, do not demean their upbringing there, but continue in the same habits; they are untru: worthy with friends and unmanly with foes, and live a life of servility or arrogance, contemptuous of their associates and subservient to their enemies. They certainly maintained Agesilaus' army for eight months at their own expense, while the forces on their own side were deprived of their pay for an equivalent time. They allotted a hundred talents to the captors of Cisthene,[33] but their own men from the expedition to Cyprus were treated with greater insolence than prisoners of war. Think of Conon, who after commanding the forces of Asia and shattering the empire of Sparta was outrageously seized for execution. Think of Themistocles, who defeated Persia at sea in defence of Greece, and was then handsomely rewarded by them. Indeed how can one accept friendship from men who punish their benefactors and show such blatant flattery of their attackers? There is no one in Greece they have not treated wrongfully. There has been no cessation of their conspiracy against the Greek people. There is nothing in the Greek world which is not at enmity with the men who in that earlier war did not scruple to pillage the sacred places and the temples, and burn them. For this reason one may praise the people of Ionia, who pronounced a curse upon anyone who should disturb or seek to restore the sacred places which were burnt – not for lack of the means to achieve it, but to secure for later generations a memorial of the impiety of Persia, a token of everlasting distrust

33. Captured by Agesilaus.

against the perpetrators of this sacrilege, and of warning to
avoid and dread them, since they are seen to have done battle,
not merely against ourselves, but against our worship of the
gods.

I could say something similar of my own fellow-citizens.
With all other states with which they have been at war they
accept reconciliation and forget their differences. But to the
peoples of the mainland they do not even offer gratitude for
benefits received, so unrelenting is the anger they feel against
them. There were many whom our ancestors condemned to
death for joining the Persian enemy, and even now at public
meetings, before any business is done, curses are pronounced
against any citizen who proposes agreement with Persia. And at
the celebration of the Mysteries the Eumolpidae and Kerykes,
by reason of this hatred, proclaim the segregation from the rite
of all non-Greek peoples as they do of homicides. So ingrained
in us is this hostility that in the realm of myth we most enjoy
dwelling on the Trojan and Persian wars, in which we can read
of their disasters. It will be found that it is the wars between
Greeks and Persians which have given rise to the composition
of triumphal odes, while wars between Greeks have inspired
laments, and that the first are sung at feasts, the second recalled
in mourning for disaster. And I think even the poetry of Homer
gained prestige from its magnificent eulogy of the warriors who
fought against the non-Greek world, and that was the reason
why our ancestors desired his art to be celebrated in musical
competitions and in the education of the young, so that our
frequent hearing of the epics should enable us to learn by heart
the hostility which was ingrained there, and so that emulation
of the prowess of the men who fought there should lead to a
desire for similar achievements.

It seems to me, therefore, that there is an overwhelming number of inducements in favour of this war, and chief among them
the present opportunity, which ought not to be let pass. It
would be contemptible to neglect it when it is here and regret
it when it has gone by. There is nothing more that we could
need for an attack on Persia beyond what is ours already.
Egypt and Cyprus are in revolt against her. Phoenicia and Syria

have been devastated by the war. Tyre,[34] which they had set great store by, has been captured by their enemies. The majority of the Cilician towns are in the hands of our allies, and the rest can easily be acquired. Lycia has never been subdued by any Persian. Hecatomnus, the governor of Caria, has actually been for some time in secession from Persia, and he will take his stand with us openly when we choose. From Cnidus to Sinope there are Greek settlements in Persian territory, which will need no persuasion to go to war, only the lifting of the ban against it. Indeed, with such bases as these at hand and a war of such magnitude already besetting Asia, what need is there for too precise a calculation of probabilities? When they are being worsted by small parts of our forces, there can be no uncertainty about their prospects if they are compelled to face the whole.

This is the situation. If Persia takes a stronger control of the seaboard towns, by stationing larger garrisons in them than before, perhaps the islands round the coast, such as Rhodes, Samos and Chios, may incline to support her. But if we take prior possession of them, the probability is that districts like Lydia, Phrygia and the rest of the inland region will come under the power of our expedition in that quarter. For this reason we need to hurry and not waste time, to avoid the fate of our predecessors, who appeared later than the Persians, lost some of their allies, and were compelled to fight at a numerical disadvantage, when they could have made their crossing with the combined forces of Greece and subdued each of the regions in turn. It has been proved that in cases of war against a mixed force of varying origins one should not wait for them to attack, but try conclusions with them while they are still dispersed. Our predecessors made this initial mistake, though they set it right afterwards, when they engaged in those tremendous battles. But, if we are wise, we shall take precautions from the start, and try to effect a surprise by establishing an army against Lydia and Ionia, in the knowledge that even the King finds unwilling subjects in the continental Greeks, and raises a greater force to surround him than any of theirs. And when we

34. Phoenicia, Syria and Tyre were attacked by Evagoras.

transport a force stronger than that, which we could easily do
if we tried, we shall be able without danger to harvest the
produce of all Asia. It is far more distinguished to fight him for
his kingdom than to wrangle with each other for the leadership.

It would be better to make the expedition during the present
period, so that our generation, which has had the losses, can
enjoy the gains as well, and not spend all their days in suffering.
The past has had enough of that, and every sort of misery
appeared in it. There are many ills that fall to the lot of human
kind, but we added to the list more than our necessary share
of them in the wars, foreign and civil, which we brought upon
ourselves, with their consequences either of violent death at
home, or wandering abroad, men, women and children as
refugees, or mercenary service for lack of other subsistence, and
death in battles fought for enemies against our own kith and
kin. Of these ills no complaint has ever been uttered. The
sufferings in the poetical realm of fantasy are thought to be
matter for grief, but the actual severe sufferings which can be
seen as due to war are so far from rousing pity that the sufferers
are more prone to rejoice at the ills of others than at their own
good fortune. Possibly my own simplicity may come in for
ridicule, if I lament the sorrows of men in the circumstances of
the present, when Italy has been devastated, Sicily enslaved,[35]
so many cities surrendered to non-Greek captors, and when the
remaining parts of the Greek world lie in the utmost danger.

I am surprised that leading statesmen in the Greek cities
think a lofty attitude suitable, though they have always been
incapable of either speech or reflection to mitigate such a
situation. If they deserved their reputation they should abandon
all else, and introduce and discuss the subject of the expedition
against Persia. They might have helped to achieve something
of value, and if they did give up before success came, at least
they would have left their oracular utterances for the future.
But men of the highest reputation spend their interest on
concerns of no importance, and have left it to men like me, who

35. Dionysius I, tyrant of Syracuse, invaded Southern Italy in 391 B.C. and
succeeding years, after being successful against the Carthaginians, who had
conquered much of Sicily a few years before.

have abandoned politics, to advise on such vital issues. Nonetheless, the more our leaders confine themselves to trivialities, the more vigorous should be the precautions which the rest of us take to avoid these besetting differences. At present peace agreements are vain. We make no settlement, only postponement of our wars, while we wait for the opportunity to do irreparable damage to each other. However, we must put these internecine conspiracies aside, and set ourselves to activities which will enable the cities to live in greater security and mutual confidence. There is a simple and easy approach to this. It is impossible to reach a secure peace without sharing in war against Persia, or to find agreement among Greek states, until we derive our assets from the same sources and engage in war against the same opponents. With this achieved, and with the removal of economic anxiety – which dissolves friendships, changes association into enmity and plunges human beings into war and dissension – we shall not fail to reach unity and enjoy good will towards each other. With this aim we should regard it as essential to lose no time in transferring this expedition into Asia, in the certainty that we shall never derive any benefit from our own internal warfare until we decide to use the experience we have acquired from it against Persia.

Perhaps it may be thought that the treaty makes it desirable to wait and avoid haste or precipitate action about the expedition. The treaty means that states set free are grateful to the King, as the author of this freedom, while those which have been surrendered to Persia are making bitter complaints, first against Sparta, and then against others who took part in the negotiations, as being responsible for their being forced into slavery. However, we should surely abolish these agreements, which have given rise to an opinion that Persia is the protector of the Greek states and the guardian of peace, while some of ourselves are concerned to injure and impair it. Most ridiculous of all, it is only the worst of the items agreed in the treaty that we continue to observe. The clauses which confer independence on the islands and the Greek cities in Europe have been long in abeyance, and, though they remain inscribed on the pillars, are invalid. On the other hand those which are to our discredit and

involved the surrender of a number of our allies are still in
existence, and we ensure their validity. These we ought to
delete and not allow to exist for a single day longer, because they
are orders given to us, and not agreements. It is universally
understood that agreements are made on a basis of mutual
equality for both parties, while orders are designed to reduce
the status of one side unfairly. We are therefore justified in
accusing the delegates who negotiated the peace on the ground
that they were sent by the Greeks, but acted for Persia. They
should have agreed either that each side should hold its own
original territory, or that each should hold its own new acquisi-
tions, or should hold what it held when peace was made. One
of these principles should have been established and made a basis
of unbiased negotiation, and finally so drafted. In the event no
consideration was allowed to Athens or Sparta, and Persia was
given complete mastery over Asia, as though it had been the
King we had been fighting for, or the Persian empire which
had been long established and we recent settlers, though in
fact this position was a late acquisition of theirs, while we had
long been the leading powers among the Greeks.

However, I think a different approach will show more clearly
the dishonour we have undergone and the rapacity of Persia.
The whole world beneath the stars consists of two parts, called
Asia and Europe, and the King has appropriated half of it under
the treaty, as though he were making a division with Zeus instead of a settlement with men. He has compelled us to have
this inscribed on stone and erected in public temples, where it
forms a far finer trophy to him than any he has won in battles.
The latter were in honour of small and isolated successes, but
this records one which covers the entire war, and has been
gained at the expense of all Greece. For this our anger is
justified, and we must take means to secure retribution and
order things properly in the future. It is a disgrace to expect
in private to think of foreigners as servants, and in public to
allow so many of our allies to be slaves to them; a disgrace that
at the rape of a single woman the Greeks of the Trojan wars
should join the victims of wrong in such universal indignation
as to refuse any compromise till they had razed the presump-

tuous offender's city to the ground, while we exact no combined retribution for the insult to the whole Greek race, though we have the power to make our very dreams realities. This is the only war which is in fact preferable to peace. It is more like a religious mission than a campaign, and desirable for the advocates both of peace and of war, the former of whom would be enabled to harvest their gains in security, the latter to acquire great wealth from the possessions of others.

There are numerous respects in which these activities will be found valuable to us. What nation ought to be the object of attack from a country which has no selfish gain to seek, but is concerned solely with sheer justice? Surely it should be the one with a history of past activity and present conspiracy against Greece, with a permanent relation towards us of the same kind. Against what nation is envy justified for men who, while not exactly lacking in spirit, have yet tempered courage with moderation? Surely against a people who have been invested with superhuman power, but have deserved less than the meanest among ourselves. Upon whom ought a campaign to be launched by men who have always set their faces towards piety, though they have a thought also for advantage? Surely upon a people who by nature and heredity alike are their enemies, who are possessed of the highest wealth and the smallest power to defend it. In all these points it is Persia which is vulnerable.

In addition we shall not even trouble the states by levying soldiers, the greatest burden to them in our internal wars. I think there will be far fewer who wish to stay at home than those who desire to be on the march. Who is there, young or old, who will be so inert as not to desire a part in this army, led by Athens and Sparta and gathered for the freedom of the allied Greeks, sent out by all Greece for retribution on Persia? How great is the renown, the memory, the glory one must suppose those who show the highest valour in such stirring deeds will enjoy in their lives or leave behind them in death! Since the men who fought against Trojan Paris earned such glory by the capture of a single city, what must we think will be the eulogies bestowed on the conquerors of all Asia? There will not be a man in the realms of action or speech who will not strive with all his power or all his thought to create a memorial of his conception and of their courage which will live through all eternity.

By now I no longer feel the same as at the beginning of my oration. I was then of opinion that I should be able to find words to fit my subject. But I cannot attain to its magnitude. Much of my intention has escaped me. So you must yourselves share my imagination of the good fortune which would be ours, if we could change the present war among ourselves to a war against the mainland, and transfer the wealth of Asia to Europe. You must go home not merely in the capacity of hearers: any who are strong in the sphere of action should raise each other's spirit to reconcile our city with Sparta; any who lay claim to oratory should abandon their futile disquisitions on subjects like money deposits,[36] and turn their competitive instincts towards the answer to the question what improvements can be made in my presentation of the subject. You must reflect that great promises preclude petty considerations and arguments which are unproductive for the audience who accept them, and demand those whose fulfilment will free them from their present impotence, and convince their hearers that they have found the road to high success.

36. Norlin (Loeb edition) quotes the suggestion that the 'deposit theme' became a recognized phrase for a hackneyed exercise in the schools of rhetoric.

ISOCRATES: PHILIP

INTRODUCTION

The address to Philip of Macedon was composed when Isocrates was over ninety, and its tone differs from the pride and optimism of the Panegyricus. *Between 380 and 346, when the* Philip *appeared, there had been many changes. The decline in the fortunes of the new Athenian League and the eclipse of Sparta by Thebes may have led Isocrates by about 370 to the belief that unity could only be established under an individual leader. He is supposed to have sent addresses about that time to both Jason of Pherae (see 119) and Dionysius of Syracuse. If so, the deaths of both very soon afterwards frustrated his hopes. But this tradition is disputed, and the letter which has been thought to make a similar approach to Archidamus, King of Sparta, can hardly have had the same intention. A different kind of change is the increasing use of mercenaries by Greek states (see 96), whose citizens became less ready to take part in wars such as that which Isocrates was advocating. On the other hand this made it easier to think in terms of any army under a single great leader, a situation which would also serve to employ them.*

The rise of Thebes was the outcome of the battle of Leuctra, which followed a Spartan invasion of Boeotia in 371. The tables were turned on Sparta in the battle, which was the first of the triumphs of Epaminondas, the general on whose brilliance the Theban supremacy rested. With this disaster the rule of Sparta ended for the time, and Thebes took steps to make sure it should not return. Apart from the expulsion of the Spartan harmosts (see introduction to the Panegyricus) *more constructive action was taken in the formation of an Arcadian League, in the foundation of the new city of Megalopolis as its capital, the rebuilding of Mantinea as a counterpoise to Sparta and the reconstitution of Messene. In addition, Boeotian invasions of Spartan territory followed; a Boeotian general, Pelopidas, made inroads into Northern Thessaly, and freed some of its states from the monarchical* rule it had suffered under Jason, in favour of a Thessalian league; and in 366 a Theban force seized Oropus from Athens (53).

In this process Thebes acquired some of the unpopularity which had once been Sparta's. Athens now began to side with Sparta (see Demosthenes, For Megalopolis), more resentment was caused by Theban attempts to overcome Achaea and, in 363, by the reduction of all Thessaly, while a year earlier Thebes earned as deep hatred as other Greek states in their times by the total abolition of a neighbour state, Orchomenus, an old rival in Boeotia. With the death of Epaminondas in 362 at the otherwise successful battle against Sparta at Mantinea, Thebes' domination began to decline, having roused as much hatred as Sparta's.

But Thebes was still a power in the Greek world, as is shown by her part in what is called the Sacred War (54). In 356 Phocis, in central Greece, having abandoned the now weakened Theban alliance into which she had been forced found herself a target for Thebes, who resented the independence of a former subordinate. Phocis included the sanctuary of Delphi (which is the reason for the title given to this war) and the centre of the so-called Amphictyonic League (74 and note). This ancient body, formed to protect the sacred site, suffered the fate of other similar institutions in offering a frequent pretext for manipulation and exploitation by its most powerful members. By means of it Thebes imposed heavy fines on Phocis for alleged sacrilege, with the implied threat of attack in default of payment. Phocis, however, under the vigorous leadership of Philomelus and Onomarchus, responded by seizing Delphi itself and its treasure, and sent appeals to anti-Theban states like Sparta. The resulting war lasted long, and by it Phocis was raised to a temporary supremacy under Onomarchus. Philip was brought into the conflict by Thessaly, and was at first defeated by Onomarchus. But his part in the war brings us to the speeches of Demosthenes, and must be included in the introduction to them (pp. 170–71).

ISOCRATES: PHILIP

You must not be surprised, Philip, if I do not begin with the thesis which is to be put before you and will follow immediately, but with one in which I discussed Amphipolis. [1] I wish to say a little about this first, to make clear that it is not due to ignorance or failure to realize my present physical decline that I have set myself the task of addressing you, but that it is a well-advised, deliberate intention.

Realizing the many ill effects of the recent war between you and Athens over Amphipolis, I set out to discuss this country and the surrounding district in terms unlike any put forward either by your supporters or by Athenian speakers, and as far removed as can be from the ideas of either. Each party uttered an incitement to war, to accord with your respective aims in it. I gave no opinion on controversial subjects, but confined myself to what seemed the line most conducive to peace. I declared that you were both mistaken in your view of affairs, and that you yourself were really fighting in support of the interests of Athens, and she of the kingdom of Macedon. It was to your advantage that this territory should be in our hands, and to ours that no attempt at all should be made to secure it. The impression of this discourse on my audience was such that none of them gave the conventional eulogy of its precision of form and purity of diction, but they admired its truth to reality. They concluded that the only way to bring competition between you to an end was, on your side, a belief that friendship with Athens was worth more than the revenues of Amphipolis, and on hers the lesson that she should avoid colonies of the sort which have four or five times been the ruin of their settlers, and look for districts further removed from the possible demands of empire and nearer to people with habits of subservience, like the region of Cyrene colonized by Sparta. In addition, you would realize that although nominally ceding the district you would actually keep control of it as well as retaining good rela-

1. On Amphipolis, see sectional introduction to Demosthenes (I) (p. 170).

tions with Athens (you will have hostages for our good behaviour in every colonist who goes into your territory), while our people would be brought to understand that their control of Amphipolis would compel them to the same good relations with Macedon as they were led to maintain with Amadocus[2] in the past by the presence of the settlers in the Chersonese.

This long discussion led my hearers to hope that the view could be disseminated, and that you would both admit your error and arrive at a beneficial compromise. Whether their idea was sense or nonsense, they must have the responsibility of deciding. But while I was engaged on this business, and before its conclusion, you made peace, and this was sensible. Any form of settlement was to be preferred to a continuance of the miseries of the war. I felt the same satisfaction at the decisions of the peace, and I thought it would be beneficial not merely to us, but to yourself and the Greek states. Yet I could not disengage my mind from the implications of the subject, but turned at once to the problem of securing the settlement and preventing my country from the quest for new enemies after a short interval. I turned the matter over in my mind, and concluded that the only way to prolong peace for Athens was a decision by the leading states to relax their own tensions by carrying the war into Asia, and to agree to merge the conflicting self-interests of different states in an attempt upon Persia, a policy which I did in fact recommend in the *Panegyricus*. With this idea in mind and with the belief that it would be impossible to arrive at a basis which would be more attractive or have broader application or greater general advantages, I was fired to write again about it. I have not forgotten my own situation, and I realize that this proposal does not presuppose a man of my age, but one in the full flower of life and of quite exceptional character. I am also aware of the difficulty of expressing the same thesis twice with tolerable results, especially if the earlier publication was of a kind to give even its critics more to imitate and admire than its fervent supporters. However, I set

2. Amadocus shared with Cersobleptes the rule of Thrace from 359 B.C., and favoured Athens. According to Demosthenes (*Aristocrates*, 183) his resistance to Philip saved Athens from war with Cersobleptes in 353.

aside these difficulties, and was ambitious enough in my old age to hope to combine what I had to say to you with a conclusive demonstration to my own pupils that to disturb general assemblies with addresses presented to the entire crowd of participants is in fact to address no one. Such disquisitions have as little effect as the legal and constitutional enactments of a degree thesis. If one is to avoid an idle waste of words and achieve something of value, and if one claims to have something of general interest to say, one must leave conferences to others and secure a figure of high reputation in the fields of both thought and action to represent one's views, if anyone is to be expected to attend to them. It was in this determination that I formed the plan of discussion with you, not for personal reasons; although I should set great store by your enjoyment of such a discussion, this was not my real intention. I observed that other men of distinction lived under the control of their state and of law, and were not in a position to exceed instructions, and in addition were quite inadequate for the ideas to be put forward. You were alone in being privileged by fortune to enter into diplomatic relations with any state you liked, and to say anything you thought fit, and also in being better equipped than any other Greek state with money and power, which are the only natural assets towards persuasion or compulsion. Indeed I regard even my project as likely to need both these, because I intend to urge you to take the lead in a movement for Greek unity and in the campaign against the non-Greek world. Persuasion will be desirable in dealing with the Greeks, and compulsion of practical use against the others. This aim covers the whole discourse.

I shall not hesitate to mention the trouble I have been given by some of my pupils, because I think it may be useful to hear it. When I revealed to them my intention to address a discourse to you, not for the purpose of display or as an encomium on your military successes, which will be done by others, but in an attempt to urge you to a more fitting, noble and valuable course of action than that on which you have lately been engaged, they were so terrified that old age might have driven me out of my wits, as to give me an unprecedented reproof: it would be

an intolerable folly to contemplate a message of advice to
Philip, who might in the past have thought himself less of a
diplomat than some, but after his recent noteworthy achievements must think himself more so than most. 'Furthermore,'
I was told, 'his entourage includes the keenest intelligences in
Macedonia, who, even if they are inexperienced in most other
matters, know better than you do where his advantage lies.
You will find a number of Greeks who have settled there, men
who are by no means without distinction or ability, and his
association with them has not at all dimmed the greatness of
Macedon. The position he has achieved is ideal. There are no
weak points in it. Why, the previous controllers of Macedonia,
Thessaly, have been brought to such close relations with him
that any section of them feels greater confidence in Philip than
in other groups of their own fellow-citizens. The states in that
district he has either brought into his own orbit by the benefits
he has conferred, or liquidated the really troublesome. He has
reduced Magnesia, Perrhaebia and Paeonia and made them
subject states. He has secured his power, official as well as
actual, over the great bulk of Illyria, except for the Adriatic
coast.³ With all this behind him do you not suppose he will
think it pure stupidity to address discourses to him, and conclude that you have a very distorted idea of the power of words
and of his own intelligence?' I will omit my initial dismay on
hearing this, and my subsequent recovery and reply to it in
detail, for fear of appearing complacent at making a neat
defence. But having, I thought, given a moderate rebuff to the
critics who had ventured to attack me, I ended with an undertaking that they should be the only people in Athens to whom
I would disclose the discourse, and that I would accept their
decision what to do about it. What their frame of mind was
when they left, I cannot tell. But after a few days, when the
text was completed and I showed it to them, they changed their
attitude enough to feel ashamed of their outspoken tone, to
regret what they had said and own that they had never made a
greater mistake. They showed more enthusiasm than my own

3. Before meddling in Greek politics Philip established his control of
Macedonia itself, of which these are divisions. (See Demosthenes Ol. *1*. 13.)

for sending the speech to you, and added their hopes that I should be received with gratitude for it not only by yourself and by Athens, but by the Greek states in general.

The reason for this narrative is to prevent anything in my initial argument, which may appear unreliable or impossible or unsuitable, from giving you a distaste for the rest and making you reject it or feel the same as my friends. I hope you will keep an open mind till you have heard the whole, because I think I shall have something to say which is both needed and valuable. At the same time I realize how much difference there is between the spoken and the written word, and how generally it is assumed that discussion of serious and urgent subjects is spoken, while a speech which is under contract and intended for display is written. This is not an unreasonable distinction. When oratory is shorn of the appearance and the voice of the speaker, and of the rhetorical transitions of a set speech, when it lacks the immediacy and intensity of a practical aim and there is no feeling of participation in actual persuasion, when the speaker is denuded of this and reads a mere list of items with an unconvincing lack of telling intonation, I think it is reasonable if his hearers find him dull. This present discourse may suffer from some such appearance of dullness, because I have not endowed it with the felicities of rhythm and decoration which I used myself in my earlier days, and demonstrated as contributing to enjoyment and conviction alike. My age precludes all this, and nowadays I am satisfied if I can achieve a simple presentation of the actual matter. In your case too I think it will be better to neglect inessentials and confine yourself to this. It will enable you to form the best and most accurate judgement as to whether there is force in my contentions if you discount the distaste connected with academic dissertations, and take each item as it is intended, without regarding them as incidentals to be treated idly, but giving each the philosophic thought of which it is said that you are also capable. Such deliberation is to be preferred to common opinion as a basis for your view. This, then, completes the preamble to what I have to say.

I shall now turn to the actual subject. I maintain that without disregarding any of your own interests you should attempt to reconcile the states of Argos, Sparta, Thebes and Athens. If you succeed in bringing these four together, there will be no difficulty in securing agreement between the rest, which are all subordinate to these, go to one or other of them for protection at any time of alarm, and derive assistance from them. Thus you have only to persuade four states to a reasonable attitude to relieve all the rest of a multitude of troubles.

You should know that it would be inappropriate for you to treat any of these states with indifference, if you view their history in relation to your own ancestors. You will find in each case a story of great good will and substantial benefits towards your people. Argos is your country of origin, and justice demands that the same precedence shall be accorded her as to your own parents.[4] Thebes is the patron town of the founder of your race, to whom she renders particular offerings and sacrifices. Sparta has conferred on his descendants permanent kingship and primacy, while Athens is credited by reliable tradition with contributing to the immortality of Heracles in a manner which is easily ascertained but would be irrelevant here, and with the preservation of his descendants.[5] Unaided, she withstood tremendous dangers in the struggle with Eurystheus, whose violence she curbed, to rid the Heraclidae of their recurrent perils. For this the survivors, not merely on that occasion, but at all times, can feel justifiable gratitude to Athens, to whom they owe their lives and the benefits they enjoy. But for the survival of the Heraclids they could never have come into being.

In view of the character of all these states you should have no disagreement with any of them. But unfortunately we are all by nature more prone to be wrong than right. So we should take joint responsibility for the past, and for the future take care to avoid repeating it. You should keep in mind the question

4. See Panegyricus, note 7. The Greeks were very conscious of parentage and descent. Perdiccas I, from whom Philip was descended, was said to have been himself descended from an Argive hero (see Herodotus V, 22), and perhaps belongs to the seventh century B.C.

5. Apparently because Athens was supposed to have offered the first sacrifices to Heracles.

what benefit you can confer, to prove clearly that your conduct does honour to yourself and to their past achievements. The moment is now yours. If you pay your debts in gratitude, they will consider after this long interval of time that you are conferring an initial benefaction. And it is fine to feel that you are a benefactor to the greatest of states, and at once to make the benefit as truly yours as theirs. Apart from this you will dissolve any ill feeling that may exist between you. In the light of immediate good offices the disharmonies of the past are forgotten. Indeed it is also an obvious truth that in all human affairs nothing is so keenly remembered as assistance in misfortune. You see the misery that war has brought these states, and the parallel between them and individuals in a quarrel, who are irreconcilable while their anger is rising, though after inflicting injury on each other they part of their own accord without out further mediation. This I think these states will do, unless you give them your attention.

It may be possible to venture objection to my proposals on the score that I am trying to persuade you to an attempt which is not feasible, because friendship between Argos and Sparta, or between Sparta and Thebes, is impossible, nor could a balance of power ever take the place of long habits of competition. When Athens held the principal power among the Greeks, and similarly when Sparta did, I do not think anything of the sort could have been attained, because each side could easily have frustrated the attempt. Now, however, I no longer take this view. All the states have, I know, been reduced by misfortune to one level, and I think they will be much more inclined to accept the benefits of unanimity than the old competitiveness. Further I agree that there would be no other figure capable of effecting this reconciliation. For you, however, these difficulties would not exist. It can be observed that you have already achieved much that seemed beyond hope or reason, which makes it not unbelievable that this may be a further union which you alone could bring about. High ideals and great ability should not confine themselves to the scope of ordinary men, but attempt what is only open to a character and a power such as yours.

I am surprised at the view that any of these proposals is

impracticable, and I wonder that those who hold it should not be aware from their own knowledge or that of others that history records numerous wars of importance whose termination has brought great mutual benefit to the contestants. There has never been more violent enmity than that of the Greek states against Xerxes. Yet the friendship which followed[6] was one which, as everyone knows, Athens and Sparta valued more than that of the states which helped to secure the power of each. There is no need to go far back in history or outside Greece itself. A full consideration of the disasters of the Greek states will show that they were a mere fraction of the misery brought to Athens by the Theban and Spartan hegemonies. Nonetheless, at the time of the Spartan campaign against Thebes and their attempt to disrupt Boeotia and disestablish its communities,[7] Athens led a force to obstruct their intentions. Then, when fortune changed, and Thebes combined with all the Peloponnesian states in a drive for the eradication of Sparta, Athens was again the only state to join in alliance with Sparta, and was in fact responsible for her survival. In view of such changes of attitude, and in the realization that the states have little thought of fixed hostility or sworn declarations or anything else except what they think is in their own interest, and that this is what they foster and preserve with the utmost eagerness, it would be sheer stupidity to suppose that this tendency will not persist, especially when they will have you to superintend better relations, as well as the impelling force of their own interest and the compulsion of their present miseries. My own opinion is that with these factors to help you everything will contribute to a satisfactory result.

6. A very hard statement to understand. As the text stands we should read 'whose friendship'. I translate to render the apparent intention. We should take Xerxes to stand for any Persian monarch and the passage to refer to the end of the Peloponnesian War or the late years of the fourth century when both Athens and Sparta turned to Persia for financial support. (See note on the passage in M. L. W. Laistner's edition of the speech.)

7. The history of Thebes constantly depends on whether the city was at any given time to be regarded as the overlord of the rest of Boeotia, or merely one among the many separate cities included in it. Thebes itself naturally tended to seek the former position, her rivals to desire the latter.

I think you can best discover whether the attitude of the states to each other is peaceable or the reverse, if we discuss, not too superficially, but not in too great detail either, the most important features of their present position.

First consider Sparta, not long ago the military and naval leaders of Greece. They have undergone such a change since the battle of Leuctra as to have been deprived of the supreme power in Greece and lose a valuable section of their Spartiate citizens,[8] who preferred to die rather than survive defeat by the previous victims of their own autocracy. In addition, they went on to see all the Peloponnesian states who had previously followed their standard against others now siding with Thebes in an invasion of their territory; they were faced with extreme danger not merely to their crops in the open, but to their wives and children in the very city and in the centre of government.[9] It was a crisis in which failure meant instant destruction, and even success brought no release from trouble. They have been under attack from the surrounding inhabitants of their own district,[10] distrusted by everyone in the Peloponnese, hated by the bulk of the Greek states, harried night and day by their own underlings. They have not a moment's freedom from campaigns, from fighting or from support of their own people in distress. Worst of all, they live in continuous fear of a reconciliation between Phocis and Thebes, who might return and subject them to greater ruin than before. In fact one cannot fail to suppose that people with this attitude would be overjoyed to see in charge of peace negotiations a man of importance capable of bringing existing warfare to a close.

Next Argos can be seen to be either in a similar case or a worse. Since the foundation of their state they have been like

8. On the true Spartiates the whole strength of Sparta depended.

9. Xenophon (*Hellenica*, VII, v.) records that Epaminondas actually entered Sparta on one occasion, but 'whether by divine agency or desperation' the Spartans repulsed him and his army.

10. Laistner thinks this phrase refers to the state of Messenia as refounded by Epaminondas in 369 (after Leuctra) by recalling and enfranchising Helots from the region, or others expelled by Sparta from Naupactus, where they had been settled by Athens. Sparta hoped to regain this reconstituted Messenia during the Sacred War (see Demosthenes, *For Megalopolis*, p. 174).

Sparta, in a condition of warfare with their neighbours, with this difference: that Sparta has operated against weaker, and Argos against stronger, opponents, which would be universally owned to be the most disastrous position. Their misfortunes in war have been such that almost every year they have had to see their country ravaged and ruined. Worst of all, when their enemies give them an interval from attack they put the wealthiest and most distinguished of their own people to death, and derive more satisfaction from it than others do from killing their enemies.[11] The reason for their disordered history is simply war, and if you can bring it to an end, you will not merely rid them of their own troubles, but enable them to initiate better relations with others.

The position of Thebes you know. After their magnificent victory and the prestige they earned from it, their misuse of their success brought them to a level with the defeated and frustrated. They had no sooner overpowered their opponents than they cast consideration aside and began to harass the Peloponnesian states, made unwarrantable inroads on the freedom of Italy, threatened their neighbours at Megara and made encroachments on Athenian territory,[12] while they sacked Euboea, and sent a naval force to Byzantium, as though sea and land alike were to come under their domination. Finally they entered upon war with Phocis in the hope of a rapid defeat of the Phocian towns and an extension of their rule over the whole surrounding district by gaining control of the Delphic treasure at the expense of their private funds. None of these hopes materialized. Instead of capturing the towns of Phocis they have lost their own, while their invasion of enemy territory does less damage than they undergo in returning to their own. In Phocis they kill a few mercenaries, who are better dead than alive, while on their retreat they lose the most distinguished and daring patriots they possess. Their affairs have taken such a turn that after cherishing hopes of universal domination they

11. An oligarchic conspiracy at Argos in 371 is said to have led to the death of 1200 citizens.

12. On Theban history of this time see sectional introduction. The Athenian territory mentioned is Oropus (see Demosthenes, *For Megalopolis*).

now depend on you for their hopes of survival. I therefore believe that they too will soon fall in with your instructions and advice.

So it would only remain for us to deal with the state of Athens, were it not that she had the good sense to make peace before the others.[13] As it is, I think she will make a positive contribution to the project, particularly if she can grasp that your arrangements are designed for the campaign against Persia.

That it is not impossible for you to unite these states I think has been proved by what I have said. I go further and say that I think I shall be able to give numerous examples to show that it will be easy. If it is shown that others in the past have made attempts which, though no more distinguished and lofty than my proposals, have yet been harder and more troublesome and have succeeded, what further argument can there be against expecting you to be quicker to achieve an easy task than a hard one?

First consider the case of Alcibiades. He was banished from Athens,[14] and found that previous victims lay down under disaster because the great name of Athens overawed them. But he refused to adopt their attitude. He thought he should attempt to force a return, and decided to make war on Athens. It would be impossible to deal in detail with every event of that time, and at this moment it would perhaps be tiresome. But he caused confusion alike to Athens and to Sparta and the rest of Greece, which brought upon ourselves the consequences which are common knowledge, while the others were involved in disasters bringing calamities whose horrors have not yet faded, and Sparta, after her apparent success, traces her present troubles to Alcibiades. It was at his instance that they were lured into naval ambitions, only to lose their military supremacy as well. Thus were one to date the rise of their present disasters from their rise as a naval power, it could not be written off as untrue. Alcibiades, then, had all these responsibilities on his head when

13. Peace of Philocrates, 346 B.C.
14. In 415 B.C. (see introduction to Andocides, *On the Mysteries*, p. 61). He returned in 407.

he returned to Athens, covered with glory, though not greeted with universal applause.

Conon's career [15] a few years later was the converse of Alcibiades'. Defeated in the naval battle at the Hellespont, not by his own fault, but that of his fellow-commanders, he was ashamed to return home. He sailed to Cyprus, where he spent some time on his private affairs, after which he learnt that Agesilaus had crossed to Asia with a large force, and was devastating the district. Being a man of great spirit, though devoid of all assets except his own person and his determination, Conon conceived the idea of a military and naval defeat of Sparta, then the leading state in Greece, and sent word to the Persian commanders with a promise to bring it about. There is no need to go further. He was joined by a fleet near Rhodes, and won a battle which overturned the Spartan empire, and brought freedom to Greece. He thus not merely led to the rebuilding of his country's walls, but to the resuscitation of her fallen glories. There could have been little expectation that a man who had acted with such humility would reverse the entire affairs of Greece, and bring their states to dishonour or to power.

Next I mention Dionysius [16] – I want to offer several instances to convince you of the ease of the proceedings I urge. He was of no great distinction in Syracuse either in birth, reputation or anything else. He indulged an unthinking, phrenetic desire for despotic power, and was prepared to do anything which could lead to it. He secured control of Syracuse, reduced all the other Greek states in Sicily, and surrounded himself with naval and military strength unequalled in his day. Cyrus [17] again, to pass to a non-Greek instance, was exposed by the roadside by his mother, but rescued by a Persian woman, and lived to change the world by becoming lord of all Asia. Thus, since Alcibiades in spite of exile, Conon of misfortune, Dionysius of undistinguished origins and Cyrus of the misery of his initial story went

15. On the career of Conon, see *Panegyricus*, 119, p. 122, note 20, and sectional introduction.
16. On Dionysius of Syracuse, see *Panegyricus*, 169, p. 132, note 35.
17. This refers to Cyrus the Great.

as far and achieved as much as they did, it must clearly be
expected that a man like yourself, of similar birth, but with the
kingship of Macedon and this widespread power to your name,
will find it easy to bring about the unity of which I have spoken.

You may well reflect how valuable it is to engage in enter-
prises whose success will set your reputation to rival the highest
in history, while, even if your hopes are unrealized, you will at
least earn good will from the Greek states, which is a far finer
achievement than the storming of any number of Greek cities. Such
successes give occasion for resentment, hostility and ill feeling,
none of which attaches to such a course as I am suggesting.
If the gods granted you a choice of the pursuit or activity in
which you would spend your life, there is no other, in my
submission, which you could prefer to this. You will not merely
win the world's emulation, you will be able to congratulate
yourself. It will surely be the acme of this kind of satisfaction
when the most distinguished representatives from the Greek
states come in deference to your power; when you join them in
deliberations for the common welfare, for which it will be clear
no one else has such deep concern as yourself; and when you
realize that all Greece is agog with expectation of your aims,
that no one is neglectful of your arbitration, some inquiring its
trend, others expressing the hope that you may not fail in your
intention, or afraid that you may be prevented by some fatality
from bringing it to its consummation. You could hardly fail to
be uplifted at such a situation, or to enjoy lasting felicity in the
knowledge of your position as leader of such a world. And no
one of even moderate intelligence could fail to urge you to a
plan of action which would bring a double harvest of outstanding
pleasure and inextinguishable honour.

What I have said on this subject might have seemed sufficient,
had I not omitted one argument, not out of forgetfulness, but
out of hesitation. Now I think I should put it forward. I believe
it is in your interest to hear it, and my duty to maintain my usual
candour and discuss it. I realize that you are misrepresented by
people who are jealous of you[18] and are apt to incite their own

18. Perhaps Demosthenes and the 'war party', though the reference is
not confined to Athenians.

states to disorder, and who suppose that general peace means war against their own individual interests. They leave everything else aside and concentrate on the subject of your power, whose rise they maintain is not in the interest of Greece, but against it. They declare that you have long harboured designs against us all; that an ostensible aim to befriend Messenia,[19] if you arrange the position in Phocis, conceals the ambition to control the Peloponnese; that initially Thessaly, Thebes and all the adherents of the Amphictyonic confederacy are prepared to follow you, while Argos, Messene, Megalopolis and numerous others are ready to join the campaign and reduce Sparta to ruin; and that once you achieve that you will find it easy to reduce all the rest of the Greek states. This is without substance, though they claim it as certain knowledge and their imaginary subjection of the world to you wins them much support; primarily among people who hold the same pernicious aims as these purveyors of rumour themselves, secondly in circles which give no real thought to international affairs, but in an entirely unperceptive attitude sympathize with any who claim to feel apprehension and misgivings about them, and again among others who do not reject the idea of your having conspired against the Greeks, but regard the charge as one to merit emulation. They are so remote from common sense as to fail to see that the same argument can be used to do damage or bring support alike. At the present juncture, for instance, the statement that the King of Persia had designs against the Greeks and was prepared for an expedition against us would not amount to any criticism against him, but would show him in a more courageous and more estimable light. But if preferred against a descendant of Heracles, who was the benefactor of all Greece, this charge would be a matter of the deepest shame. It could not fail to be a reason for resentment and hatred to be proved a conspirator against causes for whose sake one's ances-

19. On Messene see note 10 above. The Amphictyonic League was an ancient association for the protection of the sanctuary of Apollo at Delphi. Athens and Sparta were members, but it was formed largely of states in Central Greece, notably Thebes and Thessaly, until Macedon gained membership in place of Phocis after the Sacred War.

tor had elected to risk his life, and to make no attempt to preserve the good will which his achievements left behind, but instead to neglect it for the pursuit of despicable and shameful ends. You should realize and not discount the growth of this view of you, in which your enemies desire to involve you, though every friend of yours would confidently deny it. Yet in these two opinions you will find the truest indication of your interests.

Perhaps you regard it as petty-minded to pay any attention to slanderous nonsense and its followers, particularly when your conscience is entirely clear. But one should not be contemptuous of the masses or think little of high reputation in any quarter. The time when you can regard your public figure as high and distinguished, and in keeping with yourself, your ancestry and your achievements, is when you have imparted the same attitude in the Greek states towards you as you see Sparta holds towards her Kings, and your Companions[20] towards yourself. It is not difficult to achieve this, if you are prepared to be impartial towards all, to cease to be friendly towards one state and distant towards another, and if you pursue a policy which will make you trusted in Greece and feared abroad.

I hope you will not be surprised, as I also pointed out to Dionysius when he became Tyrant, at an address of unusual freedom from one who is not a military leader nor a political speaker nor otherwise a power in the land. Nature left me less well equipped for politics than anyone. I have neither the voice nor the confidence to deal with crowds, or to drag myself in the dust and abuse and hurly-burly of the public platform. But for sound and educated thinking, though it may be thought somewhat lacking in good taste to say so, I stake my claim and would set myself not among those who are left behind in the race, but among the leaders. This is the reason why I attempt to offer advice, of the kind which is within my natural powers, to Athens, to the rest of Greece and to the leaders of mankind.

You have heard fairly fully of my own theme, and of the way in which you should deal with the Greek states. As regards the

20. The Greek word 'companions' was used to refer to the Macedonian cavalry, and then officially for the King's bodyguard and advisers.

expedition into Persia, we will approach the states I called upon you to reconcile and urge them towards it, when we can be sure of their agreement. I shall now address arguments to yourself on the subject, but not in the same sense as at the period when I was previously writing about it. On that occasion I called upon my audience to hold me in ridicule and contempt if I did not show myself capable of a discussion worthy of my subject, my own reputation and the length of time the discussion occupied.[21] Now I am afraid that I may have offered a disquisition which is inadequate to all I said before. For apart from other things the *Panegyricus*, which enriched other devotees of philosophy, has impoverished me. I do not wish to repeat what I wrote there, but I am not capable of producing fresh ideas. However I must not abandon my task, but go through with my undertaking to say whatever occurs to my mind as likely to persuade you. If I make omissions and prove unable to recapture the manner of my earlier work, at least I think I shall provide a pleasant outline for others to elaborate and complete.

I think I have established this as the basis of my argument, which is essential to a plan for a campaign against Asia. One must do nothing till one has secured from the Greek states either collaboration or considerable sympathy with the project. This was neglected by Agesilaus, who appeared the most intelligent of the Spartans, from ambition rather than incapacity. He had two aims, both laudable, but inconsistent and incompatible. His design was both to conduct war with Persia and to recall his associates[22] to their cities and give them control over proceedings. The result of his arrangements with his associates was a series of difficulties and dangers for the Greeks, while that of the confusion which reigned at home was that he had no time or power for war abroad. Thus his failure to grasp the problem of that period affords a clear lesson that a correct design

21. See *Panegyricus*, 14.
22. The same Greek word as appears in 80 above, here refers to Agesilaus' friends, unless it has its semi-technical sense to refer to the political clubs, which existed throughout the Greek states (see on Lysias, *Eratosthenes*, 43), in which case Jebb thinks that Isocrates is confusing the rigid oligarchical aims of Lysander with the much more accommodating ones of Agesilaus.

will not include war with Persia without reconciliation of the Greek states and an end of the insanity which now afflicts them. This is the advice I have in fact given.

About this no thinking man would be rash enough to disagree. But if it occurred to anyone else to give advice about the expedition against Asia, I think he might have recourse to the claim that it was the experience of all who attempted war against Persia that they rise from obscurity to distinction, from poverty to wealth, from unimportance to the control of large territories and dominions. But it is not from such people as this that I draw my plea to convince you, but from the class which appears to have been unsuccessful, I mean the men who took part in the army of Cyrus and Clearchus.[23] They are admitted to have overcome in battle the entire force of Persia as completely as if they had had only their women to contend with, but when they still appeared to have the situation in their grasp they were brought to disaster by the rash behaviour of Cyrus, whose excessive exultation led him to pursue the action far beyond the rest into the middle of the enemy, where he was killed. Nonetheless, after a disaster of this magnitude the King had so little confidence in the force under his command as to summon Clearchus and the other leaders to a conference, at which he promised them large presents of money and undertook to send the rest of the army home with full pay. After leading them on with such hopes as this, and after giving the most solemn assurances normal in that country, he seized them and put them to death. He preferred to violate the sanctions of religion rather than engage in battle against those deserted soldiers. What plea, then, could have a better justification or carry a surer guarantee? Even that army would clearly have overcome the power of Persia, had it not been for Cyrus. But in your case the catastrophe of that time is easy to forestall, and the force which overcame the strength of Persia can easily be far surpassed. And if provision is made for both these demands, one can surely feel confident in undertaking the campaign.

I hope it will not be supposed that I want to elude the fact

23. On the story of the Ten Thousand see on *Panegyricus*, 144, and sectional introduction.

that I have put some of this in the same fashion as before. As I have embarked upon the same ideas, I preferred not to cause myself trouble by insisting on a second satisfactory expression of what has already been said. Were I engaged in a rhetorical display, I should attempt to avoid all such repetition, but in a discourse of recommendation to you it would be stupid of me to attend more to diction than to matter, or when others appropriate my style, to be alone in avoiding expressions of my own previous devising. Indeed I should make a successful use of any phrase of my own which meets an urgent need and is pertinent, while I would not accept a borrowed one any more than I did in the past.

So far, then, so good. Next I think I had better consider the force you will have in comparison with that of the previous expedition. Most important of all, you will have the good will of the Greek states, if you are prepared to abide by my advice about them, whereas your predecessors were led to extreme hostility by the Spartan decarchies. Indeed the Greeks thought that if Cyrus and Clearchus were successful, their own enslavement to Sparta would be intensified, while success for the King would free them from duress. And this is what happened. Secondly, as regards infantry, you will have a ready source from which to draw as many men as you like. Greece is now a land in which it is easier to raise an army, and a stronger one, from displaced exiles[24] than from active citizens. But at that time there was no permanent mercenary force. They had to collect men from the cities, and found it cost more in donatives to the collectors than in pay for the fighting force. Furthermore, if we set out to draw a comparison between you, the intended commander and chief of staff of the present army, and Clearchus, who was in command on the previous occasion, we shall find that he had never previously had charge of a force, naval or otherwise. He owed his fame to the disaster that befell him on the continent, while your own achievements amount to an enormous total, which it

24. 'The employment of mercenaries in Greece on a considerable scale began in the Corinthian War (394-390) and gradually became more and more firmly established' (Laistner). Indeed it became a difficult problem, on which see 120, 121 below.

would be well to elaborate if I were addressing other states, but in a discussion confined to yourself a catalogue of your own successes would appear superfluous and foolish.

It is worth while to make some mention of the two Kings of Persia, one whom I am proposing that you should face, and the other whom Clearchus met, to give you some knowledge of the character of each. The father [25] of the present King conducted successful wars against Athens, and again against Sparta, but the present one has never been successful against any of the forces which have ruined his country. The first acquired the whole of Asia from Greece by the treaty he made, the second is so far from control of others that he cannot even control cities made over to him. An observer would be in doubt whether he had abandoned them or whether they had adopted a lordly contempt for the power of Persia.

An account of the country itself and its condition would fill anyone with enthusiasm for attack. Egypt was in revolt about the same time as the attempt of Cyrus, [26] but was afraid that the King might raise his own force and overcome the difficulties of the Nile delta and all their other defence works. However, he relieved them of this apprehension. He gathered the largest force he could and marched against them. But he retired, not merely defeated, but a figure of derision, incapable of being a king or commanding an army. The district which includes Cyprus, Phoenicia and Cilicia, the source of Persian fleets, then belonged to the King, but has now either seceded or is in a state of warfare or other trouble to an extent which precludes his deriving any benefit from the peoples of that district, though they will be conveniently placed for you, if you conduct this expedition against him. In addition Idrieus, [27] the wealthiest potentate on the mainland, is likely to be a stronger opponent of the King than the enemies now at war with him. At least it

25. Artaxerxes II came to the throne in 405 B.C. He was not responsible for Persian successes in the Peloponnesian War, though he was, with Conon's assistance, for the battle of Cnidus. Artaxerxes III succeeded in 359.

26. Egypt revolted from Persia at the end of the fifth century, and was not finally recovered till 344. (See on Demosthenes, *Rhodes*, notes 2 and 4.)

27. Idrieus became King of Caria on the death of Artemisia in 351 B.C. (See on Demosthenes, *Rhodes*, note 1.)

would be most perverse of him if he were not eager for the dissolution of a kingdom which maltreated his brother and made war on himself, and was continually conspiring to gain control of his person and his wealth. This apprehension compels him to show deference to the King at present, and to pay him a large annual tribute. But if you crossed to the mainland, he would welcome your appearance with the feeling that you were coming to his aid, while you will gain the adherence of numerous other satraps if you promise them freedom and disseminate through Asia a word whose currency in Greece has been the downfall of the empires of Athens and Sparta alike.

I would try to go to greater length in describing the tactics which would enable you to overcome the King's power in the shortest time, were it not that I am afraid I might be subject to criticism if without previous military experience I attempted to advise a soldier of such great achievements as yours. So I think I had better say no more of that. As regards the rest of the subject, however, I think your father, and the founder of your dynasty and the originator of your race, if there were no divine or human impediment to make it impossible, would give the same advice as I do myself. I take their own achievements as evidence. Your father maintained friendship with all the countries I am advising you to keep in consideration. The founder of your dynasty had loftier aims than his fellows and desired kingship, but his designs differed from those of most aspirants to similar ambitions, who acquired the distinction by fostering party disputes, violence and bloodshed in their own states. Perdiccas[28] left the area of the Greek world severely alone, and set his eyes on kingship in Macedonia. He knew that Greek states do not usually tolerate monarchy, though other peoples are incapable of organizing their own existence without some such personal power. In fact it was his knowledge of this that gave his kingdom its personal character, which differed greatly from others. He was alone among the Greeks in not claiming to rule a racially unified kingdom, and therefore also in escaping the dangers which monarchical rule incurs. We shall find that rulers who have achieved this among Greek states have not only

28. Perdiccas of Argos (see note 4 above). Philip's father was Amyntas II.

themselves been extirpated, but their race has been obliterated from the sight of men, while Perdiccas both lived out a life of prosperity himself, and bequeathed to his descendants the distinction which had been his own.

As to Heracles,[29] others have always sung the praises of his bravery and catalogued his achievements, but his other attributes, which are qualities of mind, will prove to have had no fame accorded to them either in poetry or prose. I see this as a distinct and entirely unworked field, neither small nor barren, but abounding in fair fruit for praise and admiration, yet in need of a pen to give it adequate expression. Had I come to the task at a younger age, I should have found it easier to point to your ancestor as displaying greater pre-eminence over his predecessors in intelligence, honour and justice than in physical strength. As it is, when I turn to him and realize the great quantity of material which needs to be included, I find my present strength inadequate to the task, as I see that there would be twice as much as you have now to read. I have therefore refrained from mentioning most of it, choosing to keep a single episode, which, besides being a related and appropriate addition to my earlier argument, provides an opportunity very much in keeping with my present concern.

Heracles realized that Greece was obsessed by war, foreign and civil alike, and he brought this to an end, secured the reconciliation of the cities, and gave a demonstration to succeeding generations of their proper allies and their proper opponents in war. He carried out an expedition to Troy, then the most powerful state in Asia, and the superiority of his generalship to that of later invaders of Troy is shown by the fact that whereas they laid siege to it with the whole strength of Greece and barely reduced it after ten years, he took less than as many days with only a small force and stormed the city with ease. After this he put to death the tribal kings on the coast on either side of the Greek continent, whom he could never have extirpated had he not overcome their power. It was after these

29. On Heracles and the Heraclids see on *Panegyricus* note 7, p. 109 above. But Isocrates here does seem to show some originality, if it is not too sophistic a rationalization.

achievements that he erected the so-called Pillars of Heracles,[30] as a trophy to signalize his victory over states outside Greece, a memorial of his own prowess and triumphs, and a boundary stone to mark the limit of Greek territory.

The reason why I have dealt with this subject is to make you understand that this essay is designed to urge you to action of the kind which your forbears judged the finest there could be. All thinking men should set the highest models before themselves and try to live by them, and you most of all. The fact that there is no need to point to external examples, because there exists one in your own ancestry, must presumably stimulate you to emulation of your ancestor. I do not imply that you will be able to match all the achievements of Heracles, which would be beyond the power even of some of the gods. But in respect of the spirit that was in him, of his good will and kindly feeling towards the Greek people, you would be able to model yourself on his aims. It is in your power, if you follow the suggestions I have made, to rise to any distinction you will. The path from your present achievement to the greatest heights in the world is easier to travel than that from your original position to where you now stand. But reflect that I am calling upon you for an attempt which means that you will be conducting your campaign, not in unjustifiable alliance with non-Greek peoples against Greeks, but in alliance with Greek against non-Greek, which is the right battle for descendants of Heracles to fight.

Do not be surprised that I have tried throughout my argument to urge you to work for the Greek people in a spirit of kindness and good will. I realize that strained relations are alike painful to initiate and to endure, while good relations are found acceptable not only among human beings and animals; those gods who are the givers of good gifts to us are addressed with the title of Olympian, while the others who are invoked to deal with disaster and punishment have less attractive appellations. It is the former in whose honour temples and altars are consecrated by both individuals and communities,

30. The title was commonly applied to the two big rocks on the Straits of Gibraltar, Calpe (Gibraltar) and Abyle (Ceuta).

while the latter receive no honour either in ritual or sacrifice, but are exorcized by the human race. With this in mind you should make it your custom and persistent practice to ensure that the right view shall be universally held of you. The ambition for greater fame than others enjoy must imply an understanding grasp of action, which must meet practical demands and aspirations too, and the attempt to carry it out as opportunity offers.

Among plenty of examples to show that this is the right practice that of Jason[31] is outstanding. He had no achievements comparable with yours, yet he attained great fame, not for his actions, but for his claims. He made statements based on the intention to cross to the mainland for a war against Persia. But since Jason made such capital out of mere words, the opinion which you may expect to win must be high indeed if you carry words into action, and attempt if possible the destruction of the whole Persian kingdom: or, failing that, the annexation of as much territory as possible, the division of Asia, as some suggest, on a line from Cilicia to Sinope, and thirdly the foundation of states in this area, and the permanent settlement of those vagrants who lack subsistence and are a danger to all they meet.[32] If we do not prevent these from congregating by making sufficient provision for them, before we realize it they will reach numbers which will be a menace to the Greek world as much as abroad. We take no thought of them, but are content to ignore a reason for general anxiety and a danger to all. It remains for a man of high aspirations, an admirer of the Greek world who can see further than his fellows, to make use of these people against Persia, to cut off a large range of territory such as has been suggested, to liberate these hordes of displaced people from the hardships they both undergo and inflict on others, organize communities of them, and make them a boundary buffer state for our general protection. If you do this,

31. Jason of Pherae was a vigorous and ambitious Thessalian king, who united Thessaly before 370 B.C. and aimed at the hegemony of Greece, and even at a Greek expedition against Persia. He marched to join the Thebans in 371, but arriving after the battle, induced them to make a truce. He had far-reaching schemes to seize the rights of the Amphictyonic Council and preside over the Pythian Games, but was assassinated in 370.

32. See note 24, p. 156 above.

you will ensure both their satisfaction and the safety of us all. If, however, you fail to achieve it, there is in any case one thing that will be easy, the liberation of Greek cities in Asia.

Whatever part of this programme you can carry out, or even attempt, you cannot fail to gain greater distinction than the rest of the world, and rightly, if you yourself make the first move in this direction and urge it on the Greek states. As things are it would be reasonable for anyone to feel surprise at what has occurred and some contempt of the Greeks, when in the non-Greek world – which we have always taken to be soft, unaddicted to war and eaten up with self-indulgence – there have appeared men who claimed the control of Greece, while no one in Greece has the spirit to try to secure for her the control of Asia. We are so far behind them, in fact, that while they had no hesitation even in taking the initiative in hostility to Athens, we have not the determination to meet injury with retaliation. They admit that in all their wars they possess neither men, commanders nor any other valuable assets for an emergency, but send for everything from us. Yet we carry so far our eagerness to do ourselves injury that when we could hold secure possession of what is theirs we find petty reasons for war among ourselves, or join in the reduction of Persian rebels. Sometimes without realizing it we side with our traditional enemies in attempting the destruction of our own kith and kin.

I therefore think it is also in your interest, as the rest have so little spirit, to take the lead in the suggested campaign against Persia. But it is the duty of all others in the line of Heracles, and all who remain under the restraint of constitution or law, to retain their affection for the state in which they actually live, while you yourself, as being in a position to range at will, should look on all Greece as your country, as your ancestor did, and regard her dangers as yours and her needs as your dearest concern.

There may be criticism of me from people capable of nothing else, for calling you to this campaign against the non-Greek world and to the care of the Greek world, without reference to my own city. Had I been taking the initial step in putting forward this argument to any other country than my own, which has three times been the saviour of Greece, twice against Persia and once against Sparta, I would agree that I had been at fault. But it will be clear that she was in fact the first which I approached with this exhortation, with the greatest ardour I could command. But I realized that she had less concern for what I had to say than for the ravings of platform oratory. So I left her alone, though I did not abandon my business. I therefore deserve universal commendation for using what power I possess in continuing unbroken hostility towards Persia, in criticizing any whose view differed from mine, and in trying to urge all who seemed likely to have the power, to confer any benefit they could on the Greek states, and to seize from Persia her existing prosperity. This is the reason why I now make my address to you, because I know that, while my arguments will be liable to widespread jealousy, the same actions carried on by you will be received with general satisfaction. Words meet with no agreement, but benefits proposed in action will seem within everyone's reach.

Consider further what a disgrace it would be to allow Asia to be more successful than Europe, non-Greeks more prosperous than Greeks, to let the dynasty of Cyrus, the child exposed by his mother, win the title of the Great King, while that of Heracles, raised to the gods by his father for his virtues, is given a humbler style. None of this can be permitted. It needs to be altered to the exact opposite.

You must understand that I would have made no attempt to persuade you of any of this, had power and wealth appeared the only advantage likely to come of it. I believe you have more than enough of these already, and it is only insatiate greed which prefers to risk life for the hope of them. These are not the gains which fill my view when I address you, but the prospect of winning you the greatest and most glorious reputation. Remember that man's body is mortal, and it is upon the fair fame, the high repute, the renown and the memorial which time brings in its train, that his share of immortality depends, which it is worth any suffering, any endeavour to win. You will observe that for the noblest even of private individuals there is no other gain for which they will risk life itself, but for the sake of high repute they will accept death in battle; and in general that the desire to win ever fairer and fairer fame is universally extolled, while any other uncontrolled desire is held to show a regrettable lack of restraint. But most important of all is the fact that wealth and power may fall into the hands of enemies, whereas general good will and the other blessings I have mentioned know no legatee except our heirs by blood. So I should be ashamed not to advise you for these reasons to make this campaign and to do or die.

On this you will be best resolved, if you believe that it is not merely by this discourse that you are called to action, but by your ancestors, by Persian effeminacy, by the famous men, true heroes, who fought against Persia, and most of all by the fitting hour which finds you in possession of greater strength than any previous European, and your adversary in deeper hatred and wider contempt than any monarch in history.

I would have given a great deal for the power to blend together all the discourses I have made on this subject. Then this one might have been a worthier representation of the theme. However, you must attend to those parts of all of them whose trend and purpose is towards this war, and then you will be best advised about it.

I do not forget that many in Greece regard the King's power as invincible. It is surprising that a power set under the rule of a monarch without the blood or the understanding of a Greek, and based upon slavery, should be thought indissoluble by a Greek and a practised soldier in the ranks of freedom, when we know that construction is always hard, but destruction easy.

Remember that the highest honour and admiration goes in general to men who are capable both as statesmen and soldiers. So when you see the distinction which is accorded even in a single state to men who have both these qualities, what must you expect will be the praises sung of you, when it is realized that in the political field you have been the benefactor of all the Greek states, and in the military the conqueror of Persia? I myself regard this as unsurpassable. No achievement can ever be greater than to bring us all out of such warfare to unity of spirit, nor is it probable that any other such force could exist in the non-Greek world if you destroy their present establishment. No leader in future generations, however outstanding, can ever accomplish as much. Indeed, as regards past generations, I can cap their achievements with those which already stand to your name, without any pretence and in all honesty. When the nations you have reduced are more than the cities defeated by any other Greek state, it is obvious by a direct comparison of single instances that your achievements are greater than any of theirs. However, I preferred to keep from such an approach for two reasons: first because of the misuse that may be made of it, and secondly because I am unwilling to represent the present generation as more distinguished than the heroes of old.

You should reflect – to refer to ancient myth – that though the wealth of Tantalus, the kingdom of Pelops, the power of Eurystheus would never be applauded in prose or poetry, yet next to the outstanding character of Heracles and the valour of Theseus the army that fought at Troy and their like would win eulogies the world over. Yet we know that the most famous and the finest warriors among them held rule in tiny cities and small islands. Nonetheless, they left throughout the world a fame to transcend human glory. This is because all men give their highest esteem not to the winners of the greatest power for themselves, but to the authors of the greatest benefit to the rest of Greece.

It is not only in regard to legend that you will find this opinion is held, but universally. Even our own city of Athens would be given no praise for her maritime empire, for the enormous wealth exacted from allied states and deposited in the Acropolis, or for the numerous instances in which she assumed rights over other states – the right to destroy them, to increase their power or make what organization she chose. It was in her power to do all this, but the result of it has been a series of accusations against her. But the battles of Marathon and Salamis, and most of all her evacuation of her own country for the safety of Greece, have won her universal praise. The same opinion is held of Sparta. She earns greater admiration

for her defeat at Thermopylae than for all her victories, and
the scene of the triumph of Persia against her is one for satisfaction and contemplation, while Spartan triumphs over other
states are no matter of praise, but of displeasure, because the
first is regarded as a memorial of valour, the second of self-
seeking.

I hope you will go through and examine all I have written,
and if you find any weakness or inadequacy in it, you will put
the blame on my age, which may reasonably be excused. But if
it is the equal of my previous publications, you will, I hope,
suppose that it is the product, not of my old age, but of the will
of heaven, which has no thought for me, but for the good of
Greece, which it seeks to deliver from her present ills, while it
endows you with more than your present glory. I think you
understand how the gods deal with human affairs. They do
not directly bestow either the good or the evil which befalls
mankind, but impart a disposition to each community which
ensures that it is through each other's agency that we meet with
either. This may actually be an instance of it: they have given
me the province of speech, and you of action, in the view that
this would be your best sphere of control, while in my case
speech would be the faculty to give least trouble to hearers. Yet
I fancy that even in action you would not have succeeded in so
large a degree, had you not had some divine aid, not merely
with the aim of continuing your wars against the non-Greek
inhabitants of Europe, but in the intention that you should
benefit by that early training, gain experience, make your
character known, and then proceed to those ambitions to which
I have urged you.

I think you should respect all who speak well of your achievements, but see the finest compliment of all in the belief that
your character warrants still greater successes, and in the desire
to go beyond laudatory remarks about the present and make
future generations feel for what you have done an admiration
unparalleled in the past. I wish I could continue in this vein to
greater length, but I cannot for the reason which I have too
often given already. It remains to summarize this essay and to
give you the substance of it as shortly as may be. I maintain

that you should be the benefactor of Greece, and King of Macedon, and gain to the greatest possible extent the empire of the non-Greek world. If you accomplish this, you will win universal gratitude: from the Greeks for the benefits they gain, from Macedonia if your rule of them is kingly and not tyrannical, and from the rest of the world if it is through you that they are liberated from Persian despotism and exchange it for Greek protection.

The writing that has gone to this essay, its relevance and precision, I cannot but leave to the judgement of my readers. I think I can say this with certainty, that no one could give you better or more suitable advice.

DEMOSTHENES [I]

INTRODUCTION

Demosthenes was born in 384 B.C.*, the son of Demosthenes of Paeania, an Attic* deme. *He was taught by an earlier speaker, Isaeus, who was a leading advocate in private suits, and Demosthenes himself first came to the fore in 364, when he conducted a prosecution to preserve his own property. Thus the man who is universally acclaimed as the greatest of Greek orators began his career at an early age. Yet he was not physically robust, and was thought unsociable, puritanical and perhaps self-righteous. If so, he overcame the diffidence which this reputation implies by a strong determination, which must have been characteristic of a man who is said to have improved his vocal delivery by declaiming on the shore with pebbles in his mouth. A writer of speeches and teacher of rhetoric in his early days, he first made his name with private, i.e. forensic, speeches from 357 onwards, and the further he went, the more he seems to have moved towards politics. His first public speech in 354 was that on the 'symmories' (see* Olynthiac II, 29*). After that we have two speeches before the series for which he is most famous, which concern the relations between Athens and Philip of Macedon.*

These two speeches suggest that, though Philip was already conspicuous in the affairs of Northern Greece as an opponent of Athenian interests, Demosthenes was not yet alive to the danger he represented. (1) The first (For Megalopolis) *deals with the internal politics of the Greek states and with questions of the balance of power between them which Philip was soon to render obsolete. After the battle of Mantinea (362 B.C.) Sparta, now aided by Athens, had regained some of her old power, and in an attempt to recover Messenia had suggested a return to old boundaries, which, if agreed, would have justified her own aims. Megalopolis, feeling herself threatened by Sparta, had asked Athens for an alliance. Demosthenes is speaking on this request. His attitude may appear forced and his predictions unlikely, but there still remains some importance in the balance between the stronger states, and the political integrity of the speaker is clear.* (2) *The speech,* On the Liberty of Rhodes, *in 351, again shows Demosthenes' conception of Athens as the protector of the weak. Rhodes, with Chios, Cos and Byzantium, had revolted from the second Athenian League in the so-called Social War in 357. Afterwards Rhodes was brought under an oligarchy backed by Mausolus, the satrap of Caria. After his death Rhodes appealed to Athens for liberation.*

By 351 B.C. Demosthenes begins to deal with the subject of Macedon. He found himself in opposition to the already established Eubulus, who successfully pursued a policy of peace and prosperity. The speeches which appear in this book may be conveniently taken in two divisions, those before and those after the Peace of Philocrates, which concluded Athens' first war with Macedon. In the first of these two divisions the topics which most need analysis are the rise of Philip himself, the Sacred War and the rise and fall of Olynthus.

(1) Philip was made regent of Macedon in 359 B.C., three years after the battle of Mantinea, which brought a halt to the war between Thebes and Sparta. His ambition revolutionized a kingdom which had never played a leading part in the politics of the Greek states. He soon secured his succession by the liquidation of possible rivals, and his army by a thorough reorganization. He next made sure of his finances by a move to acquire the rich source of gold, Mount Pangaeus in Thrace, and the town of Amphipolis, which commanded the district. Amphipolis had revolted from Athens in 424, and in 357 Philip made a secret pact to conquer and restore it to Athens in exchange for Pydna, a free town under Athenian control. But the undertaking was not fulfilled by Philip. Athens continued to talk about Amphipolis, while Philip, finding Athens occupied with the revolt of her dependencies in the Social War, improved his position by gaining control of other Athenian allied cities in the north, Pydna itself as well as Potidaea and Methone, and later Pagasae, a valuable port in Thessaly.

(2) The origins of the Sacred War have already been recounted (introduction to Isocrates' Philip). Philip's entry into the war had been due to dissident factions in Thessaly since its unification under

Jason (see note on Isocrates, Philip 119). At first defeated in 353 by Onomarchus of Phocis, Philip soon regained strength, and it was in 352 that the fear of a move through the pass of Thermopylae led Athens to obstruct him there, perhaps the only time when Eubulus felt that hostile action was needed. The Sacred War dragged on under new Phocian leaders, Phayllus and Phalaecus, and it was not till 347 that a further request came from Thebes that Philip should return and crush Phocis, with the understanding that he should be a member of the Amphictyonic League in Phocis' place. Terms were negotiated between him and Athens for a treaty which carries the name of a colleague of Eubulus in the Athenian peace party. Philip was enabled to secure two great objects when he turned upon Phocis and forced her to surrender, and himself celebrated the Pythian games at Delphi.

(3) The importance of Olynthus dates from the fifth century, when cities in Chalcidice in revolt from Athens formed a league under the leadership of Olynthus, which was then too the principal town in the district. To this reference is made in the General Introduction (p. 27). The league was suppressed by Sparta in 379, but Olynthus remained an important town, which, at first a member of the new Athenian confederacy, broke away from it and was still strong enough to be the object of an Athenian attack in 364, and remained at the head of the group of neighbouring towns. In 357, alarmed by Philip's advance, Olynthus proposed alliance with Athens, but it was rejected, and instead it was Philip who, to flatter Olynthus, made an alliance which he did not mean to maintain. In 352 Philip had a hold on Thessaly as well as Amphipolis, was increasing his fleet, which attacked Athenian corn supplies coming from the Hellespont, and had actually acquired a footing in Thrace and advanced to the Propontis. The next object of attack was clearly the peninsula of Chalcidice and the power of Olynthus at the head of it. Philip had suffered from an illness, but recovered by 351, and after securing his Illyrian frontiers turned to Olynthus with a new and hostile approach. This was appreciated by Demosthenes in his Philippic I *in 351, but the full immediacy of the need for action is not apparent till 349, when Philip really turned against Olynthus. The* Olynthiac *orations were delivered while Philip was engaged against the other confederate towns of Chalcidice. But*

Demosthenes did not attain his object, and Olynthus itself eventually succumbed in 348, owing to a revolt against Athens in Euboea, which proved a fatal distraction from the force which was raised to save Olynthus. Athens had been roused by Demosthenes, but not to the extent required for two expeditions at once, and Euboea was close at hand and a more urgent problem.

DEMOSTHENES: FOR MEGALOPOLIS

In my opinion, gentlemen, both parties are wrong,[1] both the supporters of Arcadia and those of Sparta. Their accusations and misrepresentations make them appear actual members of the states they support instead of Athenians. Such proceedings may be the proper function of the visiting delegations, but a balanced discussion of the facts with a reasoned view of Athenian interests and without bias is what is demanded in a discussion of policy by our own speakers. As it is, take away known personalities and Attic speech, and I think that most people would take one party to be Arcadian and the other Spartan. I realize the difficulties of choosing the right policy, because members share their delusions and their opposed aims, and anyone who tries a middle course, if the Assembly does not wait to master it, will please neither side and be pilloried by both. Nonetheless, if this happens, I shall prefer to be told my ideas are nonsense rather than to abandon my view of Athenian interests and allow the Assembly to be hoodwinked by certain members. If you will allow me, I will leave other matters to a later stage, and begin with the common ground of agreement, which I regard as most valuable to discuss.

No one, then, would dispute the value to Athens of a weak Sparta and on this side a weak Thebes. Now the present position, to judge by frequent utterances in this assembly, is that with the re-establishment of Orchomenus, Thespiae and Plataea,[2] Thebes is weakened, while, if Sparta is to secure control of Arcadia and destroy Megalopolis, she will return to her old power. We therefore need to be careful not to allow Sparta to rise to a formidable power before the decline of Thebes,[3] not to allow the desired balance of power to alter

1. For the circumstances see sectional introduction. Rival delegations have arrived from Sparta and from Megalopolis (to which Demosthenes often refers as 'Arcadia') to invite Athenian support.

2. See note 7 on Isocrates, *Philip*, 43, p. 146.

3. This obscure sentence seems to be based on a fear of a return to Spartan domination if a Theban decline is more than counterbalanced by a

unperceived so that a Spartan rise exceeds the Theban decline. We should not take the other line of wanting Sparta rather than Thebes as opponents, which is not what we require, but that neither shall have the power to injure ourselves. This is what would give us the greatest security.

The view will be put forward that this is sound enough, but that it is scandalous if we are expected to ally ourselves with our opponents at Mantinea and render assistance to them against our previous comrades in battle.⁴ I agree, but we need a saving clause, 'provided the other states mean to play fair'. If we all intend to maintain peace, we shall give no assistance to Megalopolis, because it will not be needed, and there will be nothing to set us against our comrades in arms. We are in alliance with one side already, according to their own account, and will now be so also with the other. What more could be desired? On the other hand, if they intend to discard principle and embark on war, then, if the question is solely one of the sacrifice of Megalopolis to Sparta, this would be a contravention of justice, but I concede that we should allow it and avoid friction with our previous comrades. But if it is generally known that once in control of Megalopolis, Sparta will proceed against Messene, I ask any harsh critic of Megalopolis what his next advice is to be. There will be no answer. Indeed every man here knows that, with or without the consent of the party in question, we must oppose Sparta on two counts, the sworn agreement with Messene and the value to Athens of her existence as a state. Now I ask you to consider where you will draw the line of resistance to Spartan aggression, so as best to satisfy honour and good feeling. Will it be in accordance with the interest of Megalopolis or of Messene? The first will show readiness to assist Arcadia and confirm the peace established as a result of our efforts in war. The second will make it obvious that the motive for desiring the existence of Messene is not principle so much as fear of Sparta. We need to observe justice in our con-

_____

new Spartan rise, and exemplifies the idea of balance of power which characterizes this speech.

4. i.e. against Thebes.

siderations and our actions, but to combine it with an eye to our probable interest.

There is another argument from my opponents to the effect that the recovery of Oropus[5] is what we should first attempt, and if we gain the enmity of our potential supporters in the project, we shall have no one to help us. We must try to regain Oropus, I agree. But the idea that Sparta will be antagonistic if we make an alliance with the elements which support us in Arcadia is the one argument which is not legitimate for the party which urged our assistance to Sparta when she was in danger. This was not the kind of argument they used, when Athens was approached by the whole Peloponnese with the request to attack Sparta, to persuade us to refuse (which is what made the others take the only alternative and go to Thebes) and to pay our money and risk our lives to save Sparta. And we should probably not have been prepared to do so, had we been told that we would get no gratitude for it unless Sparta were given a free hand to do further damage. Certainly whatever may be the effect of an Arcadian alliance in cramping Sparta's plans, one must suppose that gratitude for their rescue at the last gasp should outweigh resentment at the injuries they were prevented from committing. How can they fail to assist us at Oropus, at the risk of the most extreme danger to their reputation? It seems to me impossible.

I am also astonished at the statement that an Arcadian alliance, with the policy which it implies, will mean *volte-face* for Athens which will destroy all reliance on her. My own view is the opposite. I do not think there is a man in the world who would dispute the claim that Athens was the saviour of Sparta and before that she saved Thebes, and latterly the saviour of Euboea too,[6] and that she entered into an alliance with each, with one and the same object in every instance. What object? The rescue of the victims of aggression. If this is true, the reversal would not be on the part of Athens, but of the party which

5. Oropus was captured by Thebes in 366 B.C.: see sectional introduction.
6. Athens championed Sparta against Theban attacks after Leuctra, Thebes by the alliance against Sparta in 378, and Euboea when she liberated it from Thebes in 357.

refused to abide by a just agreement. And it will be made clear that it is the pattern of events which changes with variations of self-interest, and not the city of Athens.

It seems to me that the part played by Sparta is a reprehensible one. They now say that some parts of Triphylia ought to be assigned to Elis, Tricaranum to Phlius, other parts of Arcadia to themselves, and Oropus to us. This is not with the aim of securing for each of us our own possessions. By no means. That would be a very late move towards benevolence. The aim is to give an impression of allowing all the states their various claims to territory, so as to ensure that when Sparta moves against Messene there shall be general support and a readiness to join her, for fear that in view of the successful claims of each state with the specific agreement of Sparta they will be put in the wrong, if Sparta's own claim is refused. In my view it is possible that without any arrangement to cede Arcadian towns to Sparta Athens may regain Oropus with the co-operation of Sparta, if she is prepared to be reasonable, and of others who are against Theban appropriation of further territory. But should it appear obvious that without allowing Spartan control of the Peloponnese we are not going to secure Oropus, then it would be preferable, if this view is permissible, to let Oropus go rather than sacrifice Messene, and so the Peloponnese, to Sparta. I do not think this is the only issue between us – however I will omit what I had in mind – but I think we have a number of dangers to consider.

As regards supposed action by Megalopolis taken in the Theban interest and against our own, it is absurd to make this a ground for accusation, and then, when their aim is friendship towards Athens and a return of mutual benefit, to start a policy of malignant frustration of this aim. This would be to fail to realize that their previous eager support of Thebes is the measure of the indignation these critics would earn for having taken such valuable allies from Athens, when they approached her in preference to Thebes. This, I dare say, reflects for the second time the desire to make Megalopolis look elsewhere for assistance. But I know that a calculated judgement will show what I think the rest of you will endorse, that once Sparta is in control of Megalopolis, Messene is in danger. And once she holds Messene, we shall find ourselves in alliance with Thebes. It will be far more to our credit as well as to our advantage to accept alliance with Thebes ourselves as a counterpoise to Spartan ambition than to hesitate for fear of assisting Theban allies and sacrifice Megalopolis, and later have to rescue Thebes with an added danger to ourselves. I feel no security for Athens in a Spartan absorption of Megalopolis and renewal of power. I realize that once again their leaning to war is not defensive, but is aimed at the recapture of their old supremacy. Of their ambitions when they had it, you may have still greater knowledge than I to justify apprehension.

I should very much like to ask speakers who declare their dislike of Thebes or of Sparta whether it is a dislike based in either case on a liking for Athens and her interests, or on a liking for Sparta or Thebes, as the case may be. If the latter, no support should be given to either. They are out of their senses. If they say, 'for Athens', why enhance the other two? I assure you that it is possible to bring Thebes down without increasing the strength of Sparta. Indeed it is far easier. How this is so, I will try to explain. It does not need stating that right conduct is something which everyone, even if they do not want to pursue it, is up to a point ashamed to abandon, while misconduct is openly opposed, especially by its victims. What we shall find to be the universal bane and the origin of all troubles, is the failure to stand squarely by the right. To prevent this from standing in the way of a reduction of Theban power, we should maintain the need to re-establish Thespiae, Orchomenus and Plataea, and co-operate with them, and expect it of others. This is after all the essence of honour and justice, the refusal to countenance the dissolution of ancient cities. At the same time we must not abandon Megalopolis and Messene to mal-treatment, nor allow the example of Plataea and Thebes to blind us to the destruction of already existing and established cities. If this becomes clear, the whole Greek world will desire Thebes to give up alien possessions. Otherwise, first of all we shall naturally have to expect Thebes to oppose the suggestion, when she realizes that the re-establishment of these cities means her own ruin; and secondly we shall be involved in incessant trouble ourselves. What end can there be to it, if we constantly allow the destruction of existing cities and demand the reinstatement of the destroyed?

The view which appears most constitutional demands the destruction by Megalopolis of the record of their treaty with Thebes, if they are to be firm allies of Athens. But they declare that friendship is not created by records, but by common interests, and that what constitutes alliance, in their view, is assistance to themselves. Personally, however deeply they feel this, I look at it rather in this way. I think we should both ask them to obliterate the treaty and ask Sparta to remain at peace, and if either side refuses, we should side with the one which agrees. If, while at peace, Megalopolis holds to the alliance with Thebes, it will be universally proved that Theban ambition rather than justice is what they seek to promote. If Megalopolis seeks alliance with Athens in all good faith, and Sparta refuses to maintain peaceful relations, it will be universally obvious that it is not the reconstitution of Thespiae which excites Spartan enthusiasm, but the hope that Thebes will be engaged in war while they make themselves masters of the Peloponnese. But I am surprised that there should be some who look with apprehension at the idea that Sparta's enemies should be in alliance with Thebes, but feel no anxiety at the prospect of their reduction by Sparta – especially when history has now given a practical demonstration that while Thebes always uses such allies as a makeweight against Sparta, Sparta uses them, when she has them, against Athens.

My belief, then, is that we should also remember that, if we refuse Megalopolis, her destruction and dissolution will mean the possibility of an instant access of power to Sparta; while her survival – and there have been equally surprising occurrences – will with justification make her a firm ally of Thebes. If we accept her, Megalopolis will secure her preservation at our hands, but the result must be viewed in relation to Thebes and Sparta, with a change of emphasis in the argument about risks. If Thebes is the loser, as she should be, it will not mean inordinate strength in Spartan hands, since there will be a counterpoise in their close neighbours in Arcadia. But if Thebes recovers and survives, at least they will be the weaker for our alliance with Megalopolis and her gratitude to us for her rescue. So that it is in our interest on all counts not to abandon Megalopolis, nor to allow her preservation (if it occurs) to be attributed to her own agency, nor to anyone else's but to ours.

Personally, then, gentlemen, I strongly claim to have declared my own view of the merits of the case without partiality towards either side. I urge you not to abandon Megalopolis, nor indeed any other smaller power to a greater.

DEMOSTHENES: ON THE LIBERTY OF RHODES

In a debate on so important a question, gentlemen, freedom must, I think, be extended to every participant. I personally have never considered it difficult to find the best ideas to present to you – to be candid I think they are in your minds already. The difficulty is to induce you to carry them out. A motion voted and carried is still as far from execution as before. There is one advantage for which you should thank heaven, that states which opened a war on us not long ago now see in us their only hope of survival. And the present occasion gives you some cause for satisfaction, because you will be enabled, if you make the right decision, to take up the false and slanderous accusations made against Athens and repel them in actual practice, and enhance your reputation by doing so. The charge of conspiracy was levelled at Athens by Chios, Byzantium and Rhodes, and this was the ground on which they engineered the subsequent war against us. But it will prove that the man who headed the project and pushed it through on the plea of friendship with Rhodes – I mean Mausolus [1] – ended by depriving her of her liberty, while her self-styled associates, Chios and Byzantium, gave her no support in her time of trouble; while this country, of whom she was afraid, proved her sole source of assistance. The general realization of this will lead to the universal assumption that the criterion of sound politics is friendship with Athens, and there could be no greater benefit to this country than the fostering of a state of goodwill without suspicion on all sides.

I am astonished to find in the same speakers an anti-Persian policy in the case of Egypt, [2] combined with fear of Persia in

1. Mausolus was King of Caria, but subject to Persia. He and his queen, Artemisia, are perhaps best known to us from the great monument built in his honour after his death. The Mausoleum (the name is now familiar as an ordinary noun) included work by some of the great sculptors of the day, much of which is now in the British Museum, London.

2. In 358 B.C. an Egyptian king, Nectanebos, was at war with Persia and assisted by Sparta, though it is doubtful how far Athens shared the policy, especially in view of her capture of an Egyptian ship, which was the reason for Demosthenes' case against Androtion in 355.

dealing with Rhodes. Yet the latter is a Greek state, as everyone knows, while the former is a part of the Persian empire. I think some of you remember that in a recent debate on Persia I was the first speaker, and I think I had no more than one supporter, if any, in the view that it would be wise not to base war preparations on hostility to Persia, but to direct them against your existing enemies and be prepared for defence against her as well in case of attack. And it was not a case of my expressing a view which was then rejected. The Assembly agreed. Now my present speech is a sequel to that one. If I served the King of Persia, and were asked to advise him, I would give the same advice as I do here, and urge defensive warfare against any Greek interference in his concerns, but no territorial claims outside his own realm. Now if it is your settled intention, gentlemen, to acquiesce in any accessions to Persian power which his anticipation or chicanery can achieve, it is a wrong intention in my judgement. If, however, you intend to stand for your rights through thick and thin, at the risk of war if need be, first of all the stronger your decision, the less you will be forced to undergo, and secondly, you will enhance your reputation for right judgement.

To show that there is nothing revolutionary either in my demand for the liberation of Rhodes or in your action, if you agree with it, I will remind you of some past occasions when this policy proved successful. On one occasion Timotheus was sent to the aid of Ariobarzanes, with the added proviso 'that there shall be no breach of the peace with Persia'. In view of the open revolt of Ariobarzanes [3] from Persia, and the garrison on Samos under Cyprothemis, who was sent there by the satrap, Tigranes, Timotheus abandoned the attempt to assist Ariobarzanes, but besieged and liberated Samos. And right up to the present time this has not resulted in war. No one would regard offensive and defensive operations in the same light. Anyone will fight to the utmost against dispossession, but not to secure added possessions. They may aim at this in default of opposition, but if prevented, they feel no resentment against their opponents.

3. Ariobarzanes was satrap of Phrygia. These are the disturbances sometimes referred to as the War of the Satraps.

Nor do I believe that even Artemisia would oppose such action, if Athens is bent on it. I will go a little further into the subject, and then ask you to consider whether I am right or not. It is my view that if Persian activities in Egypt were to proceed according to plan,⁴ Artemisia would make a strong attempt to secure the dependence of Rhodes on Persia, not from friendship for the King, but in the hope that, if he were a permanent neighbour, she could confer a major benefit which would secure friendly relations with her. If, however, things go as they are said to be going, and the Persian objective is lost, she would rightly regard the island as having no further value for Persia at present, but as a threat to her own power and as an obstruction to any movement there. It therefore seems to me that she would prefer Rhodes to be in our power without any open surrender on her part than to be acquired by Persia. Indeed I do not think she will send a force, or, if she does, it will only be a poor and ill-mounted one. As regards the intentions of Persia, for that matter, I will not claim any knowledge, though I would maintain decidedly that Athenian interest demands that the King should make it clear whether he intends to lay claim to Rhodes or not. It is not only the benefit of Rhodes that we shall have to consider when he does, but our own and that of Greece as a whole.

Yet even if the present holders⁵ of Rhodes were in full control of their own city, I would not have recommended taking their part, for any undertakings they might have made. I know that in the first place they incorporated some of the citizen body with them to dissolve the democracy, and, when that was done, expelled them again. People who have not shown good faith with either party cannot be regarded as valuable allies of ours either. Nor would I ever have made this proposal out of consideration solely for the populace of Rhodes. I do not represent them, nor am I personally acquainted with anyone there. And indeed, even if I were, I would only make it with a view to the interest of Athens, because the position of

4. Though Persia succeeded against the satraps, the revolt of Egypt from Persia was not reduced till a good deal later.
5. i.e. the oligarchy established by Mausolus.

Rhodes is one in which, if this is consistent with support of them, I sympathize with the Athenian view. It is from resentment at Athenian insistence on her own rights that Rhodes has lost her liberty. They could have maintained alliance on terms of equality with Greeks who are their superiors, yet in fact they have become the slaves of foreign slaves, whom they have themselves admitted to their own inner fortifications. I would almost say, if we want to assist them, that what has happened has been good for them. Had they enjoyed success, I am not sure whether a place like Rhodes would now have been prepared to learn good sense. But experience and admonition having taught them the many ills that folly brings to most of mankind, they may, with luck, acquire wisdom for the future. This I regard as no small benefit. In fact I maintain that we should try to save them without feeling resentment, and remember the many occasions when we ourselves have suffered from conspiracies, for none of which you would say we deserve to be penalized.

Observe a further point, gentlemen. Our country has been engaged in numerous wars, against democracies as well as oligarchies. You know this well enough. But the motive of each of these encounters is perhaps a thing on which no one reflects. What is that motive? Against popular governments it has either been a matter of private grievances which could not be solved by public negotiation, or of partition of land, of boundaries, of community feeling or of leadership. Against oligarchies none of these considerations has applied; it has been an ideological matter or a question of liberty. Indeed, I would not hesitate to maintain that I think it better that all the Greeks should be our enemies under democracy than our friends under oligarchy. In dealing with free states, in my view, there is no difficulty about regaining peace, while with oligarchy even friendship is precarious. There can be no good feeling between oligarchy and democracy, between the desire for power and the aim at a life of equality.

It is surprising that the idea should not be current that with the oligarchies at Chios or Mytilene, or now at Rhodes, indeed I might say in any instance in which men are induced to submit to this sort of subjection, the constitution of Athens itself shares the danger, surprising that the inference should never be drawn that in a world organized oligarchically Athenian democracy can never be allowed a place. Her enemies realize that there is no other state to bring freedom back into the world, and the origin of so much potential injury to themselves is what they will seek to destroy. In general, injury may be supposed to lead to the hostility of the injured party. But the subversion of a political way of life and its change into oligarchy should be regarded, I urge, as fatal to all aspiration to freedom. Besides, a democratic community like ourselves should be seen to have the same feelings towards victimized peoples as we should expect others to have towards ourselves in the event of our suffering a fate which we should all deplore. Even if the view is held that Rhodes deserved its fate, this is not the moment for satisfaction at it. In the uncertainty of the future for anyone, the fortunate should always show consideration for the welfare of the unfortunate.

I hear frequent reference to the fact that when disaster overtook our democracy[6] in this country, we yet had sympathy from well-wishers. At present I intend to refer briefly to one of them only, Argos. I should not wish this country, with its reputation for aid to the unfortunate, to be shown less forward in this respect than Argos. Living as neighbours to Sparta, who was in open command of land and sea alike, Argos showed no fear or hesitation in declaring her friendship towards Athens, and when Spartan representatives came, we learn, to demand the extradition of Athenian refugees, the decree of Argos was that they should leave before sunset on pain of being treated as enemies. It would be a disgrace, gentlemen, that when the people of Argos showed no fear of Spartan authority and power at such a time, we as Athenians should be intimidated by a non-Greek power, and a woman at that. Indeed Argos would agree that she has been often worsted by Sparta, while we have had frequent victories over Persia and never a defeat, either from his subordinates or from the King himself. Or, if he has ever won success against Athens, it has been by bribery

6. During the rule of the Thirty at Athens.

of the most despicable of Greek traitors and by no other means. Even that brought him no benefit. You will find that the period in which he used Spartan power to weaken Athens coincided with his own perils from Clearchus[7] and Cyrus. So there has never been either an open victory or a successful conspiracy against us. In some quarters I gather that Philip is often disregarded as unimportant, and Persia held in awe as a powerful opponent at any time. If the one is to be left unopposed as negligible, while we treat the other with universal deference as a danger, what enemies are there for us to confront?

There is a class of people in Athens, gentlemen, who excel at voicing the rights of others in this assembly. To them my recommendation would be simply this; they should make it their aim to do justice to Athens when speaking to others. Then they will begin by doing their own duty. It is paradoxical to assert the rights of others when one has failed to stand for one's own. And it is not right for a citizen to consider arguments against his own country and not for it. Why, I ask you, is there no one in Byzantium to speak against their appropriation of Chalcedon, which is the property of Persia, though it was in our hands, and has no connexion with Byzantium? Or again, to forbid the transference of Selymbria, previously an Athenian ally, to become a tributary of theirs, and the appropriation of this district in contravention of the sworn agreement which laid down the autonomy of these cities? Again, there was no one to point out to Mausolus in his life-time, and after his death to Artemisia, that they should not appropriate Cos and Rhodes and other Greek states from which Persia, their previous master, withdrew in favour of Greece by agreement, and which were the subject of many armed conflicts of distinction on the part of the Greeks. Or if there is anyone to point this out to these two, there is apparently no response to it. Personally I regard it as right to restore the Rhodian democracy. Nonetheless, even if it were not the right course, when I consider the conduct of the others I have mentioned, I think it expedient to

7. Clearchus was the Spartan leader of the Ten Thousand. See the sectional introduction and note 30 to Isocrates' *Panegyricus*. The reserved reference to Philip here is somewhat surprising in the same year as *Philippic I*.

do so. Why? If the world set its face towards right it would be a dishonour that Athens alone should stand apart. But when the rest of the world is preparing for iniquity, that Athens alone should lay claim to right without any positive action, seems to me not exemplary, but cowardly, because it is men's actual effectiveness which determines the validity of their claims. I can offer you an example known to everyone. There exists an agreement between Greece and Persia made by this country and universally commended, and a later one made by Sparta which met with condemnation.[8] The two pacts did not lay down the same rights. Private rights were defined by law for separate communities on a basis of equal participation for weak or strong alike. But now the rights of Greek cities are laid down for the weaker by the stronger.

Since, then, you are primed already with the rights of the case, consider how it is in your power to put them into practice. It is so, if we are understood as accepted champions of the freedom of mankind. But it is reasonable to suppose that our duty is very hard to achieve. Other countries have in all cases a single issue to settle, between themselves and their obvious adversaries, whose defeat leaves no obstacle to the attainment of their ends. For us in this country there are two, of which one is the same as for others, but there is an additional and greater issue. We need by our deliberations to get the better of the party[9] which has set out to oppose our interests. When they make it impossible to do what is our duty without a struggle, it is natural that we may fail where we might succeed. The ease with which many take up this political position may be due to the assistance of corrupt supporters, though some blame may with justification be laid at your door. You ought to adopt the same view of political as of military loyalty. What view? A man who abandons the post in which his commander places him is declared to be a citizen no longer, nor have any of a citizen's rights. The same view should be held of the man

8. The so-called Peace of Callias in 448 B.C. (see note on Isocrates, *Panegyricus*, 118), and the King's Peace in 387–6, when Greek states were dictated to by Persia and Sparta.

9. i.e. the party of Eubulus.

who betrays the duty bequeathed to him by past example, and joins the ranks of oligarchy. He should be deprived of the right to join your deliberations. As it is, in dealing with allies you find the highest loyalty where the oath has been sworn to hold to the same friends and the same foes, but in home politics it is the very men who are known to rank themselves with our greatest enemies on whom is conferred the assumption of loyalty.

Nonetheless, grounds for accusation of such people, or for reprimanding the rest of the country, are not hard to find. What is hard is to devise words or actions to put right what is wrong. Perhaps this is not the moment to refer to everything that is relevant. But if you can set the seal on previous decisions by some action of value, there may well be a thorough advance. My own view is that a strong grip on the situation is needed, and action worthy of Athens. Remember how you enjoy praise of her past greatness and the distinction and military achievements of previous generations. Reflect that these were achieved and dedicated not merely for your admiring contemplation, but for the imitation of the virtues they enshrine.

DEMOSTHENES: PHILIPPIC I

WERE it a new question, gentlemen, which lay before us, I should wait until most of the regular speakers had made their contribution, and if I were satisfied with the views expressed, I should add nothing; if not, I should try to voice my own. But as it is the reconsideration of a subject frequently discussed by speakers before, I hope I may be pardoned for speaking first. Had my opponents urged the right policy in the past, this discussion would be superfluous.

First, then, we must not be downhearted at the present situation, however regrettable it seems. The worst feature of it in the past is the best hope for the future. What feature? The fact that it is plain dereliction of duty on our part which has brought us to this position. If it followed on a period of exemplary conduct by the people of Athens, there would be no hope of improvement. Next we should reflect upon what history or our own memory can tell us of the greatness of Sparta not so long ago, and of the glorious and honourable part played by Athens in maintaining the war against them in the cause of right.[1] Why mention this? To set this fact firmly before your minds, gentlemen, that if you are awake, you have nothing to fear, if you close your eyes, nothing to hope for. To prove this I point to two things, the past power of Sparta, which we defeated by sheer attention to business, and the present aggression of Macedon,[2] which alarms us because our attitude is wrong. If the belief is held that Philip is an enemy hard to face in view of the extent of his present strength and the loss to Athens of strategic points, it is a correct belief. But it must be remembered that at one time we had Pydna, Potidaea, Methone and the whole surrounding district on friendly terms, and that a number of communities now on his side were then autonomous and unfettered, and would have preferred our friendship to his. If Philip had then adopted this belief in the invincibility

1. i.e. in the Corinthian War, 394–387.
2. i.e. after the defeat of Onomarchus in the Sacred War.

of Athens in view of her control of points commanding Macedonian territory, while he himself lacked support, he could not have achieved any of his present successes nor acquired the strength he has. As it was, he observed with insight that these strategic points were the prizes of war, that they were open to the contestants, and it is a natural law that ownership passes from the absentee to the first comer, from the negligent to the energetic and enterprising. This is the spirit which has won him the control of what he holds, in some cases by the methods of military conquest, in others by those of friendship and alliance. Indeed alliance and universal attention are the rewards to be won by obvious preparedness and the will to take action. If, then, this country is prepared to adopt a similar outlook and to break with the past, if every man is ready to take the post which his duty and his abilities demand in service to the state, and set pretences aside, if financial contribution is forthcoming from the well-to-do, and personal service from the appropriate group, in a word, if we are prepared to be ourselves, to abandon the hope to evade our duty and get it done by our neighbours, we shall recover what is our own with God's will, we shall regain what inertia has lost us, and we shall inflict retribution upon Philip. You must not imagine that he is a super-human being whose success is unalterably fixed. He has enemies to hate, fear and envy him, even in places very friendly to him. His associates, one must suppose, have the same human feelings as anyone else. But now all this is beneath the surface. It has nowhere to turn because of the slowness, the inactivity of Athens. It is this that I urge you to lay aside. Consider the facts, gentlemen, consider the outrageous lengths to which Philip has gone. He does not offer us a choice between action and inaction. He utters threats, according to my information, in overbearing terms. He is not content to rest on his laurels, but is continually adding to the haul he collects in the net in which he ensnares our hesitant, inactive country. When are we to act? What is to be the signal? When compulsion drives, I suppose. Then what are we to say of the present? In my view the greatest compulsion that can be laid upon free men is their shame at the circumstances in which they find themselves. Do you need to go round and ask each other whether there is any startling news? What could be more startling than a Macedonian fighting a successful war against Athens, and dictating the affairs of Greece? 'Philip is dead', comes one report.³ 'No, he is only ill', from another. What difference does it make? Should anything happen to Philip, Athens, in her present frame of mind, will soon create another Philip. This one's rise was due less to his own power than to Athenian apathy. But I might add that if anything did happen, if chance, which is always the best friend we have, could give us this added service, you may be certain that by being close at hand in a position to control a disordered situation we could turn it to our advantage. As it is, even if circumstance offered it, we could not take over Amphipolis, detached as we are both materially and mentally.

As regards the need to be ready and willing to act I think my point is clear, and I pass on from it. I shall now try to say something on the nature of the expedition which I think would rid us of our troubles, its size and how its financial requirements and other needs could best and most quickly be organized in my view. But I have one initial request to make. Wait to criticize till you have heard it all. Make no assumptions in advance. And if it appears an unusual force from the outset, do not suppose that I am attempting to delay it. 'Here and now' is not always the best advice. What is done cannot be undone even by immediate measures. The best expedient is a precise account of the nature and size of the force needed to hold the position until we can end the war by arbitration or by the defeat of our opponents. That is the only means of ending our disasters. I consider myself able to offer this, though without prejudice to any other proposals suggested. My undertaking is as big as that. But the proof of the pudding is in the eating, and of that you shall yourselves be the judges.

First, then, gentlemen, I declare the need to provide fifty triremes, and secondly to arouse a spirit in the men of this country which will recognize that, if need be, they must serve in them in person. Further, transports and sufficient smaller craft for half the cavalry must be provided. This I maintain

3. This report of Philip's death was current in 352.

should be a standing force to use for immediate moves away from home, to Thermopylae, the Chersonese, Olynthus or where you will. The idea must be implanted in Philip's mind that Athens has abandoned inaction, and may make a sudden move, as she did to Euboea and earlier, we learn, to Haliartus and finally the other day to Thermopylae.[4] The idea is not altogether a matter for contempt, even if it were improbable that my proposal would be carried out. He will either be too unnerved to take action in the knowledge of our readiness (and he will know of it well enough – there are plenty to inform him, unfortunately) or if he neglects to act, he exposes himself to surprise attack, with nothing to withstand an Athenian landing in his territory, if he gives us the chance. This, then, is the decision which I maintain should be taken by the people of Athens, and this is the provision which is needed. But before that a further force needs to be equipped for continuous service in attacks on Macedonian territory. I am not asking for mercenary forces running into five figures, nor for the forces of diplomatic correspondence. I demand an establishment which shall be the possession of Athens and obey the orders of whatever commander is appointed, be there one or many, be he this man or that. I demand also the funds to maintain it. What, then, is to be the nature and the size of this force, its means of subsistence and the will to do its work? Let me take each of these points separately. I mean a mercenary force, but I do not make the mistake repeated in the past, when nothing has seemed large enough, and enormous figures have been voted which in practice have gone completely unimplemented. We should begin on a small scale and then increase it, if it seems inadequate. My proposal is a matter of two thousand men in all, but it should include five hundred Athenians, of whatever age group you decide. They should serve a stated term, not a long one,

4. An Athenian expedition regained Euboea from Thebes in 357. Athens had previously helped Thebes at Haliartus in Boeotia in 395, the occasion of the death of Lysander. The expedition to Thermopylae was in 352, when Philip threatened a descent through the pass into southern Greece, in connexion with his Thessalian campaign. But it does not seem sufficiently clear at what point Athens took action and how on this occasion alone they were able to do it effectively.

but whatever is decided, and on a basis of successive shifts. The rest should be mercenaries. They should be supported by two hundred cavalry, again including fifty Athenians at least, and on the same system of service. They must have transport provided. What else? Ten warships. Philip has a war fleet, so Athens must match it, to ensure the safety of this force. And the source of supplies for them? I will pass to the elucidation of this point when I have made clear my reasons for advocating a force of this size and a citizen contingent as part of it.

As regards numbers, the reason for what I propose is that it is not open to us now to provide a field force to stand up to Philip's. We must be content with a raiding force, and that in the first place must be our strategy. It must not be of excessive size, for which we lack the funds, nor entirely contemptible. There must be a citizen contingent to accompany the force for this reason. In the past I believe Athens maintained a mercenary force at Corinth under the command of Polystratus, Iphicrates, Chabrias and others, and accompanied by citizen troops. I understand that a defeat was inflicted on Sparta by this force together with its Athenian units.[5] But since our mercenary forces have been self-subsisting, it is our friends and allies who have suffered defeat while our enemies have regrettably increased. These forces take a passing glance at the task Athens has for them, and then are off overseas to Artabazus or anywhere else, with their commander after them. This is not unnatural. You cannot command without pay to offer. My demand therefore is to remove such pretexts from commander and men alike, by issuing pay and providing the surveillance of a parallel citizen force, our present conduct of affairs being ridiculous. Suppose you were asked the question, 'Are you at peace?', 'No,' you would reply, 'we are at war with Philip.' But surely ten Athenians were appointed to command divisions of various kinds, and two to command cavalry. What are they all doing?

5. This appears to have been the first instance of the use of mercenaries in Greece (see Isocrates, *Philip*, 96). Polystratus is little known. Iphicrates earned distinction in 390 B.C. against Spartan hoplites, and Chabrias was his successor, and won a naval victory at Naxos against a Spartan fleet in 376.

Except the individual you actually send to the theatre of war, they are conducting the ceremonial processions with the Festival Committee. They are like clay figures voted for civilian appearance,[6] not for war. Shouldn't we have had our own commanders of infantry and cavalry, an Athenian staff, to make it our own force? But our own cavalry commander has to sail to Lemnos,[7] while the cavalry engaged in the fight for Athenian possessions are under Menelaus. I intend nothing against him personally, but his post, whoever was to hold it, should be occupied by an Athenian appointment.

This may appear true enough, but what you want to hear is the extent and the source of the money needed. Let me go on to this. First, finances. Maintenance, in the form of supplies alone, for this force will amount to upwards of ninety talents. Ten warships account for forty talents, at twenty *minae* per ship per month. Two thousand men need the same amount again, to allow ten *drachmae* a month each ration money, and two hundred cavalry at thirty *drachmae* a month makes twelve talents.[8] If this is thought a very small start, to provide rations for the men serving, it is an incorrect view. I am quite sure that, given this, the force will provide itself with the rest in the field, without inflicting damage on other Greek states, and make up its pay in that way. I am prepared to sail as a volunteer, and to accept any penalty if this does not prove true. Next, the source of the funds I propose to raise.

(A Bill of Ways and Means is read)

That, gentlemen, is the extent of the money we[9] have been able to raise. When you vote it, if you decide to do so, you will

6. Literally 'in the market place', through which processions passed. They were in the charge of army officers, who, Demosthenes suggests, were like *terra cotta* figures, intended for ornament rather than use.

7. A special officer was always appointed to command cavalry in Lemnos.

8. 100 *drachmae* = 1 *mina*, 60 *minae* = 1 talent. These figures give 2 obols per day as the estimated pay for each man, which was normally doubled to provide ration money in addition, and may be compared with a figure of 3 or 4 obols as the pay of an unskilled labourer. Demosthenes expects pay to be supplemented by raids on the enemy country.

9. The plural indicates some kind of assistance in drawing up the details.

be giving your vote for action against Philip, and action not confined to the words of manifestos and despatches.

It seems to me that your deliberations on the subject of war and its entire equipment would be rendered more effective by consideration of the country in which it is to take place. You must recognize that it is by careful attention to winds and seasons that Philip gains considerable advantage. He waits for the Etesians[10] or for winter before making moves by them beyond our reach. With this in mind we should avoid a war of single expeditions, which will always be too late for their effect, and resort to a standing force. We can command winter harbourage at Lemnos, Thasos and Sciathos and other islands in the neighbourhood. There are harbours there and ready supplies and all necessities for an army. And at the right time of year, when coastal operations are safe and winds not dangerous, there will be easy access to trading ports.

The use that will be made of this force, and the moment to choose, will be settled as opportunity arises by the commander appointed. What we need to provide is the subject of my proposal. Make this available, first the finances I have proposed, then the rest, men, ships and cavalry, the whole force complete and clamped down to the business of war, with the control of this assembly over finance, and a general required to submit a report, and you will be at an end of continuous debates on the same subject, unsupported by action.[11] And in addition, Philip's greatest asset will be lost to him. What is this asset? The fact that he makes use of our own allies in the war against us by piratical raids on sea transport. What else? Athens will be clear of damage. It will not be like past occasions, when he made descents on Lemnos and Imbros and went off with Athenian citizens as prisoners, when he cut off Athenian shipping and appropriated untold wealth, when finally he made a landing at Marathon and possessed himself of the state galley,[12]

10. North-easterly winds regular in the Aegean in July and August (see *On the Chersonese*, 14).

11. Demosthenes' tone does not yet suggest immediate urgency.

12. This was called the Paralus. Among official functions it conducted the sacred mission to the sanctuary of Apollo at Delos, in the course of which it touched at Marathon.

which he removed from her station. It proved impossible for Athens to prevent these depredations, or to bring force to bear at the proposed moment. Yet why is it, do you suppose, that the festivals of the Panathenaea and the Dionysia always take place at the correct time, whether the task of managing them is allotted to experts or laymen – and these are things which run into greater expense than any military expedition, and probably demand greater trouble and preparation than anything else at all – whereas our expeditions are invariably too late, like the ones to Methone or Pagasae or Potidaea?[13] The reason is that the festivals are regulated by law. Everyone knows long beforehand who is to head the tribe in the theatre or the games, and when he is to receive what from whom, and what he is to do. Nothing is left vague and unspecified there.[14] But in the military field and in preparation for it there is no order, no organization, no precise control. The result is this. It is not till the news of the actual emergency comes that we appoint commanders. We then proceed to property exchanges,[15] consideration of ways and means, later on to a decision to use alien troops, later still to change to citizen troops, then to adopt others after all. And in the time all this takes, the object of our expedition is lost before it is begun. The time for action is squandered in preparation, and opportunities for action will not wait for procrastination and pretence. Then resources which we imagine we possess throughout are proved inadequate at the critical moment. Meanwhile Philip's insolence goes to the length of a despatch of this sort to Euboea.

(*The text of a despatch is now read*)

Most of what has just been read, gentlemen, is unfortunately

13. See sectional introduction, p. 170.
14. The Panathenaea were in charge of special officials, chosen by lot, the Dionysia in the first place were under the archon, who had a staff of ten for the purpose.
15. The trierarchy (see glossary s.v. Leitourgia) was one of the public services undertaken by individuals. But if anyone nominated for one of them thought that a wealthier man had been passed over, he could claim to exchange property with him or else demand that the other should take over the task.

true. Yet it does not, perhaps, make pleasant hearing. Now if the omissions made by speakers to avoid unpleasantness are going to be repeated in the actual course of events, there is a case for political ingratiation. If, on the other hand, ingratiation out of season brings actual loss, then it is despicable to pursue self-deception and postpone unpleasantness at the expense of sacrificing realities. It is a failure to realize that the proper pursuit of warfare does not mean following in the trail of events, but being in front of them. One would claim that a commander should be ahead of his men, and so should statesmen be ahead of events, and not be compelled to follow them. The citizens of Athens, however, possessed as they are of the greatest power of all in ships, fighting men, cavalry and monetary resources, have never to this day made a right use of any of them. The war against Philip exactly resembles the methods of an untaught foreigner in the boxing ring. If he is hit, he hugs the place, and if you hit him somewhere else, there go his hands again. He has not learnt, and is not prepared, to defend himself or look to his front. So it is with the policy of Athens. If news comes of Philip in the Chersonese, an expedition there is voted, if it is Thermopylae, it is sent there. Wherever he goes, we hurry up and down at his instance, controlled by his strategy without any constructive military plan of our own, without foresight to anticipate news of what is happening or has happened. If this was, perhaps, a possible course in the past, that time is now at an end. There is no longer room for it. It must be some divine providence, gentlemen, which is ashamed of the conduct of this country and has implanted this busy spirit in Philip. Had he been content with his initial captures and gone no further, some people here would probably have been satisfied with circumstances which brought the stigma of shame and disgrace on the whole nation. But his continual attempts to add to his gains may stir us to action, unless all spirit is lost to us. It is astonishing that there is not a man in Athens to reflect with indignation that a war which opened with the aim of bringing deserved retribution upon Philip of Macedon should now be ending in an effort to escape disaster at his hands. Yet it is certainly clear that he will not stand still unless his advance is

impeded. Is this what we are to wait for? Are some unmanned
ships and a few optimistic ideas enough to satisfy us that our
ends are secured? Can we stop short of manning our own fleet,
sending out a force of Athenians, at least in part, now that the
time has almost run out? Can we stop short of an expedition
overseas? The question is asked where we are to anchor. The
war will of itself find out his weak points, if we press on with
it. If we stay at home and listen to abuse and recrimination
between speakers, never shall we enjoy any success. I assure
you, where part of our citizen army is sent overseas, even if not
all of it, the favour of providence and of fortune goes with it.
But when the expedition consists only of a commander, an
unimplemented decision and the hopes which are expressed
from this platform, nothing is achieved, our enemies deride us,
while our allies are frightened to death of such expeditions.
It is impossible, quite impossible, for one man to accomplish
our every hope. Promises and statements and accusations against
this person or that are only too possible, and the ruin of our
affairs. When the commander is given a few miserable men
without pay, when his every action can be misrepresented with
ease at home and random decisions are made on a basis of
hearsay, what can be expected?

How is this state of things to be ended? It will end when this
country gives its citizens a triple function, to serve in her armies,
to witness the conduct of the campaign, and, on their return,
to judge the report, so that it is not a matter of hearing news of
it, but of eyewitness knowledge. In our present shameful state
every commander risks his life two or three times in court, but
they none of them dare risk it in battle. They prefer to risk the
lives of slavers and privateers than perform their proper function. A criminal's true death is a sentence executed, a general's
is in battle against the enemy. But as for us, we go about saying
that Philip is plotting with Sparta for the break-up of the Theban
confederacy,[16] or that he has sent representatives to Persia, or
that he is engaged on fortifications in Illyria, or any other
invention that anyone likes to disseminate. I do not think this
is likely. I think he may well be intoxicated with what he has

16. On the Theban confederacy see Isocrates, *Philip*, 43, and note 7.

achieved, he may have many such dreams in the manifest absence of any opposition and in the exaltation of success, but I do not think it likely that he chooses to act so that the merest fools in Athens know his intentions. And the merest fools are the purveyors of rumours. If we can say good-bye to all that and realize one thing, that this is our enemy, who is stealing from us our possessions and has long defied all right, if we see that every hope we have indulged of help from others has been proved to be the reverse, and that the future lies in our hands alone, if we realize that to refuse to fight him on his own territory is perhaps to be compelled to do so on ours, then we shall have reached a proper decision, and be emancipated from empty words. What we need is not speculation on the future, but the certainty that it will be disastrous if we lack the proper outlook and the will to action.

I have never elected to seek public favour by policies which I did not believe expedient. On this occasion too I have spoken simply and bluntly without reservation. I wish I were sure it would benefit me to speak the truth as much as you to be told it. I should feel much happier if I were. As it is, I must rest in uncertainty of the effect it will bring on me, but the certainty that these convictions are to the benefit of the nation, if they are carried out, is the basis upon which I choose to speak. May the decision be one which will prove the best for us all.

DEMOSTHENES: OLYNTHIAC I

You would give a great deal, I fancy, gentlemen, for a clear understanding where your interest is likely to lie in the affairs under consideration. This being so, you should be ready to pay keen attention to such proposals as are made. Not only can you secure the advantage of hearing any considered suggestion which may be offered here, but it may be your good fortune, I imagine, to find that valuable ideas occur impromptu to speakers, which may make it easy, from the whole range open to you, to choose the wisest path.

Gentlemen, this moment of history cries out to declare that it is time to take a positive grip of affairs, if we have any thought for their security. But our attitude is one which I can scarcely describe. My own view calls for an immediate vote for an expeditionary force, for the speediest possible provision of the means to implement it (to avoid a repetition of the past), for the despatch of representatives to announce it and to maintain liaison on the spot. The greatest danger is that concessions or threats which may carry conviction, or misrepresentation of our absence, may enable an unscrupulous and clever opportunist like Philip to secure important advantages for himself. Nonetheless, it is reasonably true that the hardest feature to contend with in Philip's position is also our greatest asset. His personal control of all activities, open or secret, his combined position in command of the army, state and exchequer, his invariable presence with his forces, give him a real superiority in military speed and efficiency. But in regard to the exchanges he would like with Olynthus the reverse is true. It is clear to the people of Olynthus that it is no longer their own credit, no longer a territorial matter which is at issue in this war, but the destruction and enslavement of their country. They know what was the fate of the betrayers of the state at Amphipolis, of Philip's sponsors at Pydna. It is a general truth that autocracy is suspect among free states, especially if it appears on their boundaries.

With this knowledge at heart, and with other considerations

in mind, we should in my submission set our will and stir our spirit at this eleventh hour to war, with a readiness for financial contribution and personal service without stint. We have no sort of excuse now for reluctance. Yesterday it was common talk that Olynthus must be set to war against Macedon. Today this has come about of itself, and in a most advantageous manner for this country. Had it been at our instance that Olynthus entered the war, she might have been an uncertain, not a whole-hearted ally. But as her own complaints are the basis of her enmity, it should be a lasting hostility based on her own fears and grievances. An opportunity has fallen to us, and we must not let it slip, we must not succumb to the same fate as so often before. On the occasion of the aid we sent to Euboea,[1] when Hierax and Stratocles stood on this platform and urged us to move overseas and take over their city, had we shown the same enthusiasm in our own interest as we did for the safety of Euboea, we should have been in possession of Amphipolis and have been saved all subsequent trouble about it. Again, when news came of the siege of Pydna, Potidaea, Methone, Pagasae[2] and the rest, to cut a long list short, had we then in one single instance taken the field with proper spirit, we should now have a far humbler and easier Philip to meet. As it is, our refusal to seize the fleeting moment, and our assumption that the future will look after itself, have effectively turned Philip into the greatest monarch who has ever appeared in Macedonia. Now at last we have our opportunity in Olynthus. It has come to us unsought, and it is the greatest in our history. Indeed I think a fair reckoning of the favours of fortune to Athens, even though much is not as it might be, should inspire deep feelings of gratitude. The many losses war has brought may properly be attributed to our own neglect. Their occurrence recently instead of long ago, and the appearance of an alliance to balance them, if we are ready to make use of it, can only be put down to her favour. This has a parallel in finance. Keep what you gain and you will feel a debt to fortune. But let it evaporate, and the gratitude disappears with it. And in politics

1. In 357. See *Philippic I*, 17 and note.
2. See sectional introduction.

failure to make good use of opportunity means that fortune's favours too are forgotten. It is by the ultimate result that the initial assets are estimated.

It is therefore vitally necessary to think of the future, to enable us to set our ways straight and wipe out the discredit of past conduct. If we are to abandon Olynthus too, and Philip is to become its master, what is to prevent him, I should like to know, from moving wherever he chooses? Do any of us reckon and fully realize the methods which have brought Philip from initial weakness to his present stature? First the capture of Amphipolis, then of Pydna, next Potidaea, then Methone, then the move into Thessaly. Next came Pherae, Pagasae and Magnesia, and after securing the whole position as he wanted it, he was away to Thrace, where he expelled or established the princes of the district. Then came his illness, but when he recovered, there was no decline into inactivity. He at once attacked Olynthus. I say nothing of his excursions into Illyria and Paeonia, or against Arybbas[3] and the rest.

Why point this out now? It is to bring to your knowledge and realization two things: first the disaster of squandering your interests one by one, and secondly the restless activity which is Philip's life and which never allows him to rest on his laurels. If it is to be his motto that every move must be an advance, and ours that we are never to take a grip of reality, I urge you to contemplate what is the likely result. Indeed who could remain in blind ignorance, or fail to realize that the war at Olynthus will be on our own territory if we neglect it? If that is to happen, I am afraid we shall find ourselves in the position of the easy borrower at high rates, who after a fleeting moment of prosperity has to surrender principal as well as interest. We may find that our inertia has been bought at high cost, that the unvaried quest for pleasure may bring us to the necessity of much that is the opposite, to the jeopardy of our very possessions at home.

Destructive criticism, I shall be told, is easy and anyone can make it. It is particular and positive proposals which demand the

3. Arybbas was a king in Epirus, defeated probably in 352 at the time of Philip's third expedition against the Illyrians.

statesman. I am perfectly aware, gentlemen, that it is often on the last speaker that your anger descends, and not where the responsibility lies for what you find unsatisfactory. But I do not think one should allow consideration of personal safety to make one hesitate to speak out. My declared view is in favour of intervention to preserve the members of the Olynthian confederation by sending a force for that purpose, and by inflicting damage on Macedonian territory with a second naval and military force. Neglect either of these, and I am afraid the campaign will be ineffective. Confine it to attacks on Macedonia, and Philip will reduce Olynthus and then have no difficulty in defending his own territory. Confine it to assistance to Olynthus, and he will realize that there is no threat to Macedon, and lay siege to Olynthus and maintain his threat to the position till in time he gains control of the besieged cities. Our force must be considerable and must be in two sections.

That is my view about the expedition. As regards the finances of it, you are in possession, gentlemen, of a source of revenue unparalleled in the world.[4] You receive it in the form you like. If you are prepared to use this for the expeditionary force, you have no need to look further. But if not, you do need resources, indeed you have none at all. Is it, then, my proposal that this fund should be appropriated to military purposes? No,[5] it is not. My view is that a force must be equipped, and that a single organization ought to cover payments received and expenditure required. The normal view favours money to spend at the festivals without any trouble in acquiring it. The only alternative is a universal subscription, the amount depending on the need. But the money is needed, and is indispensable to the performance of the smallest part of our duty. There are various suggestions for the means to raise this fund. Choose which you like,

4. This refers to the so-called Theoric Fund, a subject which Demosthenes clearly treats with some uneasiness. It had been created to provide the poor with the means of attending the festivals, and had gradually appropriated all the surplus revenue. It was jealously preserved by popular opinion, and an attempt made shortly before this speech to secure some of the fund for war purposes had been met by an indictment for illegality.

5. Demosthenes is careful not to call this a proposal, but merely a statement of opinion.

so that while the opportunity is there, you keep your grip on the situation.

It is worth while to make a considered judgement of Philip's present position. It is not what it appears, it is not, as a casual glance might suggest, an easy or ideal situation for him. He would never have provoked this war, had he thought that actual fighting would be necessary. His hope was that he had only to approach, to be master of every situation. But his hope has been vain. This is his first anxiety. It was unexpected and is a great disappointment. His second is Thessaly.[6] It is by nature unreliable and it has proved so to everyone. Philip is no exception. Thessaly has passed a resolution to demand the return of Pagasae and prevented the fortification of Magnesia. I have even heard mentioned the proposal to deny him the benefit of open markets and ports, which should supply the general needs of Thessaly, and not be appropriated to Macedon. And if he is to be kept from this source of supply, he will be in dire straits for the provisioning of his forces. One must indeed suppose that the peoples of Paeonia and Illyria and the rest would prefer autonomy and freedom to servitude. They are in no habit of submission, and Philip is a harsh master, it is understood, and it is not hard to believe. Undeserved success is the road to folly in unbalanced minds, which makes it harder to keep than to win prosperity. For us then, gentlemen, his inopportune acts must be our opportunities to join in the contest, by representations where necessary, by personal service, by incitement of others. If Philip had such a chance against Athens, remember how ready he would be to attack us, if war came to Attica. Should we not then feel ashamed to lack the courage, when the opportunity is there, to do to him what he would do to us if he could?

One point more. You must not forget that your choice must be made now between a war conducted by you on his territory

6. Philip occupied Magnesia, a district of Thessaly, in 352, after which he was granted the right to levy market dues there. But it was later restored to Magnesia (see *Olynthiac II*, 7, and *Philippic II*, 22). It must be admitted that this section and the last show an inclination to wishful thinking on the part of Demosthenes, which is perhaps a regular characteristic of democratic communities in their dealing with autocracy.

and one conducted by him on yours. If Olynthus holds, you will be engaged on Macedonian territory and do damage to it while enjoying the fruits of your own in security. But if Philip captures Olynthus, what will stand in the way of his advance against ourselves? Thebes? It may seem harsh to say it, but Thebes will join the invasion. Phocis then? She cannot protect her own territory without help from us. Some other champion? No one will be prepared to do it. For Philip, on the other hand, it would be astonishing if the threats he gives vent to at the expense of his reputation for sanity are not put into action when he has the power. Indeed, the difference between fighting here and fighting there hardly needs emphasis. If an Athenian force had to spend a mere month in the field, and live on the country for all the needs of an army, without an enemy at all, your farmers would lose more than the expense of the whole of the last war. If war comes here, what must be the extent of their losses? Add to that the violence, and last but not least the ignominy of our position, as great a loss as any on a balanced view.

These are the facts we must focus, and so advance to the attack and thrust the scene of war into the territory of Macedon. We have our motives. The wealthy must seek to spend a little of the wealth they are lucky enough to possess so as to enjoy the rest in security. The young and strong should seek military experience on the soil of Macedon, and so make formidable protectors of their own. The politicians should hope to make it easy to face investigation of their political careers so that the experience of the nation may colour its criticism of their conduct of office. And for every reason may it be for the best.

DEMOSTHENES: OLYNTHIAC II

GENTLEMEN, there have been many indications of the goodness of Providence towards Athens, and our present position is one of the clearest. Potential enemies of Macedon have appeared, neighbours possessed of some power and, most important of all, an attitude towards war which makes them feel that their relations with Macedon have been first unreliable, then disastrous to themselves.[1] This has all the appearance of an intervention of Providence on our behalf. So it is for us ourselves to ensure that we do not lag behind circumstance in support of our own position. It is to our discredit, indeed to our deepest discredit, to surrender our hold not merely on states or districts which were once ours, but on the assistance and the opportunities which fortune provides.

A long account of the power of Macedon as a means to urge Athenians to their duty I regard as a mistake, for this reason. Anything that can be said to this effect increases Macedonian prestige and damages this country. The more Philip's successes exceed his deserts, the greater his reputation as a world's wonder. The more Athenian statesmanship falls short, the lower stands Athenian credit. I will say no more of this. A proper estimate will show that here lies the reason for his rise to power, not in any resource of his own. The debt he owed to his collaborators, for which Athens should demand justice, I am not disposed to discuss now. But there are subjects apart from this which are of greater value to put before this assembly, and which on a true reckoning constitute a damaging charge against him. These I shall try to present.

Merely to decry his perfidious breaches of faith without factual evidence may rightly be written down as empty abuse. But an account of his actions up to the present, with a detailed examination of the points against him, needs no great length and appears desirable for two purposes: to display his true weakness and to prove to people who are dismayed at his invincible

1. This of course refers to Olynthus.

205

strength that he has exhausted the whole catalogue of falsehood
which has made him great and that his position is on the verge
of ruin. I should emphatically agree that Philip was an object
for our fear and our wonder, if what I saw were a power based
upon right. But long and full consideration shows the truth.
His first success was at the expense of our own folly, when the
Olynthian representatives were denied the negotiation they
wanted by the tale of Philip's intended transfer of Amphipolis,
and the much discussed secret pact.[2] He next secured the adherence of Olynthus by unjustifiable treatment of a former ally,
in seizing Potidaea from us and transferring it to Olynthus.
Finally Thessaly was persuaded by a promise to surrender
Magnesia and undertake a Phocian war for her own benefit.[3]
There is not a state which has tried to make use of him without
falling victim to his duplicity. In every case he deceived them,
and exploited their folly and ignorance for his own advancement.
He has risen on their shoulders, each time they have seen in
him a means to their own advantage. He should owe his destruction to the same forces, now that his invariable self-interest
has been proved against him. This is the point to which Philip's
fortunes have been brought, and I challenge any speaker to
prove to me, or rather to this assembly, either that my contention is false, or that anyone who has once been trapped is likely
to trust him again, or that anyone once reduced to slavery will
not delight in the hope of freedom.

If you suppose this is true, yet believe that the King of
Macedon, by his capture of strategic points and harbours, will
have power to dominate the world, it is an unsound belief.
Unity based upon good will and common interest gives men
the spirit to toil, to endure and to stand. But the power which
like his is rooted in greed and violence will fall in ruin at a word,
at the first false step. Never, gentlemen, never can a lasting
power be founded on broken promises and lying words. Such

2. Amphipolis was to be restored to Athens in exchange for Pydna.
3. On Thessaly see *Olynthiac I*, 22. There seems to be no inconsistency,
such as has been suggested, between this and the present passage and 14
below. The uncertainty of Thessalian politics is looked upon as a potential
danger to Philip's position, and so an advantage to Athens.

empires stand for one short hour. They may blossom with fair hopes, but time finds them out, and they fade and die. In a house, in a ship, in any structure, it is the foundation which most needs strength. So it is too with the actions of men's lives, which must be founded on truth and justice. And this is not true of the achievements of Macedon.

My view is that we must assist Olynthus. The better and the speedier the help that is suggested, the better I shall be pleased. Secondly we must send to Thessaly to provide information and a spur to action. The present decision there is to demand the restoration of Pagasae and negotiations about Magnesia. But it is essential that our representatives shall not be confined to words, but shall have some action to point to in the shape of an expeditionary force in keeping with Athenian prestige, and to show that we mean business. Words without actions are vain and empty, especially from Athens. The readier we seem to use them, the more we are distrusted. Great is the change, the altered attitude we need to show, by contributions of money and of service, and by general readiness, if we are to command attention. If you are prepared to carry your obligations into actual reality, it will not only expose the frailty and uncertainty of Philip's alliances. It will find out the weakness of his whole power and position at home.

Broadly speaking, the power and the empire of Macedon, as a supplementary force, is no small asset, as indeed it was to Athens against Olynthus at the time of Timotheus,[4] or again to Olynthus against Potidaea as an addition to their strength; or recently when they assisted a decadent and divided Thessaly against the royal house. Even a small added power is always of value. But in itself it is weak and fraught with troubles. In fact all the activities in which Philip's greatness might be thought to lie, his wars and expeditions, have made his position still more precarious than nature made it. Do not imagine for a moment, that one and the same set of circumstances brings satisfaction both to Philip and to his subjects. His aim and ambition is glory. His way is the way of action and accepted risk, his goal the greatest renown in the history of the kings of

4. Timotheus took Torone and Potidaea for Athens in 364.

Macedon. He prefers that to safety. But they do not share these
ambitions. They are torn by marching from end to end of the
country, and reduced to misery and continuous hardship. They
are kept from their own pursuits, their personal affairs, and
even what opportunities chance allows cannot be organized,
because ports in the country are closed by the war. This affords
clear indication of the relation of most of Macedonia towards
Philip.

As to his paid soldiers and his *corps d'élite*, who have the
reputation of being a superbly welded military force, I have it
from an irreproachable informant, who has been in that country,
that they are no more than ordinary. Men of military experience,
I was told, are discarded by a selfish leader who wants all the
credit himself, because his ambition is as outstanding as anything else about him. On the other hand men of restraint and
integrity in other fields, who cannot endure a life of drunkenness
and debauchery and indecent dancing, are rejected and passed
over by a man like Philip. The rest of his *entourage* are bandits
and flatterers, capable of taking part in drunken revelry which
I hesitate to describe. This is clearly true, because the outcasts
of our society, who were thought lower than mere street-
entertainers, creatures like the slave, Callias, who do comic
performances and write low songs at the expense of others to
get a laugh, these are the people he likes and keeps around him.
This may seem little, but it is in fact a great proof of this contemptible character on a right estimate. At present, no doubt,
this is obscured by success. There is nothing like success to
conceal dishonour. But at any moment of failure it will be put
to the test. And it will not be long, in my view, granted the
consent of heaven and the determination of this country, before
it begins to show signs. In physical health a man who is strong
may go for a time without noticing anything amiss, but in time
of illness troubles extend everywhere, to any past fracture or
strain or underlying weakness. It is the same with a state,
whether democratic or monarchical. In time of external war
weaknesses are not commonly apparent. But war on its frontier
brings them to light.

If anyone here observes Philip's prosperity and supposes him a formidable opponent, it is the view of good sense. Fortune is a powerful force, indeed it is everything, in all human affairs. Nonetheless, given the choice, I would prefer the fortune of Athens, granted her will to follow the call of duty in detail, to that of Philip. There are many more ways open to her than to him to command the favour of heaven. Yet here we sit inactive. He could not remain inactive and still demand the assistance of his own friends, let alone the good will of heaven. No wonder that with his expeditions, his energy, his personal control of detail, his opportunism at every juncture, he gets the better of democratic hesitation, deliberation and inquiry. I am not surprised. The opposite would be surprising, if neglect of our duty in war brought success against his complete fulfilment of it. What does surprise me is this.. In the past, against Sparta, this country went to war for the rights of Greek states,[5] declined numerous opportunities of self-seeking and for the rights of others sacrificed her wealth in war expense and her security in war service. Now she is slow to offer money and slow to serve in defence of her own possessions. We saved others on many occasions collectively and singly, but the loss of our own possessions is something we do not stir a finger to prevent. This is what surprises me, this and one other fact, that there is not a man capable of reckoning the length of the war against Philip, and asking what this country has been doing in all this length of time. You know the answer. She has passed it in procrastination, in optimism, in recrimination, condemnation and yet more optimism. Is this assembly senseless enough to hope that the proceedings which turned the scale in the country's affairs for the worse will now have exactly the opposite effect? It is not in reason, it is not in nature. It is natural that it should be easier to preserve than to acquire possessions. Now however the war has left us nothing to preserve, and acquire we must.

And this is for our own initiative to achieve. The essential is enthusiastic contribution to war funds, and war service, and a truce from recrimination until control is ours. Then we can judge by realities, give honour where honour is due, and demand

5. In the Corinthian War, 394 B.C. See *Philippic I*, 3.

retribution for misconduct and an end to excuses and deficiencies. You cannot make bitter criticism of the part played by others except on the basis of unfailing integrity in your own. After all, if you want realities in connexion with your commanders, what do you suppose is the reason why all those you send overseas hurry to abandon their country's war, and discover private wars of their own? It is that in that field the prizes of war belong to the country (if Amphipolis falls, it will soon return to Athens) while the risks are personal and rest on the commanders, and pay is non-existent. In their field the risks are less, while captured booty falls to the commanders and their men. Lampsacus,[6] Sigeum and the ships they capture are instances. They go where it pays them to go. As for ourselves, when we take a look at the disastrous state of our affairs, we put our commanders on trial. Then, when we invite their comments and appreciate their overriding difficulties, we acquit them. Ultimately the result for us is dispute and division between this view and that, in a deteriorating situation. Some time ago the committees were the basis of war contributions. Now public affairs are on a committee basis.[7] Each party has its leader in the orator, a military commander to support him, and their *claqueurs*, who correspond to the rest of the three hundred. The rest have been distributed to one party or another. We must abandon this method, we must be ourselves again now at this eleventh hour, and unite for organization, speech and action alike. If you assign to one set of men an almost tyrannical control of the state, to another the compulsory task of naval commands, financial support and military service, while to a third is allotted merely that of criticism without

6. Occupied by Chares in 356, perhaps with the consent of the satrap, Artabazus.

7. One of Demosthenes' earliest public speeches (354 B.C.) had been concerned with the organization (initiated in 378) of syndicates of 300 for the payment of war tax and later the financing of ship building. Here he compares the divisions and disunity between political parties with the disputes between these committees. Each committee had a chairman, the wealthiest of them, and a manager, who organized the raising of the money in the interest of the committee, as did the political parties with their orator, the general they favoured, and their supporters.

participation, you will never have the efficient control you need. Any section that is slighted will fail to play its part, and then you will have the satisfaction of punishing them instead of the enemy.

Let me summarize our requirements: universal money contribution according to means, universal service in detachments till all have served, universal freedom to speak and a choice of policy not confined to that of one or two particular politicians. Carry this out, and instead of immediate applause for the last speaker, bestow it on yourselves for a general improvement in the whole position.

DEMOSTHENES: OLYNTHIAC III

I AM moved by different feelings, gentlemen, when I turn to the actual course of events, from those which arise from what I hear said here. Speakers, I observe, are concerned with retaliation on Philip, but the march of events has created the prior need to forestall danger to our own country. Speeches of this kind appear to me to make the mistake of suggesting the wrong subject for your deliberations. There was a time when this country had it in her power to combine her own safety with retaliation on Philip. I know that well enough. Both possibilities existed within my own experience here. But I am now convinced that it is enough to hope initially to secure the preservation of our allies. Once that is assured, we can begin to consider retaliation, and ways and means to it. But until a sound beginning has been laid down, discussion of the end is useless.

This present moment, beyond all others, demands deep consideration. It is not present policy that I regard as the main difficulty. My problem is how to address this meeting. The evidence of my own eyes and ears convinces me that this lack of grip upon affairs is more a failure of will than of intelligence. I beg you therefore to tolerate directness on my part. You must consider the truth of what I say with the aim of improvement in the future. You must realize that it is the ingratiating method of certain speakers which has brought our whole position to so low an ebb.

I must first, I believe, go back a little over the past. You remember when the news came three or four years ago that Philip was besieging Heraeon Teichos in Thrace.[1] It was the month of November. Amid an outburst of speeches and excitement the decision was taken to launch forty ships manned by a citizen force of the under-forty-fives and raise a sum of sixty talents. The year ended.[2] July came, August and September,

1. The occasion cannot be exactly determined. Presumably in 352, when the rumour of Philip's death was current.
2. The Athenian year began in June. The mysteries took place in early October.

and then at long last ten ships were despatched under Chari-
demus, unmanned, and the sum of five talents was voted. News
had come of Philip's illness or death (both were reported) and
therefore it was thought that there was no occasion for an
expedition, and it was abandoned. Yet that was the decisive
moment for it. Had we then carried out with energy the operation which was voted, Philip would not have survived to
trouble us now.

That occasion is now beyond recall. The present war has
offered another opportunity, which has led me to mention the
first, so as to avoid a repetition of it. What are we to make of it?
If we are not to go into action 'to the utmost of our strength'
and 'with all power',³ observe how our tactics will all have
played into Philip's hands. There stood Olynthus with a
certain strength, and the position was that neither she nor
Philip viewed the other with confidence. Peace was negotiated
between us and Olynthus.⁴ Here was a troublesome obstacle to
Philip, to have a considerable state threatening his interests, and
a state in good relations with this country. It seemed desirable
on all scores to engineer a war between them, and what was so
often talked of before has now come about by one means or
another. What course is therefore open but to take strong
and enthusiastic action in support of Olynthus? I see no alternative. Even apart from the dishonour of any compromise, the
danger of it is considerable, in the present position of Thebes,
the bankruptcy of Phocis, and with Philip, once he has control
of the present situation, unhindered by any obstacle from
turning in this direction. If anyone here desires to postpone the
action we need, then it is his desire to witness calamity at home
when he might hear of it elsewhere, to crave aid when he might
offer it. That it will come to this if we neglect the present we
must surely all realize.

I hear the rejoinder, 'Yes, the need for action is accepted,
and it will be taken.' But how? Do not be surprised if my
answer is an unexpected one. Establish a legislative committee.
But pass no new enactment. You have plenty. Repeal what

3. The phrases belong to a formula used in treaties.
4. 352 B.C.

you have that are detrimental. I refer specifically to that regarding the Theoric Fund[5] and to some military enactments, which either appropriate military funds to unmilitary purposes or establish immunity for indiscipline, and so turn all patriotic feeling to despondency. It is by breaking this barrier, by making the way safe for public-spirited proposals, that you really initiate the quest for the universally acknowledged benefit of the nation. Meanwhile do not keep looking for men who will court destruction by making such proposals. None will be forthcoming, especially as the only likely outcome of doing so is undeserved injury without any valuable result, and an increased premium on public spirit. The repeal of such enactments must be demanded of the very men who passed them. It is unwarrantable that their proposers should win popularity to the public detriment, while the unpopularity which can herald better things stands as an obstacle to the public-spirited proposer. Till you have set this position right, gentlemen, you must not demand from anyone the character to break the law with impunity, or the insensibility to put himself into manifest danger.

Nor must it escape you that a vote is valueless without the will to carry it out whole-heartedly. If measures passed had power in themselves to compel us to action, or to bring the substance of them into reality, we should not have a history of numerous enactments and little or no action, nor would Philip so long have defied restraint. If enactments alone were enough, he would have been penalized long since. No, in the order of events action follows speech and decision, but in effect it has the priority and the greater validity. We need this addition to what is already available. We have in plenty the capacity to speak, the perspicacity to judge the spoken word. We shall be able to add action to these, if we play our true part. There can be no time, no moment better than the present. When can we act as we should, if not now? Has not this Macedonian stolen a march on us and captured our possessions?[6] We are faced with the greatest ignominy, if he proceeds to seize power also over this territory of Chalcidice. The friends we promised to

5. On the Theoric Fund see on *Olynthiac I*, 19.
6. Contrast the way in which Isocrates refers to Philip in *Philip*, 3, p. 139.

preserve in case of war are at war now. He is our enemy, in possession of our property. He is an uncivilized intruder, he deserves any appellation you give him. And yet we let it all pass, we virtually assist the process, and then, I suppose, we shall demand to affix the responsibility. We shall not lay it at our own door, I am sure. It is not only during the perils of war that runaways fail to accuse themselves, but prefer to arraign the High Command, or their neighbours, or anyone else. But the failure has been due to the army which has run away. The accuser could have stood firm, and if all had done so, victory would have been theirs.

Our case is the same. If one proposal is unsatisfactory, another can be offered without attacking the first. If a second is preferable, put it into action and good luck to it. But perhaps this is an unattractive proposal. If so, it is not the fault of the proposer, unless he has omitted the obligatory prayer. Prayer is easy, gentlemen. We can summarize in it our every wish. But choice, when we have political questions before us, is not so easily made. It must be the choice of right policy, and not the easy road, if the two cannot be combined. Yes, comes the reply, but if it is possible to leave the Theoric Fund and provide another source for military expenses, surely that is better. I agree, if it is possible. But I doubt if it has ever been or will be the fortune of anyone to spend his all unjustifiably, and then be financed out of the deficit to do his duty. This is wishful thinking, and self-deception is the easiest of pitfalls. Where the wish is father to the thought, the truth is often different. You must consider the problem in terms of an expedition that is practical, manageable and financially viable. Good sense and right feeling forbid us to make some financial shortage affecting the war an excuse for lightly accepting a position of disgrace, forbid us to fly to arms against Corinth and Megara,[7] and, for lack of money to transport our forces, allow Philip to enslave Greek cities.

7. There is no need to look for a particular reference here. Demosthene is contrasting the quick resentment which may be roused by immedi differences at home with reluctance to take an honourable path at a gr distance.

I do not speak from an irresponsible desire to give offence. I am not so senseless or ineffectual as to seek offence without benefit. But I think the true citizen must put the reality of survival above the gratification of rhetoric. This was the method, this was the character of political dealing, I understand, as perhaps you all do, practised by the speakers of the past, who are extolled by members of this assembly, but not imitated by them; the method of the great Aristides, of Nicias, of my namesake[8] and of Pericles. Since the appearance of our modern speakers, who ask 'What are your wishes? What proposal would you like? What can I do for your gratification?', Athenian strength has been squandered for immediate popularity. This is what happens, and as their stock rises, that of the nation sinks. Think, gentlemen, what summary could be given of affairs in the past and in your own time. The account will be short. You know it well enough. The examples which could lead us in the path of success are not taken from foreign history, but your own. Your predecessors had no flattery from speakers, and no love from them, as you do. But for forty-five years they were the accepted leaders of the Greek states.[9] They amassed over ten thousand talents on the Acropolis. The king of this district of Thrace was their subordinate, and stood in the right relation for a non-Greek to a Greek state. Many and great were the victories they won by land and sea as citizen fighters, and they were alone of mankind in leaving by their achievements a reputation high above carping envy. Such they proved in the sphere of Hellenic affairs. Look now at the character they bore in our city itself, in public and private relations alike. In the first the architectural beauty they created in sacred buildings and their adornment was of a quality and an extent unsurpassable by later generations. Their private lives were of such restraint, and so well in keeping with the character of the community, that if the type of house lived in by Aristides or Miltiades[10] or any of the great men of that day is known nowa-

8. Presumably the Demosthenes who commanded in the north-west in the
Peloponnesian War and was executed at Syracuse after the retreat.
. i.e. between the Persian and Peloponnesian Wars, though it seems
ful how the reckoning is made.
aders of Athens during the period of the Persian Wars.

days, it can be seen to be no grander than its neighbours. No one then made capital out of public affairs. It was felt that the community should be the gainer. But their integrity in the conduct of Hellenic affairs, their devotion in that of religion, their equity in that of private concerns, gained them the highest happiness. So stood the state in the past under the leaders I have mentioned. What is the position now under our present splendid administrators? Is there any similarity, any comparison with the past? I cut short a long list of instances. You can all see the degree of helplessness to which we have come. Sparta is finished. Thebes is fully occupied. No other state is strong enough to bid for the supremacy. We could retain our position in safety and hold the scales of justice for the rest of the Hellenic world. And yet we have lost territory of our own, we have spent over fifteen hundred talents to no purpose, the allies we made in the war have brought us down in the peace,[11] and we have brought an adversary of such magnitude on the stage against us. I invite any man present to tell me here and now, what other source there is of Philip's power than ourselves. 'Well,' I am told, 'that may be very unfortunate, but at home, at least, we are better off.' What is the evidence of this? Plaster on the battlements, new streets, water supplies. These are trivialities. Turn your eyes on the pursuers of these political ends. They have risen from beggary to riches, from obscurity to prominence, and in some cases have houses which outshine the public buildings themselves, while their consequence rises with the decline of the nation.

What is the reason for all this? Why was Athenian history then so glorious? And now why is so much amiss? Because then the people of Athens had the courage to act and to serve in person, the people were the master of the politicians and the controller of all its assets. Then it was a matter of satisfaction to every man elsewhere to be admitted by the people to share its honour, its power and some of its benefits. Now the reverse is true. It is the politicians who control assets, and through whose agency all action is taken. We, the people, are enervated

11. i.e. in the period 378–362 B.C., during which the new Confederac arose.

and our revenues and our allies whittled away. We are incidental, subsidiary, content to be allowed a little from the Theoric Fund and a procession at the Boedromia,[12] and, our finest moment of all, to feel gratitude for what is our own. It is these men of our own city who keep us down to this level, who cosset us till we eat out of their hands. But never, I am sure, was a high and virile spirit attained through petty and contemptible practices. The character of men's habits is reflected inevitably in their spirit. These are words which may well bring down greater detriment on my head for saying this than on others for causing it. Free speaking is not permitted here on all subjects, and I am surprised that it has been allowed now.

This is our last chance to rid ourselves of such habits, to serve the nation, to act like Athenians, to use what is superfluous at home as a stepping-stone to gains abroad. If we can do this, perhaps, perhaps, gentlemen, we may make some finished, some great achievement, and say goodbye to these petty doles. They resemble the diets imposed by doctors, which neither bring strength to the sick man nor let him die. The distributions we receive are not enough to bring any satisfying benefit, nor allow us to turn our back on them and look elsewhere. They merely serve to encourage individual inaction. Do I imply their appropriation to the army? Yes, I do, and at once on a single organization for all, so that every individual may have his share of public support and provide the services needed by the state. If the situation permits inactivity, a man is best at home where he is not driven by want to illicit action. Suppose a situation like the present. Then he can serve in person and draw his pay from the same source, as is only right for public service. Or take the case of a man outside military age. The unorganized and unearned payments he now receives he will get under the new system for work of superintendence and organization. In a word, without any more than slight addition or subtraction I bring Athens from a lack of system to a systematic arrangement of universal application, under which are included payment, military and judicial service, the performance of public tasks of all kinds according to capacity and circumstance. In no in-

12. It is doubtful which festival is here meant.

stance do I advocate passing the earnings of the active to the inactive. In no case would I have citizens in idleness and leisure receiving news of the successes of some general's mercenaries, as happens now. I make no criticism of any who are engaged in the necessary service of the state. I merely demand that the nation perform for itself the tasks for which it now commends others, and not abandon the lofty post secured and left for her by your predecessors in the ranks of nobility and danger.

I have attempted to speak as I think desirable. Let your choice be made in accordance with the best interests of our country and all her citizens.

DEMOSTHENES [II]

INTRODUCTION

The interval between the fall of Olynthus in 348 B.C. *and the last speech which appears in this book,* Philippic III, *in the summer of 341, includes two main sets of events, those centring round the Peace of Philocrates in 346, and those of the period of indecision after it, which ended when Philip finally attacked Athens in 338.*

(1) After the fall of Olynthus Demosthenes' views were effective in sending a delegation to Peloponnesian states to stimulate efforts against Philip. But Eubulus and his associates knew that peace was financially necessary. Philip also was ready for it, but could afford to insist on two demands, that he should be free to deal with Halus in Thessaly, whose dispute with Pharsalus Philip had been invited to settle, and with Phocis. These were not mentioned in the actual terms negotiated. Athenians tried to pretend that they knew of a 'gentlemen's agreement' to let Phocis live. But Philip had no such idea, and at once destroyed it; and followed this by realizing his other great desire, to preside at the Pythian games at Delphi. There was much dispute and recrimination between Athenian representatives on the peace delegation which is the subject of Demosthenes' long speech against Aeschines, which is not included in this volume. The circumstances of the negotiations as a whole, coupled with the feeling aroused by Demosthenes over Olynthus, almost caused Athens to repudiate the Peace, and Demosthenes in the speech On the Peace *in 346 had to advise acquiescence in it.*

(2) After the Peace, despite professions of friendly feeling towards Athens, Philip's diplomatic aims were in favour of Thebes against Athens and Sparta, and already in 344, in Philippic II, *Demosthenes points out that this is merely an interval before a final struggle.*

Meanwhile Euboea had been established as independent after the revolt in 348, and Philip did little to encourage hopes that he intended to return it to Athens. He expelled the democrats from Eretria, forcing them from the nearby Porthmus, and treated Oreus similarly, as Demosthenes describes in Philippic III.

But the next scene of Philip's operations was Thrace, whether to prevent attacks on his territory by Thracian princes, or to gain greater control of the Bosporus and Hellespont. It was an area of great importance to Athenian trade, and was largely in the hands of princes like the undependable Cersobleptes, with whom Athens had conducted some ineffectual negotiations in 356 for the control of the Chersonese. In 352 Cersobleptes had been subjected to the power of Macedon, but revolted two years later, and Philip was again engaged against him in 346 during and after the peace negotiations. In the Chersonese (the tongue of land in Thrace more recently called the Gallipoli peninsula), Athens had claimed sovereignty and set out cleruchies (see Isocrates, Panegyricus 107 p. 120). These were under the command of Diopeithes, and the venture was fairly successful apart from the town of Cardia, which had always been anti-Athenian and was claimed as an ally and garrisoned by Philip. Diopeithes retaliated by various irregular proceedings against Macedonian possessions on the Propontis, but he was not provided with enough men or money to maintain effective hostilities. Philip wrote a protest in threatening terms, and this was the situation in which Demosthenes' speech On the Chersonese was delivered in 341. It was followed after a short interval by Philippic III, with war imminent once again. We have no actual evidence of the effect of this fine speech, but from diplomatic activities among the Greek states it appears that the danger from Macedon was now fully realized, and the policy which Demosthenes represented regained the ascendancy in Athens. In 340 an alliance of Athens, Corinth, Megara and other states was formed, and the war was resumed. Demosthenes' final diplomatic triumph was to win over Thebes in 339. But by now it was too late.

DEMOSTHENES: ON THE PEACE

I REALIZE, gentlemen, the degree of ill will and confusion aroused by the present situation, not merely from the extent of our losses, which oratory has nothing to offset, but from the lack of a generally agreed policy in regard to what remains to us, about which there is varying opinion. The framing of policy is always a tiresome and difficult business, but the citizens of Athens have rendered it still more difficult. In the normal course deliberation comes before action, but with us it comes after it. Hence the commendation and applause invariably bestowed, in my experience, upon criticism of past mistakes, which fails to secure the real aim of debate. Yet despite this I stand here in the firm conviction that we have only to abandon partisan demonstrations, as is demanded by the needs of the country and the importance of the issues before us, to find the ability to frame and advocate policies to improve the present and redeem the past.

I am perfectly aware that it is an outstandingly profitable practice, if one has the face, to make oneself and one's previous utterances the main theme. But I regard it as so contemptible and tiresome a habit, that I hesitate to use it, even when I realize the need. But I think it will give you a better understanding of what I am going to say, if I remind you a little of what I have said in the past. First, then, at the time when, in view of disorders in Euboea, this country was induced to follow Plutarchus[1] in raising a war that was as expensive as it was inglorious, I was the first and the only speaker to oppose the project. I was almost torn in pieces by the party which urged on the country a number of serious losses in return for diminutive profit. After a very short interval, at the cost also of disrepute and of treatment of their benefactors unparalleled for a generation,

1. Philip's intrigues in Euboea, which distracted Athens from aiding Olynthus, are referred to in the sectional introduction, p. 171. Plutarchus of Eretria appealed for Athenian aid, and was assisted by Eubulus and his par̄ but proved to be a turncoat.

the lesson was learnt that the advocates of this expedition were unprincipled, and that mine had been the right policy. Again, there was the case of the actor, Neoptolemus. I became aware that under the pretext of official protection afforded by his art he was gravely damaging the interests of Athens, by favouring Macedon in his conduct of proceedings as your representative. I therefore raised the subject in this assembly, without a semblance of personal or other propaganda, as was proved by the result. I am not intending any reflection on the supporters of Neoptolemus. There were none. It is this assembly I blame. If it had been a performance in the Theatre which was under consideration instead of the position and security of Athens, he would not have met with so lenient a reception, nor I with such hostility. Yet I think this is universally realized, that, while his journey into enemy territory was nominally designed to secure payment of debts in that country, in order to honour his public obligations here, actually he made a great deal of the claim that it was outrageous to be blamed for bringing wealth from Macedon to Athens; yet no sooner did the Peace secure his immunity, than he realized the property he had acquired here and absconded to Macedon with it.

These are two of the predictions I made, which are evidence of honest accuracy in the facts. There is one third example, and then I really will embark on my subject. After those of us who formed the delegation returned from the ratification of the Peace, there were numerous promises in the wind, of a new foundation for Thespiae and Plataea,[2] of Philip's intention to preserve Phocis, if he secured control, and to disestablish Thebes;[3] that Oropus was to be awarded to Athens and Euboea exchanged for Amphipolis, and other chimerical hopes, which led you to disregard both interest and equity by abandoning Phocis. But it will be clear that I did not mislead the country either positively or negatively. I said what I thought, as I am sure you remember, namely that I had neither knowledge nor

2. Thespiae and Plataea had been dispossessed or destroyed by Thebes in '73.
3. See Isocrates, *Philip*, 43. On Oropus see Demosthenes, *For Megalopolis*, and sectional introduction.

expectation of anything of the kind, and I thought such statements were nonsense.

These instances, in which I clearly showed better foresight
than others, are not to be put down to any superior ability that I
can boast. I shall not claim that intelligent prediction is due to
anything but the two causes I have put forward. The first,
gentlemen, is good luck, which I realize has more power than
all the ingenuity and wisdom of men. The second is that my
judgement and my reckoning are free of self-interest. No one
can point to any gain to me attaching to any policy or any
utterance of mine. I can therefore take an unbiased view of the
national interest, based solely on the facts. Once financial profit
is put in the scale, the balance is upset and intelligence out-
weighed, and there is no further hope of right or sound judgement about anything.

The first prerequisite, in my view, is that any alliance or
contribution which anyone wishes to secure for Athens shall be
secured without breaking the peace. Not that it is anything
remarkable, or in any way worthy of Athens. But whatever can
be said of it, better for our position that it had never been made,
than made and then broken by this country. We have lost many
assets whose retention would have made war safer and easier
then than it is now. Our second need is to avoid giving the
assembly of the so-called Amphictyonic Council[4] the need, or
a common pretext for, war against us. Personally, in the event
of a fresh war between us and Philip over Amphipolis or on
any other private ground not shared by Thessaly, Argos or
Thebes, I do not believe any of them would take part against
Athens, least of all – please keep your protests till you hear
what I have to say – least of all Thebes, not from any friendly
feeling towards us, or from anti-Macedonian views, but because
they fully realize, for all their reputation for slowness of wit,
that in a war against Athens they will get all the kicks and none
of the halfpence, which will be kept under someone else's close
control. They will not let themselves in for this without a general
cause and occasion for war. Again, in the event of a further war
with Thebes on the score of Oropus or any other private bone

4. See Isocrates, *Philip*, 74 and note.

of contention, I do not think that Athens would have anything to lose. Supporters of either side would go to arms in defence against an attack on their own territory, but would not support either in aggression. This is the way of alliances of any significance, and it is a natural way. There is no one whose relations with Athens and Thebes are equally poised between defence and offence. All would share a defensive aim to maintain the integrity of both, but not an offensive aim to secure the success of one which involved a threat to themselves. What then do I regard as the danger we should guard against? The danger that a future war may provoke a general pretext and a common complaint against us. Suppose Argos, Messene, Megalopolis and other Peloponnesian states which share their view, take exception to an *entente* between Sparta and ourselves and the idea of our making some capital out of Spartan activity.[5] Suppose Thebes increases the hostility she normally shows, on the ground of our offering asylum to Theban fugitives and our general ill feeling towards her, and Thessaly for our rescue of Phocian refugees, and Philip for our exclusion of him from the Amphictyonic League, then I am afraid that individual resentments may give occasion for a general war, on the claim of the Amphictyonic decrees. These may lead everyone beyond their own best interests, as happened in the Phocian war. You must realize that Thebes, Philip and Thessaly did not share common aims, though their course of action was in accord. Take the case of Thebes. Philip's appearance and his control of the pass was something they could not prevent, any more than his coming last in the field and stealing the credit of their labours. At the present time Thebes has made some territorial gains, but her prestige, her credit, is low, since but for Philip's arrival the gain would never have been made. This was not at all what she wanted, but her desire to acquire Orchomenus and Coronea, which she could not secure, compelled her to submit to it. As to Philip, there are people who go so far as to say that he was against ceding Orchomenus and Coronea to Thebes, but was compelled to. They can enjoy this notion if they like, but of one thing I am sure, that he was

5. See in general the speech on Megalopolis (p. 173 seqq.) seven years ⸆ier.

not so concerned with this as with his desire to control the pass, to secure the prestige of making it appear that the decision of the war had lain in his hands, and to put the Pythian games at his disposal. This was his particular aim. Finally, Thessaly had no wish for an increase of power on the part of either Thebes or Philip, either of which they regarded as damaging to themselves. They wanted a place at the Council and in the control of Delphi, two considerable assets. This aim meant furthering the other activities. You can see therefore that in each case it was the pursuit of private gains which led on to the acceptance of losses. And that, exactly, is what this country needs to forestall.

'So we must do as we are told in a dangerous situation. Is that your contention?' I am asked. Not at all. My contention is that we should avoid reaching a position unworthy of Athens, and also avoid the onset of war, that we should cultivate a reputation for good sense and a right view. But the unthinking acceptance of every loss without any thought of war is the attitude I wish to consider. We are allowing Thebes to hold Oropus. And if we are asked what is our real and genuine reason for this, the answer is, to avoid war. And the reason why we have ceded Amphipolis to Philip by the agreement, why we allow Cardia[6] to stand apart from the rest of the Chersonese, and Caria to include the islands of Chios, Cos and Rhodes,[7] and Byzantium to enforce customs dues,[8] is clearly our belief that we can expect greater benefit from peace and tranquillity than from conflict and self-interest in the fields I have mentioned. It is therefore an act of folly and downright perversity, when our relations with individual states as they bear on our closest interests are what they are, to try conclusions with them all for the sake of the shadow show at Delphi.

6. Cardia had remained detached even after the Chersonese, at the northern end of which it stood, had been secured for Athens in 353, and in 346 Philip gained recognition of it as an ally.

7. On Chios and the other cities of the Social War see Demosthene speech *On the Liberty of Rhodes*, p. 180. These states were still dependen Caria, now under Idrieus (see Isocrates, *Philip*, 103).

8. i.e. on Athenian corn ships from the Euxine.

DEMOSTHENES: PHILIPPIC II

GENTLEMEN, when debates are held on Philip's intrigues and deliberate breaches of the Peace, the Athenian point of view is conspicuous for its correct and humane attitude. Attacks made on Philip are invariably commendable, but there is nothing to commend in the action taken, nothing to justify the arguments used. Indeed the whole position for this country has reached a point at which the more strongly and openly Philip is convicted of breaches of the treaty with Athens, and of designs against the Greek states in general, the harder it becomes to advise on policy. The reason is twofold. At a time when practical measures, not words, are essential to curb aggression, we, your advisers, avoid action, legislation and practical proposals, because we are afraid of public resentment, and prefer tirades on Philip's unjustifiable proceedings. Our audience here on the other hand is better equipped than Philip to impart and listen to justifiable argument, yet against his present course of action offers complete inertia. The result is inevitable, I suppose, and perhaps right. We each succeed best in the field of our greatest activity and interest, Philip in the field of action, Athens in that of words. If you are still content merely to have right on your side, there is no difficulty. It will cost you no exertion. But if means are to be taken to improve the position, to prevent a still further unsuspected deterioration, and the rise of a force against us which we cannot begin to match, then our old approach needs to be entirely changed. There must be a movement on the part of speakers and audience alike towards effective practical measures, and away from the path of ease and complacency.

First, then, if any feeling of confidence exists in the face of Philip's present power and the extent of his influence, any belief that this represents no danger to Athens and does not constitute a general menace to this country, I am astonished, ~~nd~~ I want first to ask everyone here to listen to a brief account ~~the~~ reasoning which leads me to take the opposite view and ~~d~~ Philip as our enemy. After that, you can adhere to

whichever view you prefer, the forecast which I offer, or the
policy of confidence and trust in Macedon. My inferences are
these. What was the first gain made by Philip after the Peace?
The control of Thermopylae and Phocis. What use did he make
of it? He preferred the interests of Thebes to those of Athens.[1]
Why? It was his own advantage and the control of all Greece
which was the aim of his calculations, not peace and quiet, and
certainly not justice. He realized quite rightly that he could
offer no inducement to the city of Athens or to men of your
character which could tempt you to secure your own benefit
at the cost of the betrayal of other states to him, that you would
take thought for right and shun the dishonour such a course
involves, that you would take all proper regard for the future
and oppose any attempt of his of this sort as strongly as if you
were at war with him. His view of Thebes, on the other hand,
which was borne out by events, was that in return for their
own advantage they would leave him a clear field for the rest,
and not merely refrain from interference or opposition, but join
in hostilities, if he gave the word. It is on the same assumption
that he is now giving assistance to Messene and Argos. This
indeed is a high compliment to this country, which is judged
on this basis to be the only one which would accept no profit
for herself to betray the common interests of Greece, no private
satisfaction or gain in exchange for the good will of the Greek
states. This was a reasonable assumption in your case, as the
opposite was in the case of Argos and Thebes, in the light of
present and past history alike. His observation and his researches
tell him that a previous generation of Athenians had the power
to be rulers of the rest of Greece on condition of being themselves subservient to the King of Persia. Not merely did they
refuse to tolerate such an idea, on the occasion when Alexander,
the ancestor of these kings of Macedon, came to offer terms,[2]
but preferred to evacuate their territory and face any fate, and
ultimately achieved glories which are the envy and the despair
of every orator – and I will myself omit what is beyond words to

1. i.e. in destroying Phocis, which was at enmity with Thebes and friendl*
to Athens.
2. i.e. in 480 B.C., after the battle of Salamis.

express. He knows, too, that that generation in Thebes and Argos either joined forces with the invader or did nothing to resist him. Hence he realizes that both these states will pursue their own advantage without any regard for the common interests of Greece. He therefore supposed that if he chose to turn to Athens, he would secure her friendship on terms consistent with justice, but if he joined the others, he would be acquiring accomplices in his own self-seeking. That is why he set, and will set, his choice on them rather than on us. It is not that he can look to a stronger navy there than here, or that he has discovered a land power that enables him to turn away from navies and harbours. Nor has he forgotten the terms and the promises which gained the peace for him.

Perhaps I shall be told, on supposed inside knowledge, that his motive was not one of self-interest or anything of the kind I have criticized, but simply that he thought Thebes had a better case than Athens. This is the one argument which it is impossible for him to use. The man who orders Sparta to relinquish Messene, can hardly surrender Orchomenus and Coronea to Thebes and pretend that his motive was equity.[3]

The only plea that remains to him is that he was under compulsion, that he acted against his own wishes, but found himself caught between the Thessalian cavalry and the infantry of Thebes, and was therefore led to make concessions. Excellent. So we are told he is likely to be suspicious of Thebes, and the story is going round that he intends to fortify Elatea.[4] This may be his intention, and an intention it will remain in my opinion. But there is no question of intention about his link with Argos and Messene against Sparta.[5] He is sending troops and money now, and is expected in person with a large force.

3. For Sparta to relinquish Messene would be division of territory anciently undivided; to incorporate Orchomenus and Coronea would mean creating a united Boeotia. Compare, however, Demosthenes, *For Megalopolis*, and Isocrates, *Philip*, 43.

4. Elatea was a town in Phocis, whose walls had been pulled down in 346. It commanded the road between Phocis and Thebes, and if its walls were restored could block a Theban move into Phocis. Similarly its capture Philip in 339 opened for him the way to the south.

See back *On the Peace*, 18.

Is it to be supposed that he is out to undermine Thebes' actual enemy, Sparta, and at the same time preserve his own victims in Phocis? This is quite beyond belief. I scarcely imagine that even if Philip had been compelled in the first instance to act against his wishes, or if he were now set on abandoning Thebes, he would be in constant opposition to her enemies. To judge by his present course, his previous actions were obviously just as much a matter of policy, and a true estimate of them shows that every movement has been directed against Athens. Just consider. His aim is empire, and he sees Athens as the only obstacle to this aim. He has been in the wrong for a long time, as he is perfectly aware. It is his seizure of our possessions which has won him the safety of his other gains. Had he given up Amphipolis and Potidaea, he would never, he imagines, have been safe at home. He fully realizes both that his designs are aimed at Athens, and that Athens knows they are. He sees us as intelligent people whose hatred of him is justified, and he is on tenterhooks for fear of damage in the event of a move on our part, if he fails to anticipate it. This is why he is so much on the alert, so much on the spot, why he cultivates anti-Athenian support from Thebes or his Peloponnesian adherents, whose self-interest is expected to make them favour the present, while their stupidity prevents them from foreseeing the future. Yet on a sensible view there are fairly obvious indications to be seen, which it fell to me to point out to Messene and Argos.[6] But perhaps it is as well that they should be indicated here again.

'With what resentment,' I said to Messenian representatives, 'do you suppose Olynthus would have received any criticism of Philip in the period when he let them hold Anthemus, which every former king of Macedon laid claim to, when he presented them with Potidaea and expelled its Athenian colonists, making himself responsible for our hostility while he had given them the benefits of possession? Do you suppose they foresaw their ultimate fate, or would have believed any prediction of it? Yet,' I pointed out, 'after a short spell of prosperity at others' expense they have had a long run of deprivation themselve

6. i.e. on a mission of propaganda against Philip.

they have been ignominiously expelled, not merely overwhelmed, but betrayed and sold by each other. There is no safety for free states in such over-familiarity with dictators. And what about Thessaly?' I went on. 'Do you suppose they imagined that the Philip who abolished their tyrannies and presented them with Nicaea and Magnesia[7] was the man to impose their present partition, and that the leader who gave them their seat on the Amphictyonic Council would be likely to curtail their own revenues? Of course not. Yet this is what happened and is there for all to see. And you yourselves,' I warned them, 'as you observe Philip's presents and promises, should pray, if you are wise, that you may not come to see him as a liar and a deceiver. There are numerous contrivances for the safety and protection of states, there are palisades, fortifications, field works and the rest. They are all the work of men's hands, and a drain on wealth. There is one safeguard alone which is afforded by the nature of human wisdom, and brings safety and protection to all. What is this? Distrust. Keep it secure and clasp it to your hearts. For its preservation is your defence against all harm. What,' I asked them, 'is your greatest desire? Freedom? Then is it not obvious that Philip's very titles are diametrically opposed to it? Every king and every tyrant is an enemy to freedom and an opponent of law. Take good care that in your eagerness to avoid war you do not acquire a despot.'

They heard my speech and applauded it, as well as a number of other speeches from representatives, both in my presence and, apparently, afterwards. But they are no more inclined to resist Philip's offer of friendship and his promises. Indeed, it is not surprising that Messenian and Peloponnesian states should abandon in practice what reason tells them is in their interest. You are Athenians, who have your own intelligence besides the warnings of speakers to convince you that you are the victims of deception and strategy, that inactivity now will betray you into disaster. So true it is that immediate ease and complacency

7. Magnesia: a district of Thessaly, not to be confused with either of the two well-known towns of the same name in Asia Minor. The translation ('partition') neglects a reading ($\delta\epsilon\kappa\alpha\delta\alpha\rho\chi\iota\alpha\nu$ – government by a board of ten) which is not precisely accountable, and may be wrong. See back on *Ol. I* 22.

present a stronger inducement than thoughts of future advantage.

Our best course for the future is a thing you will discuss further by yourselves, if you are wise. But the reply that will provide your best immediate decision, I will now suggest to you.

(The reply is read)

It would be right, gentlemen, to call in evidence the bearers of Philip's promises which induced you to accept the Peace. I myself would never have agreed to serve on the delegation, and I am quite sure your countrymen would never have put an end to the war, if they had supposed Philip would act as he did after securing peace. There was a wide discrepancy between his word and his actions. There is also a second class of witnesses we should call. Who are these? The party who after the Peace and my return from the second delegation sent to ratify it, when I realized how Athens had been misled and was loud in denunciation of the betrayal of Thermopylae and Phocis, then declared that I was a man who drank water instead of wine,[8] bound to be awkward and difficult, whereas Philip, once past Thermopylae, would do everything we wanted, fortify Thespiae and Plataea, check Theban misdemeanours, dig a canal through the Chersonese at his own expense, and grant us Euboea and Oropus in exchange for Amphipolis. These were all statements made on the platform, as I am sure you remember, reluctant though you are to recall your own injuries. The most shameful thing of all was that in your optimism you voted that the same terms should be binding on a future generation. To such a degree was this country led astray. Why do I choose this moment to introduce this fact and demand testimony of it? I will tell you the absolutely candid truth without concealment. I have no wish to embark on abuse and acquire notoriety in this assembly at the price of giving my original opponents fresh scope for earning their fee from the enemy.[9] Nor is it idle talk. No, it seems to me that this country will have greater

8. See Demosthenes, *De Fals . Leg.*, 46.
9. i.e. for their services in replying.

cause to regret Philip than it has now. This is the thin end of the wedge. I hope my guess is wrong, but I am afraid we are already regrettably close to the point of danger. When, therefore, it is no longer open to you to disregard the trend of events, when it is no longer a matter of hearing from me or someone else of the perils of Athens, but they are there for all to see and know, I suspect that you may incline to be angry and violent. I fear that members of that delegation may fail to reveal the corrupt practices of which they are themselves conscious, and then any attempt to set right what has been their responsibility may be visited by recrimination on your part. For I realize that there are often critics who vent their antagonism, not on those responsible, but on the nearest victims. So while we are faced by a period of hesitation and delay, and listening to speeches, I want to remind every one of you, however well he may know it, who it was who urged the abandonment of Phocis and Thermopylae, the command of which set Philip on the road to Attica and the Peloponnese, and made the issues before this assembly not those of abstract justice and of foreign affairs, but of our own safety and of war on Attic soil, which will bring misery to each of us when it comes, and is indeed upon us today. Had this country not been led astray, there would have been no problem. Philip would have secured no naval success or penetrated into Attica, nor passed Thermopylae and Phocis by land. Either he would have kept to his legal rights, and adhered to the terms of peace and remained inactive, or else he would at once have been involved in a similar war to that which made him then desire peace. I have said enough to give a reminder. That this reminder should be put to the ultimate test, I pray may be avoided. I have no wish that anyone's penalty, however deserved, should be exacted at the price of the peril of the community.

DEMOSTHENES: ON THE CHERSONESE

OUR situation, gentlemen, ought to ensure that speakers discard all bias for or against any party, and each urge merely the view he regards as soundest, particularly in a debate on public issues of the highest importance. But as some speeches are inspired by the spirit of competition, or other motives of whatever kind, members of this assembly in general should set everything else aside, and vote and act as the national interest demands. The subject of greatest concern is the position in the Chersonese and the campaign which Philip has now been conducting for ten months in Thrace. But most of the speeches deal with the activities and intentions of Diopeithes.[1] As regards any accusations against members of this force, who can be legally brought to book at any time, I regard this as open either now or later, and there is no need for me or anyone else to make statements about it. But it is Philip's hostility to this country, his presence in the neighbourhood of the Hellespont with a considerable force, and his attempts to gain advantages at our expense (advantages which we shall lose the chance to recover if we are too late) that is the subject, in my view, which requires instant discussion and action, and which must not be sidetracked by irrelevant disputes and accusations.

I am often surprised at the choice of topics in this assembly, but one of the most astonishing was the claim I heard made a few days ago, that the duty of a statesman was to make a clear-cut choice either of war or peace. But the fact is this. If Philip's proceedings are peaceable, if he is not in possession of our property in contravention of the peace, if he is not engaged in wholesale propaganda against us, then there is nothing to be said. We should maintain peace, and it is clear that Athenians are quite ready to do so. But if the terms of peace to which we are sworn lie before us in black and white, and it has been manifest from the very beginning, before the expedition of Diopeithes and the cleruchs, who are now charged with

1. See sectional introduction, p. 222.

responsibility for war, that Philip has without justification appropriated a number of our possessions, which are the subject of resolutions of protest passed by this assembly, that he has been continually guilty of depredations from other Greek and foreign states and of anti-Athenian activity, then what is the meaning of talk about clear distinction between war and peace? We have no choice. We are left with the one most just and unavoidable course, which speakers like this deliberately overlook. What is that? Resistance to aggression. Unless it is meant that if Philip holds off Attica and the Peiraeus, no wrong is being done, no act of war committed. If this is the boundary whereby rights are laid down and peace defined, it is universally clear how wrong, how intolerable, how dangerous an idea this is. At the same time it stands in direct opposition to the accusations made against Diopeithes. What is the logic of giving Philip a free hand outside Attica, and refusing Diopeithes even assistance to Thrace on pain of calling it an act of war? Or it is admitted that the case here is disproved, but the action of the mercenary army in ravaging the district of the Hellespont, and of Diopeithes in imposing dues, was still unjustifiable and ought not to be tolerated. Very well. I won't dispute it. But I do think that if this opinion is really given in all good faith, the demand to disband the existing force of Athens, which is sustained by propaganda against its commander and his provision of supplies, ought to be balanced by a proof that Philip's armaments will be disbanded, if it is allowed. Otherwise it amounts, it should be observed, to a return for Athens to the position which proved so disastrous before. You are fully aware that nothing has done more to make Philip's successes possible than his command of the initiative. With his standing army on the spot and his anticipation of his aims, he can attack where he likes in a moment. We have to get our information, and it is not till then that agitation and preparation begin. The result is that he achieves his objects without trouble, while we are too late and find that our expense has been wasted. We present a display of hostility and the desire to obstruct him, but we have the added sense of failure to act in time.

It must not escape you, then, that now at this very time all else is empty words and mere pretence, but this aim is real and is actually being put into operation, the aim that Athens shall remain inactive at home and undefended abroad, while Philip secures his every object without hindrance. Look first at the present. At this moment he has a considerable force in waiting in Thrace, besides sending for large reinforcements according to opinion there. Suppose he waits for the winds and then moves against Byzantium, first of all, do you imagine that the same absurd attitude will prevail in Byzantium as before, and that they will not expect either to call us in or to maintain their own defence? Not they. They will introduce even troops they mistrust more than ours rather than surrender to Philip, unless he can steal a march on them. Then, if we cannot sail a force out, and there is none in readiness out there, there will be nothing between them and disaster. It may be that they are insanely improvident. All the same they must be preserved, because it is in the interest of Athens. Again, it is not certain that he will not attack the Chersonese. To judge by the despatch sent to this country, he intends operations against the district. In that case, if a standing force is in existence, it can either operate in defence of the district or in attack on the Macedonian position. But once it is disbanded, what can we do in face of an attack on the Chersonese? File a suit against Diopeithes! What good would that do? Is it suggested that we should send an expedition from here? Suppose the winds[2] prevent it. 'Well,' I am told, 'it won't happen.' Who will give a guarantee of that? Do you gentlemen realize and reflect upon the time of year that is approaching, during which it is thought reasonable to leave the Chersonese undefended and hand it to Philip? Then again, suppose he leaves Thrace without moving against the Chersonese or Byzantium – you must reckon with this possibility too – and advances on Chalcis and Megara in the same way as he did previously against Oreus,[3] which is our best policy then? To

2. See *Philippic I*, 31.

3. Chalcis and Oreus in Euboea had been among towns which were the object of Philip's intrigues, which distracted Athenian attention from activity in defence of Olynthus. See sectional introduction to Demosthenes (1), p. 171. There was similar activity in connexion with Megara at the same time. See also 36 below, and *Philippic III*, 12, 17, 27, 74.

defend ourselves against him here and allow the war to come to Attica, or to create a diversion for him at home? Surely the latter.

We should all realize this, reckon with it and reverse our judgement, and instead of depreciating and seeking to disband the force Diopeithes is trying to raise for Athens, we should make a spontaneous effort to add our own force to his, to help his financial stability and co-operate readily in other activities. If Philip were asked whether he would prefer that the troops under Diopeithes, poor though they may admittedly be, should be in good trim and in good standing in Athens, and should be increased by the collaboration of the state, or be decimated and ruined by disparagement and accusation, his answer, surely, would be the latter. So Philip's most heartfelt prayers are being granted by the actions of some of us. If so, you cannot have far to seek for the cause of Athenian disasters.

I now wish to make a candid appraisal of the present situation of the country and our activities and our conduct of affairs. We are not willing to pay money contributions, not prepared to serve in the forces, unable to keep from public spending.⁴ We refuse either to grant Diopeithes the League's assessment⁵ or to approve his own financial arrangements. We merely run him down and ask how and when he is going to act, and so on. And holding the attitude we do, we do not even carry out our own duties. In debate we applaud eulogies on Athenian prestige, while in practice we assist the opposite view. Periodically speakers are asked the question, what policy ought to be adopted. My question of members of the Assembly is what language ought to be adopted. If everything alike, contributions, service, spending restrictions, the assessment, Diopeithes' finances and citizen duties are to be refused, there is nothing left to say. When it comes to a free hand for adverse propaganda, to the extent that even his supposed intentions are condemned in advance amid public agreement, what can one say?

4. i.e. the Theoric Fund, on which see *Olynthiac I*, 19 and note.
5. The Greek word is used elsewhere in Demosthenes of the contributions of the allies under the second Delian League, and it seems to be set in contrast to what Diopeithes raised unofficially.

What this policy amounts to is a thing some members need to realize. I shall give a candid account of it. There is no other alternative. Every commander who has ever led an expedition from Athens – I will stake anything on this – extracts money from Chios or Erythrae or anywhere he can on the Asiatic seaboard. It is exacted in different amounts according to the scale of the expedition. Whatever the amount, states that grant it are not so insane as to do so for nothing. They buy immunity for their traders, safe conduct, exemption from harbour dues and so on, under the heading of goodwill, which is the word used to cover these exactions. It is the same in the case of Diopeithes. He has an army, so obviously he will be paid by all these people. Where else can it be supposed that troops can be financed from, by a commander who gets nothing from Athens and has no resources of his own to provide pay? From the sky? No, he subsists on what he can collect, beg or borrow. So all that is achieved by his accusers here is a general warning not to give him anything, because he will be punished for his mere intentions, without reference to any activity or exaction. What is asserted is that he is intending a siege, or that he is betraying Greek citizens. Is anyone so interested in the Asiatic Greeks? If so, they evidently take better care of others than of their own country. The proposal to send a second commander to the Hellespont amounts to just this. If Diopeithes is acting un-justifiably and exacting dues, it needs no more than the shortest of despatches to prevent it. The law allows for indictment of such offenders, not for an expensive expedition with triremes to keep watch on them ourselves, which is sheer madness. It is against our enemies, who are not touched by law, that we can and must maintain troops, despatch triremes and contribute money, while against ourselves we employ decrees or indictment or the official warship.[6] This is the method of sensible dealing, the other, now in vogue, of ruinous perversity. That examples of such an attitude should appear here is bad, but not the worst. You yourselves, members of this assembly, adopt an attitude which means that speakers have only to declare that Diopeithes

6. This ship, called the Paralus, was sent to bring back criminals from Athens.

is the cause of all our ills – or Chares or Aristophon[7] or anyone members may mention, and there is a clamour of agreement. But if you are truthfully told, 'Nonsense, gentlemen, all our failures and troubles are due to Philip. If he were inactive, we should have none,' you cannot dispute the truth of the statement, but you appear resentful and you feel deprived. The reason is – and I urge you most strongly that I must be allowed freedom to say what I want in defence of our best interests – the reason is this. A certain section of the nation has rendered this assembly intimidating and intractable in debate, but in military preparation inert and contemptible. Consequently, if a culprit is named whom you know you will have power to indict, you agree and acquiesce. But if it is one whose punishment depends on armed power alone, you have no answer, and are annoyed that your position is exposed. The exact opposite ought to be the case. In political life it is in debate that a kindly forbearance should be shown. There you are dealing with yourselves and your allies. But military preparation is the field in which to inspire fear or stubbornness, where the issue lies between you and your enemies and opponents. But the process of popular oratory, with its excessive ingratiation, has brought a spirit of self-satisfaction and complacency in debate, where we are told nothing but what we want to hear, while the active world of public affairs has brought us to the extreme of peril. Imagine some of the Greek states whose interest our passivity has neglected, demanding an account of our activities. 'Gentlemen of Athens,' they might say, 'you are always sending us manifestos to the effect that Philip has designs against us and the rest of Greece, and is a person to guard against, and so forth.' We should have to agree. That *is* what we do. 'Then you are the most contemptible of supporters. Philip has been kept away for ten months by war or illness or winter, and cut off from home, and you have done nothing either to liberate Euboea or to recover your own possessions. He has been active, while you were at home in idleness, though in perfect health (if such an

7. Chares, a vigorous Athenian admiral, first became noteworthy in 357 by his capture of Sestos. He was supported by Aristophon, the orator, in a charge of bribery against his colleagues in the Social War in 355.

attitude of mind can be called healthy), he has established two tyrants in Euboea,[8] one to provide a fortified post against Attica, the other against Sciathus, while you have made no attempt to abolish these, if nothing else, but have simply acquiesced. You have obviously stood aside for him and made it perfectly clear that even if he dies ten times over, you will never stir a muscle. In that case why bother us with delegations and accusations?' What answer shall we give to that, gentlemen? I see none at all.

Now there are certain people who think they can refute a speaker by the question, 'What is our right course?' I will give them the best answer both in justice and in truth, when I reply, 'Not your present one.' However, I will speak in further detail. And I urge such claimants to be prepared to act on the reply with as much vigour as they ask the question. First, then, my recommendation is that you take full cognizance of the fact that Philip is at war with this country, that he has broken the peace – you may as well put an end to recrimination on this point – that he is an ill-wisher and an enemy to our whole city, to the ground on which it stands, and to every man in it, even those individuals who most imagine they gratify him. Look at Euthycrates and Lasthenes of Olynthus, who appeared his firmest friends when they betrayed their country to him, but came to the worst end of all. This free country is the supreme object of his enmity and his designs, and its destruction is his dearest wish. This is not unnatural. He knows very well that even with complete control of all the rest he can have no security while democracy remains in Athens, that in the event of a single setback, which can often occur in human affairs, every element under the sway of force will come to Athens for refuge. You who are her people are not a people naturally given to the selfish pursuit of power, but strong to prevent it in others or wrest it from them, a thorn in the flesh of despotism, and willing champions for the liberation of mankind. Therefore he does not by any means desire the freedom of Athens to mount guard over his interests. Nor is he guilty of false or careless thinking. Our first need is to assume that he is an irreconcilable

8. See 18 above. The tyrants here referred to are the tyrants of Eretria a~ Oreus.

enemy to free and democratic institutions. If we are not convinced in our hearts of this, we shall not be prepared to take
action on it in reality. Secondly, we must clearly understand
that his every practice and manipulation is a design upon this
country, that every act of defence against him is a defence of
this country. No one is naïve enough to suppose that dismal
holes in Thrace – what else could one call them? – like Drongilus
and Cabyle and Masteira, which he is now engaged in reducing,
form an attraction whose capture is worth the effort, the winter
campaigns and the hardships which he undergoes, while the
harbours and dockyards and warships of Athens, her silver
works and her income, are nothing to him; and that he will
leave all this to us, while he winters in the trenches to secure
the millet and spelt in Thracian grain-pits. Of course not. That
and everything else is aimed at the control of what is ours.
What then is the reaction of sensible people? To realize this
and make up our minds to it, and to abandon our excessive,
our irreparable inactivity, to contribute funds and expect our
allies to do the same, to ensure in actual practice that this
standing army remains in being, so that his force, which is
held in readiness for the injury and enslavement of all Greece,
may be countered by ours in equal readiness to preserve and
assist her at every turn. Emergency armaments never succeed.
It is essential to organize a force and provision it, to appoint
commissariat and subsidiary staff who can take whatever steps
are possible for accurate financial organization, and to exact
responsibility for the finances from them, and for the action
from the commander. If you do so, if you are really prepared to
do so, you will compel Philip to maintain peace with justice
and to keep to his own territory, which would be an inestimable
benefit, or else you will meet him in warfare on equal terms.

   If this appears to anyone to be a matter of great expense and
considerable labour and perseverance, he is entirely right. But
let him reflect on the future of Athens without it, and he will
see the benefit of a ready acceptance of the way of duty. If there
exists some divine guarantee – no human one could give
sufficient security – that inactivity and general drift will not be
llowed eventually by a Macedonian attack on Athens itself, I

moşt solemnly declare that it is a disgrace and dishonour to our
people, their traditions and the achievements of the past, to let
our personal inertia betray and enslave the peoples of Greece.
I myself would rather forfeit life than so much as speak of it.
Yet if there is anyone who does advocate such conduct and can
persuade you to it, so be it, abandon resistance and let all our
greatness go. But if there is not, if, on the contrary, every man
of us can tell that the more we allow Philip to control, the more
intractable and the stronger we shall find him, then why hold
back, why wait? When shall we be ready to do what is required
of us? I suppose, when necessity compels us. What free men
would call necessity is not merely upon us now, it is long past.
And the necessity of slaves we must hope may not come to us.
What is the difference? The free man's greatest necessity is
his shame at what takes place around him. Greater than that
probably does not exist. The slave's necessity is the whip, and
physical torture, which I hope may be as remote from our
experience as it is intolerable in imagination.

I should have been glad to enlarge on the whole subject and
demonstrate the way in which certain people are pursuing the
political ruin of the country. But I will omit the bulk of it. When,
however, the question of relations with Philip arises, the cry is
at once heard of the benefits of peace and the difficulty of
maintaining a large force. 'The revenues are being plundered,'
we are told, with arguments calculated to produce delays at
home and freedom of action for Philip. In consequence we gain
leisure and inaction, which I fear you may think has been won
at great cost, and our objectors win the resulting popularity
and profit. In my view, first it is not in *our* competence to urge
peace. Here we sit, convinced already. It is in that of the author
of acts of war. Once he is convinced of it, your agreement is
secured. Secondly, what we ought to find intolerable is not the
necessary measures for protection, but the results of failure to
take them, and the plunder of the revenues should be halted by
the provision of a safeguard to preserve them, not by abstaining
from the duty of a citizen. Nonetheless I also feel resentment
that such concern is felt at plunder of the revenues, when it ˙
in your own power to preserve them and punish malversati˙

while none is aroused at Philip's wholesale plundering of all Greece, which is done at your expense.

What is the reason, then, why a leader who is openly in arms in contravention of right, and seizing towns, is never stated to be at war, while statesmen who urge that he should not be given liberty to do so are accused of making war? I will give it you. The object is that the resentment which Athenian citizens are likely to feel, if they are injured by the war, may be turned against speakers whose desire is for her good, to cause indictment of them instead of resistance to Philip, while the culprits stand as accusers instead of submitting to justice. This is what is meant by their statement that there is a party in the Assembly which wants war, and that this is the subject of their counter-claim. But I am fully aware that without any proposal of war from an Athenian citizen Philip holds numerous other possessions of ours, and has just sent an expedition to Cardia. Yet, if we are anxious to pretend that he is not at war, he must be the greatest fool in the world, if he proves it untrue. What shall we say when he actually attacks us? He will say he is not at war, as he declared to Oreus, when his men were actually in her territory, or earlier to Pherae,[9] when he was engaged in an attack on their walls, or to Olynthus in the first place, until his army was there on Olynthian soil. Shall we go on even then with our claim that the policy of resistance to him is a policy of war? The only other policy is slavery. There is no other alternative, if self-defence and peace are both denied us. Indeed the issue is not the same for us as it is for others. It is not the reduction of Athens that he desires, but its total destruction. He knows we shall refuse slavery, and even if we accept it we shall be incapable of it because we are accustomed to supremacy, whereas we shall have greater power than anyone to cause him trouble, if we have the chance.

We must take it that the ultimate issues of our destiny are at stake, that men who have sold themselves to Macedon deserve of us every degree of hatred and of violence. It is impossible to overcome our enemies outside the state, till we have exacted

9. Pherae was the Thessalian city whose tyrants included Jason (see ...rates, *Philip*, 119, p. 161).

punishment from those who are here among us. What do you suppose is the reason of his insolence to us (I can call it nothing else), the reason why he treats other states with consideration, even if it ends in deceit, while to us he offers plain threats? In the case of Thessaly, for instance, his many friendly actions ended by betraying them into their present enslavement. The miseries into which Olynthus was deluded after being presented with Potidaea and a good deal more, are beyond description. Now Thebes is being led astray by being accorded the control of Boeotia¹⁰ and freed of a troublesome war. They have all been offered a bait for their personal satisfaction, and have suffered a fate which is common knowledge, or will be faced with it in due course. In our instance I say nothing of losses in the war, but in the actual course of the peace consider the extent to which we have been hoodwinked and deprived. Think of Phocis, Thermopylae, Thrace, Doriscus, Serrium, even Cersobleptes.¹¹ Does he not have and admit that he has Cardia? Why did Philip choose one treatment for the others and a different one for ourselves? Because this is the only state in which licence is given to speak on his behalf, in which it is safe to accept bribes from him and still address you, even after your many deprivations. It would have been unsafe in Olynthus to speak on Philip's behalf except when the bulk of the population had enjoyed the benefits of the possession of Potidaea. It would have been unsafe in Thessaly, except when the majority had enjoyed the benefit of Philip's expulsion of the tyrants and his award of membership of the Council.¹² It would have been unsafe in Thebes, until he handed over Boeotia and destroyed Phocis. But at Athens, despite Philip's rape of Amphipolis and Cardia, despite the armed strong point he has established against her in Euboea, despite

10. See Isocrates, *Philip*, 43, note 7, etc.

11. See sectional introduction. These are instances of Athenian setbacks due to dilatory methods, after the Peace of Philocrates. The position of Cersobleptes at that time is not clear. His loyalty to Athens had never been dependable, and whether his reduction to a vassal state of Macedon in 346 could have been prevented does not seem certain.

12. The tyrants of Pherae are meant. On the Amphictyonic Council see Isocrates, *Philip*, 74, and note there. Also sectional introduction to this speech.

his immediate move against Byzantium, it is still safe to speak for
Philip. Some who have done so have risen from poverty to
riches, from remote obscurity to fame and reputation, while this
country herself has turned honour into dishonour and wealth
into bankruptcy. For I maintain that a city's wealth lies in its
allies, its credit, its good will, of all of which we are bankrupt. As
a result of our feckless disregard of all these it is he who wins the
envy, respect and fear of Greek and non-Greek alike, while
Athens is deprived and humiliated, outstanding in all that
money will buy, but, in the proper realm of wealth, contemptible.
And some speakers, I notice, hardly adopt the same attitude
towards fellow-citizens as towards themselves.[13] They urge you
to rest inactive, even at the cost of injury. But they are unable
to accept inaction themselves, though far from suffering injury.

Then I am told by the next speaker, 'You won't take the risk
of positive proposals, you haven't the courage to stand up to it.'
A daredevil without shame or principle I sincerely hope I am
not, but I credit myself with greater courage in this assembly
than many of our action-party politicians. Gentlemen, when a
man carries on the process of judgements, confiscations, grants,
indictments, without an eye to the probable benefit of the country, such action is not a display of courage. He holds a guarantee
of indemnity in the popularity he secures by his politics and
his expression of them. He can be violent without danger. But
the genuine pursuit of good policy, which may oppose the
general desire, which involves no quest for popularity, but
always for the highest ends, yet holds itself responsible for
both, that is where real courage lies. This is the true citizen
of his country, not the gentlemen who will forfeit the highest
interests of the state for the sake of a momentary popularity.
So far am I from any admiration of such people or any belief
in their worth as Athenians that if I were asked the question
what benefit I had ever conferred on the country, I would
forgo the many claims I could make, from the financing of
triremes and theatrical products, the furnishing of money for
revenues or ransom, and other acts of public spirit, in favour
of the statement that I pursue no such policy as that. I could do

13. i.e. they are active supporters of Philip.

as others do, I could bring accusations, court popularity, secure confiscations and the rest, but I have never lent myself to any such pursuits, nor been led to them by profit or ambition. I have persisted in a policy which has lessened my standing in the public eye, but would raise that of the state itself. So much I can perhaps say without offence. And I do not regard it as consistent with true citizenship to seek a policy which might lead me straight to the highest place in the state, while it brought her to the lowest among her neighbours. The state should grow to success with the wisdom of her best citizens, while all uphold the highest, not the easiest ends. This will be the path of Nature herself, and along this path the words of true statesmanship should lead.

I have even heard this said, that my speeches are indeed always admirable, but I offer nothing but words, while what the country needs is positive action. I will state my position on this without reservation. I did not consider that the statesman is called upon for any action except the advocacy of good policy. The truth of this can easily be demonstrated. You know, no doubt, that Timotheus,[14] of recent fame, made an oration in this assembly, urging us to arms to save Euboea from enslavement by Thebes. Words were his means of expression, and to this effect. 'Are you holding a debate, when Theban troops are in Euboea, wondering how to deal with them, and what action to take? Will not your action be to fill the sea with your warships, to rise and march to the Peiraeus, to get the troopships afloat?' Timotheus produced the words, and the citizens of Athens the actions. Both took part in the completed achievement. If he had spoken to the greatest possible effect, as he did, and they had been inert and unresponsive, nothing of what Athens achieved on that occasion could have taken place. It is the same now, in regard to the words which I or anyone else utters. The actions must be expected from yourselves, the right policy, and the knowledge to urge it from the speakers.

Before I sit down, let me summarize my position. I contend

14. Timotheus, son of Conon, a leader in establishing the second Athenian League. This episode belongs to 357, when Thebes was trying to secure power in Euboea. Demosthenes had himself served on that occasion.

that money must be raised, our existing force maintained and any faulty details rectified, but without injury to the whole on the score of chance accusations. We should send representatives to all states for information, exhortation and action. At the same time corruption in the state's affairs should be punished and universally condemned, to make it possible for moderates of proved integrity to have the wisdom of their ideas approved to themselves and others. Pursue this policy and put an end to general neglect, and perhaps, perhaps there might be a change for the better. But if you merely sit in this assembly and let valour go no further than shouting and applause, while you shrink from necessary action, I see no suggestion which without the performance of duty can ever save this country.

DEMOSTHENES: PHILIPPIC III

In *Philippic III* there are several passages which do not appear in the text of the best manuscripts, but in the margin only. It is uncertain whether they indicate an alternative version of the speech or are later additions to it. All these passages can be cut without damage to the sense, and most, but perhaps not all, weaken rather than strengthen the urgency of a fine piece of oratory. But they are included here, because the additions, if they are not genuine, are at least early, and may actually have been in Demosthenes' text. These passages are marked with the symbol [   ].

A NUMBER of speeches have been delivered, gentlemen, at almost every meeting, about Philip's proceedings since the peace, and his illegal actions not only against this country, but against others. And everyone would join, if they are not already doing so, in the statement that words and action are alike needed to put an end to his unjustifiable conduct and inflict penalties. But, as I see it, the whole situation has been taken so far and left so uncontrolled, that, unpleasant as it may be to say so, I fear it is true that, had every speech and every proposal been aimed to secure the worst possible result for Athens, it could not have been arranged to less advantage. This may perhaps be assigned to a variety of causes. It is more than a few isolated reasons that have brought things to this pass. In particular a proper investigation will show that it is due to a preference for popular over true values among speakers, in some cases to the protection by individuals of their own fields of distinction and power to the exclusion of forethought, [which they prefer the country to avoid.] In other cases unjustified attacks are made on responsible officials, which results merely in Athens penalizing herself and being occupied in doing so, while Philip has a free hand to do what he likes. This sort of government is in our bones, but it is also the cause of our troubles. And I do ask you, gentlemen, not to loose your anger on me at the truth which my candour may reveal. Look at it in this way. Free speaking is something which in most fields is so generally expected in Athens, that it is allowed to foreigners and slaves, and one can often find servants here speaking their mind with more licence than citizens in some other countries. But in politics it has been completely extirpated. The consequence is complacency and flattery in this assembly, where gratification is all we are offered, while in the actual world of affairs we are driven to desperate danger. Now if this attitude persists, I have no more to say. But if you are prepared to listen to sound policy without wishful thinking, I am ready to offer it. However desperate a condition affairs are in, whatever opportunities have been wasted, it is still possible, given the will to do our duty, to remedy it. One thing I can say, which may seem contradictory but it is true. The worst feature of the past is the best basis for future hope. What feature? The fact that it is complete and total dereliction of duty on our part which has brought us to this position. If it followed a period of exemplary conduct by the people of Athens, there would be no hope of improvement. But in fact it is the neglect and inertia of Athens which Philip has worsted. She has not been defeated. She has never stirred a finger.

[If it were universally admitted that Philip is at war with Athens and has contravened the terms of peace, the only course for speakers to urge or advise would be to take the easiest and most certain method of defence against him. But as the strange attitude exists which, despite his action in capturing towns, in holding Athenian possessions and in wholesale unwarrantable conduct, yet tolerates frequent statements at meetings of the Assembly that it is a section of this country which is responsible for the war, it is necessary to take precautions and correct this position. The danger exists that proposals and recommendations of defence may lead to an accusation of provoking war.[1] . . .]

If, then, it is open to this country to remain at peace, and this alternative is in our power (to begin at this point) then I maintain that we should so do, and the author of such a proposal should promote legislation and act in this sense without deception. But if someone else is under arms, if there is someone else with a strong force at his command who offers the pretence of peace to this country, while his actions are those of war, what is left us but resistance to him? If a pretence of peace is

1. A further sentence is omitted by the Oxford text.

what you want, as he does, I will not argue with you. But any idea
that peace is a situation in which Philip holds the rest of the
Greek world with the intention of proceeding against Athens is
first of all insane and secondly means peace enjoyed by Philip
and not by Athens. And this is the situation purchased with all
the money he has spent, the situation in which he makes war
on Athens, but not Athens on him.

Indeed, if we are going to wait for the moment when he admits
he is at war, we must be the greatest optimists in existence. If
he marches on Attica or the Peiraeus, he will never make such
an admission, to judge by his treatment of others. When he
was forty *stades* from Olynthus, he proclaimed to her people
the alternative that either they must abandon Olynthus or he
Macedonia, when up till then any such accusation against him
had been greeted with indignation and protestations of innocence. Again he marched to Phocis ostensibly as to an allied
power, and Phocian representatives joined the march, while the
majority here contended that his advance through the pass
would do no good to Thebes.[2] Yet again there was the case of
Pherae the other day. Philip entered Thessaly in the guise of a
friend and ally, and seized Pherae, which he now holds. The
last instance is that of the unfortunate city of Oreus.[3] Philip
stated that he had sent his force as a benevolent measure of
surveillance. He had heard that they were in a state of trouble
and dissension, and it was a matter of genuine friendship on
the part of an ally to assist at such a time. Can we then suppose
that in the case of people who would never have taken the
offensive against him, but defensive measures at the most, he
preferred deception to open force, and yet in ours he is likely
to make an open declaration of war, particularly while we
continue to invite deception? It is unthinkable. It would be
unparalleled folly on his part if without any complaint from
his victims, but an actual tendency to blame some of our own
number, he were to dissolve internal differences and rivalries

2. In 346. Though Philip never agreed to any mercy towards her, Phocis
apparently expected it, even when Philip passed Thermopylae.

3. On Oreus see the speech *On the Chersonese*, and sectional introduction
to this speech, p. 221.

of ours and warn us against himself, and remove all pretext for his employees to mislead us with the argument that he is not 'at war.

But I ask you, could anyone in his senses judge of war and peace on a basis of words and not of actions? Of course not. Very well, then, from the first days after the signing of peace,[4] before the appointment of Diopeithes or the despatch of the force now in the Chersonese, Philip was engaged in the capture of Serrium and Doriscus, and the expulsion of the garrison placed by the Athenian commander in Serrium and the Sacred Mount.[5] What did this action amount to? Peace had been his sworn undertaking. Don't say, 'What does that matter?' or 'How does that affect us?' Whether this was a minor matter or one which did not concern us is perhaps a different question. But right and justice, be the breach of them small or great, are one and the same. Think of the Chersonese, agreed as ours by Persia and all the Greek states.[6] When he sends a force there and admits to running an expedition and gives orders for it, what is he doing? He asserts that he is not at war. But I cannot for a moment agree that such actions on his part are in accordance with the peace made with Athens. I declare that even in interference with Megara, in the manipulation of a tyranny in Euboea, in his recent movement into Thrace and his intrigues against the position in the Peloponnese,[7] in all the designs which his power activates, he is breaking the peace and is at war with Athens – unless you are prepared to say that to erect siege artillery is a peaceful occupation, until it is set in action against the walls. No, no. A man whose actions and calculations are designed for my capture, is at war with me before he ever discharges a weapon. What events are there whose occurrence would be a danger to this country? The alienation of the Hellespont, the control of Megara and Euboea by an enemy, or

4. Strictly speaking these attacks of Philip's did not occur after the signing of peace, but during the negotiations for it, a period, however, during which he had undertaken not to attack the Chersonese. But he took characteristic advantage of some uncertainty as to what was included in the Chersonese.

5. These were places in Thrace, but hardly in the Chersonese itself.

6. This statement is not supported by any known authority.

7. See *On the Chersonese*, 18 (Megara), 36 (Euboea), etc.

a tendency in the Peloponnese to side with Philip. This is the artillery aimed against Athens, and how can the man who erects it be said to be at peace? The day of his destruction of Phocis is the day I lay down as the first of his war against Athens. Defend yourselves against him, and I say you will show your good sense. Leave him alone, and you will be unable to do so when you want to. I am so far removed from your other advisers, gentlemen, that I do not advocate consideration of the Chersonese and Byzantium. I advocate assistance and prevention of harm to them, [and a vote of all necessaries to the troops now there]. Your deliberations should be about all the Greek states. They are in dire danger. But I want to make clear to you the cause of these fears about the present, to enable you, if I am right, to share my reasoning and exercise some forethought for yourselves, if for no one else, and if you think it is nonsense and moonshine, never again credit me with a single sound idea.

Philip's rise to power from small and humble beginnings, the distrust and division within the Greek states, the fact that such a rise on his part was much more extraordinary then than the control of all the rest would be now that he has so much already, and all else of this kind which I could enlarge upon, I pass over. But I can see that everyone, beginning with this country, has conceded to him what has throughout the past been the bone of contention in all Greek wars. What is this? The power to do what he likes, to encroach on and pillage the Greek states piecemeal, and to attack and enslave their cities. We have been the leaders of the Greeks for seventy-three years, and Sparta for twenty-nine.[8] Some power has also lain with Thebes recently after the battle of Leuctra. But never yet, gentlemen, has this country or Thebes or Sparta been granted this power by the cities of Greece, to do what they choose, never by a long way. In our case, or rather that of the Athenians of that day, when there was an opinion in some quarters that their conduct was beyond toleration, everyone, even states with no ground of complaint, thought it right to join in the war against them. There is no need to multiply instances. Athens and Sparta,

8. i.e. Athens 477 to 405, Sparta 404 to 376 B.C. (battle of Naxos).

without needing any initial injustice of each other's to complain of, always felt an obligation to take arms in support of a victim of injustice. Yet all the offences committed by Sparta in those thirty years, or by our ancestors in their seventy, are less than the acts of injustice against Greek states committed by Philip in less than thirteen years of his power. They are not a fraction of these, as it takes only a short time to demonstrate. I omit Olynthus, Methone, Apollonia and thirty-two towns in Thrace[9] which he destroyed with such virulence that it is hard for a visitor there to be sure they were ever inhabited. I say nothing of the destruction of the large population of Phocis. But what about the people of Thessaly? They have had their constitution and their units of government taken from them and tetrarchies established, to make their slavery extend not merely to cities, but to whole regions.[10] The cities of Euboea are under a tyranny, a tyranny in an island close to Thebes and Athens. In his letters he says in so many words, 'I am at peace with all who are prepared to accept what I say.' And he does not write this without carrying it out. He has marched to the Hellespont, as he did previously against Ambracia,[11] he is in possession of the considerable city of Elis in the Peloponnese, there has been a recent plot against Megara; neither the Greek nor the non-Greek world is big enough for his rapacity. All the Greek states can see and hear this, and yet there are no deputations of protest sent out between us, no indignation. Our morale has been so undermined in individual cities, that to this moment we are incapable of any action for our advantage or our prestige, we cannot combine, we cannot do anything by way of support or mutual assistance. We look on, indifferent to his rise. Each of us has the idea of making a profit out of the moment of another's destruction, as far as I can see, instead of taking thought or action to secure the survival of the Greeks. It

9. The 32 are the cities of the Confederacy of Olynthus. But Apollonia was not one of them, nor is it certain in what circumstances it fell to Philip.

10. See *Philippic II*, 22.

11. See below, 34, 72. Ambracia in the north west of Greece was one district in which Athens checked Philip's advance from Epirus in 343. In Elis an oligarchic faction declared for Philip.

is like the periodic onset of fever or some other epidemic, and attacks even the apparently remote, as everyone knows. There is another thing which is common knowledge: that any troubles inflicted on the Greek states by Sparta or by ourselves were at least injuries inflicted by genuine inhabitants of Greece, and one would look upon them in the same way as on a true-born son, who had come into considerable property, but made some mistake or injustice in the administration of it. In itself this might deserve criticism or accusation, but it would be impossible to de.ıy that it was a relative and the heir to the property who had done it. But had it been a slave or an illegitimate claimant who had lost or damaged what did not belong to him, goodness knows how much more heinous, how much more resented his action would have been. There is no such feeling about Philip and his present proceedings. He not merely does not belong and is not so much as related to the Greeks, but is not even of respectable foreign descent; he comes of that Macedonian riff-raff which could not even offer a good slave for sale in days gone by.

There is no limit to our degradation. He caps his destruction of towns by celebrating the Pythian Games,[12] the festival of the Greeks alone, and if he is not there himself, he sends his slaves to organize the celebrations. [He commands Thermopylae and the gate to Greece, and his garrisons and mercenaries control thesc places. He holds the right of first access to the oracle of Apollo,[13] and has brushed us aside as well as the Thessalian and Dorian peoples and the rest of the Amphictyonic states, and debarred us from a right which is not even open to all Greek states.] He dictates to Thessaly her form of government. He sends mercenaries to Porthmus to expel the democracy of Eretria, and to Oreus to establish Philistides as tyrant. And the Greeks see all this and put up with it. They seem to me to regard it like a hailstorm, which everyone prays to be spared, but no one takes steps to prevent. It is not only the insults to Greece which are left unrequited, it is the injuries to themselves, and this is the final humiliation. He has encroached on

12. Philip was President in 346 and 342.
13. This privilege was conferred on Philip at Delphi by the Amphictyons in place of Athens for his vigour against Phocis.

Corinthian preserves at Ambracia and Leucas. The Achaean post at Naupactus he has sworn to deliver to Aetolia. Thebes owned Echinus, which he has now captured, and Byzantium, against which he is marching, is his own ally. This country itself has lost (to omit other places) the principal city of the Chersonese, Cardia. The same thing happens to us all, but we hesitate, we are benumbed, and turn our eyes on our neighbours in mutual distrust, instead of on the author of all our injuries. Yet, when he has treated the whole body of us so outrageously, what can we expect from him, when he has separate control of each one?

What is the cause of this? It is not without any basis, not without good reason, that the Greeks had in the past a natural tendency towards freedom, or now towards servitude. There then existed something, an element in the spirit of the people, which today is there no more, but which in those days overcame the wealth of Persia and led Greece to freedom, which was never defeated in battle by land or sea, but whose loss now has brought everything to ruin, and turned the affairs of Greece upside down. What is this? [Nothing subtle or remote but the sheer fact that] bribery in the desire to rule or destroy Greece met with universal hatred, that a conviction for bribery was a matter for intense feeling and attended by the most severe punishment, [without any appeal or any lenience]. Never was the critical decision, which chance often puts in the hands of the neglectful instead of the conscientious, open to a price offered by speakers or commanders, nor was their feeling of solidarity or their distrust of tyrants and foreigners, or indeed anything of that sort. But the present provides a market for the sale and export of everything, and the corresponding imports lead to the decay or contamination of Greece. What are these? Envy of gain, ridicule of openness [sympathy with wrong laid bare,] resentment of criticism, and all the apparatus of corruption. Yet warships and men and supplies of money and materials, and everything which would be judged to contribute to the power of cities, are present in greater numbers and abundance now than then. But it is all rendered useless, ineffective and without value by venality.

That this is true you can presumably see for yourselves, and have no need of any evidence of mine. That the past was the opposite I will demonstrate, not by means of any words of my own, but by the written records of your own ancestors, inscribed by them on a bronze tablet on the Acropolis, [not for their own benefit – their true spirit was there without any inscription – but to provide you, their descendants, with a reminder and an example of the need to set the same values in your hearts. The words are these] 'Arthmius, son of Pythonax, of Zelea is without rights and declared an enemy of the people of Athens and their allies, together with his dependants.'[14] There follows the reason: 'because he carried Persian money to the Peloponnese'. This is the inscription. And I beg you most earnestly to consider the attitude of the Athenians of that time in doing this, and the claim they were making. Here was a man from Zelea called Arthmius, an underling of Persia (Zelea is in Asia), and because in the service of his master he carried money, not to Athens, but to the Peloponnese, the city of Athens declared him an enemy to themselves and their allies, together with his dependants, and without rights. This is not the ordinary way of disfranchisement. It has no application to our citizen of Zelea, if he was to have no part in Athenian affairs. There is, however, a clause in the laws of homicide, that where a man is not permitted trial for homicide [and his killer is indemnified against penalty] he shall die without rights. The meaning of it is this, that the killer of such a man is free of guilt. The authors of this enactment thus took the view that they had a duty to protect all Greeks. Only on this assumption would they have been concerned with a case of bribery and corruption in the Peloponnese. But they imposed punishment and retribution on any such instances they knew, to the extent of inscribing their names. The result is naturally that the Greek world inspired respect outside it, and not the other way about. It is not so now. Our present outlook is not the same in these or any other respects. What is this outlook? [[15] You know well enough yourselves.

14. The date and occasion of this decree, which is mentioned again by Demosthenes elsewhere, are not known. Nor can we be sure that his interpretation of it is correct, though presumably his hearers accepted it.

15. Some editors would exclude this passage, which at best must be a variant version.

There is no point in general accusation. And similarly the rest
of the Greeks know it equally well, which is my reason for the
claim that the present situation demands both eager activity
and sound advice. What advice?] Do you want to be told
details? And will you accept them without resentment?

(A list is read)

There exists a naïve argument intended to offer consolation to
Athens by urging that Philip is not yet what Sparta was when
she held command of the sea as well as all the land area, while
Persia was in alliance with her, and there was no power to stand
against her. Nonetheless, this country stood up to her then
without being torn to pieces. In my view, while there has been
considerable and virtually universal advance, so that nothing
remains as it was in the past, there has been no advance, no
revolution greater than that in warfare. First of all I learn that
in those days Sparta, and the rest equally, for the four or five
months of full summer would invade and ravage the country
with heavy-armed troops in a citizen army, and then return
home. So old-fashioned were proceedings, or rather so much
on a citizen basis, that there was no bribery at all, but warfare
was regular and open. Nowadays you can see, of course, the
extensive ruin caused by treachery, and the absence of organization or set battles, and you learn that it is no close formation
whose leadership enables Philip to go where he will, but light
troops, cavalry, archers and mercenaries, and this is the kind
of army he puts together. But when on these lines he attacks a
state which is rotten at the core and whose power of resistance
is sapped by distrust, he brings up his artillery and besieges it.
I say nothing about summer and winter, and the fact that no
difference is made between them, no season set aside for an
interval. But we should know all this and reckon on it, and not
admit war into the country, nor be brought crashing by a regard
for naïve ideas of the Peloponnesian War in the old days. It is
essential to maintain a watch on affairs and on armaments at as
long a range as possible, to prevent his leaving his own territory,
and not to be involved in a war at close quarters. When it comes
to warfare, gentlemen, we have many advantages, assuming

that we are prepared to play our part, such as the nature of the country with its wide possibilities for raiding and guerrilla tactics, and many more. For a pitched battle he is better trained than we are.

But the decisions you need are not confined to this, nor to active measures of military defence. Your thoughts, your feelings should be feelings of detestation towards speakers in this assembly who take Philip's side. You must understand that it is impossible to overcome the enemies of Athens till you have brought his supporters in your own city to book. And I most solemnly declare that you will never achieve it. The insensibility, the insanity of this assembly – I don't know what to call it, I am sometimes led to believe we are under the malign influence of some evil power – is capable of allowing abuse, jealousy, satire or any other motive to make us demand a hearing from men in the pay of the enemy, some of whom would not even deny this description, and show amusement at any abuse we may give vent to. Bad as it is, this is not the worst. You have made politics a safer thing for men like that than for true supporters of Athens. Observe the disastrous results of listening to such ideas. They are events well known to you.

Political circles in Olynthus contained one party of support for Philip and subservience to him in every instance, and one of genuine support for their country and concern to avoid its enslavement. Which party was it that caused the fall of Olynthus? Which betrayed the cavalry whose loss led to the fall? Philip's supporters, whose misrepresentations of the patriotic party, while the city still stood, even induced the Olynthian people to banish Apollonides.[16] And this is not a single isolated instance in which this practice has done endless damage. In Eretria after the eviction of Plutarchus[17] and his mercenaries and during the democratic control of the city itself and of Porthmus, there were two parties, one favouring Athenian influence, the other Macedonian. It was largely, if not solely, the latter who gained the ear of that wretched, unlucky people,

16. Democratic leader in Olynthus, later made a citizen of Athens.
17. On Plutarchus see back on *The Peace*, 5 and note, and sectional introduction here.

who were eventually induced to expel their own best advisers. Philip, their supposed ally, sent a thousand mercenaries under Hipponicus, pulled down the walls of Porthmus, and established an autocratic council of three, Hipponicus, Automedon and Cleitarchus. He has since twice suppressed attempts by Eretria to secure freedom, [first by sending the force under Eurylochus, then that commanded by Parmenio].

It is hardly necessary to go into all the instances. But at Oreus, as everyone knew, Philip's supporters were Philistides, Menippus, Socrates, Thoas and Agapaeus, who control the city now, while one individual named Euphraeus, who had lived here in Athens, stood for freedom and against subjection to anyone. In his case the abusive and insulting treatment he received from the people throughout would make a long story. But a year before the capture of the town he exposed the treachery of Philistides and his associates, whose activities he discovered. Whereupon a large gang under the protection and general direction of Philip rushed Euphraeus off to prison as a subversive influence. At this the democrats of Oreus, instead of rescuing Euphraeus and forcibly expelling the others, showed no resentment towards them, and stated with satisfaction that Euphraeus had deserved what he got. After which the conspirators enjoyed complete freedom to secure the capture of the town, and proceeded to set the plan on foot. Any of the populace who realized the truth were terrified into silence by their memory of the fate of Euphraeus. They were reduced to such an abject condition that despite the impending calamity not a man dared speak a word before the enemy had completed their designs and were at the gates. At that point there was some attempt at resistance, and also a movement towards surrender. After the shameful and disastrous capture of the town these conspirators exercised despotic control over it, turned upon their previous preservers, who had been prepared for any measures against Euphraeus, and exiled or executed them. Euphraeus himself committed suicide, and so gave active proof of the honesty and unselfishness of the stand he took against Philip.

You may wonder what is the reason why the people of Olynthus, Eretria and Oreus were more favourably inclined to speakers in Philip's interest than in in their own. It is the same reason as arises in our own case. Speakers in the genuine interest of Athens, even if they wish it, sometimes find it impossible to say a word to gratify popular opinion, because it is inconsistent with care for the city's welfare. For the others popularity is itself co-operation with Macedon. On those occasions the first party kept asking for money, the others denied the necessity; the first demanded war and distrust, the second peace, until the trap closed. Everything else, to omit further details, seems to have run on the same lines. One party argued with an eye to popularity, the other as the means of survival. But eventually for the most part it was not due to ingratiation nor in ignorance that the majority were led that way. They subsided, because they thought they had altogether the worst of the struggle. And I declare most emphatically my apprehension that this may happen to our own country, when there comes the calculation and the realization of being at the end of her resources. Heaven send that things may never reach this point. Death is many times more to be desired than subservience to Philip [and the betrayal of some of your best advisers]. It was a fine sort of reward the people of Oreus enjoyed when they entrusted themselves to Philip's friends and rejected Euphraeus, and the people of Eretria when they discarded Athenian representatives and surrendered to Cleitarchus: to be subjected to slavery, violence and massacre. It was a fine sort of forbearance that was shown to Olynthus on the appointment of Lasthenes to the cavalry command and the expulsion of Apollonides. It was criminal stupidity to indulge such hopes, to pursue false policies and refuse the path of duty, to listen to the suggestions of enemy agents and imagine that the importance of the city they lived in preserved them from any kind of misadventure. This is what is abject, to say 'Who would have thought it? Of course we ought to have done this and not that.' There is a great deal that could be said in Olynthus now which it would have saved them to foresee, a great deal in Oreus or Phocis, and in all the states which have been lost. But that is no consolation to them. While the ship is still afloat, be she big or small, is the time for sailors, steersmen and every member of the crew to do his utmost to prevent any design or any accident from capsizing her. Once the sea closes over her, the effort is vain. So it is now, gentlemen, with this country. While we are still ourselves preserved, while we still possess a great city with enormous resources and the highest honour, what action are we to take? Perhaps this is a question many of this audience have long wanted to ask. I will answer it, and add a proposal which you can further if you like it. You must make your own defence, take your own measures. I mean this in terms of ships, money and men. Even if the whole world submits to slavery, Athens must fight for freedom. This is what we must in our own persons bring to reality and to clear vision, and then we can call upon others, and send our representatives to point it out [everywhere, to the Peloponnese, to Rhodes, to Chios and I would add to Persia, whose interests are also concerned with refusing to allow Philip to subdue the world]. If they are convinced, there may be more to share any danger or expense that is needed, if not, at least events may be delayed. Since it is a single individual and not the combined strength of a community against which this war is being fought, even delay has its value, as had last year's talks conducted by my good friend, Polyeuctus, Hegesippus and the others as well as myself, in our canvass of the Greek states, which caused Philip to hesitate instead of moving against Ambracia or towards the Peloponnese. I do not ask that we should call on others, if we are not prepared to do what is vital for ourselves. It would be naïve to neglect ourselves and claim concern for others, or to forget the present and rouse alarm about the future. This is not what I want. I call for supplies for the force on the Chersonese and the fulfilment of their other requirements, for personal preparation on our own part and a summons to all Greeks for their unification, instruction and incitement. This is the part a city with our reputation should play. The idea that Greece will be rescued by Chalcis or Megara, while Athens eludes the issue, is wholly wrong. It will be enough if these cities themselves survive. It is we who must do it, we whose ancestors gained the glory and bequeathed it in the course of great perils. And if each of us is to sit idle and press for his own requirements and his own exemption from duty, first of all he will never find anyone to do it for him, and secondly, I fear that all that we seek to avoid will be forced upon us.

That is my declaration and my proposal, which, in my belief, might yet set our house in order. If any speaker can offer a better, let him urge it, and may the decision of this assembly, I most earnestly pray, secure our best interest.

GLOSSARY OF TECHNICAL TERMS

L, A, I, D refer to the speeches, in this selection, of Lysias, Andocides, Isocrates, Demosthenes. Numbers refer to sections.

ACCOUNTS. (A 77) All holders of office had at the end of their year of duty to submit an account of their tenure of office, which was examined by auditors chosen by lot from the Council and subject to a legal case in the event of any question.

AGORA. The market place. Most frequently mentioned is that at Athens, where it was the centre both of business and of general intercourse.

ANAKEION. (A 45) The temple of the Dioscuri on the north side of the Acropolis at Athens.

APATURIA. (A 126) The festival celebrated by the members of 'phratries' (brotherhoods) in Athens, at which the young were enrolled into the phratry.

ARCHONS. (D. *Philippic I*, 36, note) In the earliest times the principal magistrates of Athens. There were originally three, the Basileus dealing with religious matters, the Polemarch with war and the Archon with administration. Later six junior archons were added, called Thesmothetae. They had wide judicial and executive duties, but never dominated politics after the rise of the Strategi in 487 B.C. with the decree enacting the appointment of the archons by lot.

AREOPAGUS. (L 69) The oldest council in Athens, associated with the early powers, both political and judicial, of an aristocratic constitution, together with the archons (q.v.) who continued throughout to be members of it. But its importance declined with theirs from 487 B.C., and its general functions of supervision were formally removed in 462–461. (But see A 83 and note.) It remained a highly venerated body connected with jurisdiction for homicide, whose name and fame remained to the days of St Paul ('Mars' Hill') and of Milton's *Areopagitica*.

ASSEMBLY. (*passim*) The Athenian Assembly (Ecclesia) was the meeting of all citizens to which were addressed discussions of major issues introduced by the Council (Boule). Any citizen could attend and speak. The total number of citizens may have been as much as 40,000 in about 430 B.C., but the oligarchs in 411 claimed that the attendance on the Pnyx hill, where the Assembly was held, never reached more than 5000.

BASILEUS. (A 77) See Archons. The Basileus presided over the Areopagus and had charge of religious ceremonies, his jurisdiction including cases of impiety and homicide.

CADMEIA. (I *Panegyricus*, 55) The citadel of Thebes.

CLERUCHIES. (I *Panegyricus*, 107) See note on p. 120.

COLLECTORS. (A 77) Officials in charge of collecting money due to the State treasury.

COMMISSIONERS OF INQUIRY. (A 36) Members of a commission established for the special investigation of an incident or incidents (e.g. the case of the Hermae).

COUNCIL. (*passim*) The Council (Boule) at Athens consisted of 500 members, fifty from each tribe, elected by lot and serving for a year, which formed an executive body of wide scope for day-to-day purposes. All citizens over thirty were eligible, but none could serve more than twice, and not in successive years. It provided its own presidents and also those of the Assembly, for whom it prepared business. See also *Prytaneis*.

CYNOSARGES. (A 61) A gymnasium, i.e. a sports ground, east of Athens, sacred to Heracles.

DARIC. (L 11) Persian gold coin equivalent in value to twenty Attic *drachmae*.

DECARCHY. See sectional introduction to I, *Panegyricus* p. 100.

DELPHINIUM. (A 77) Temple of Apollo and Artemis in S.E. Athens. Used for certain cases of homicide.

DIONYSIA. (D *Philippic I*, 35) Athenian festival in honour of Dionysus held about April, and particularly associated with the dramatic competitions. Visitors attended it in large numbers.

THE ELEVEN. The body of police commissioners instituted by the Thirty Tyrants.

EPHETAE. (A 77) A commission of the Areopagus for the judgement of minor cases of homicide. Though the name remained, regular members of the law-courts (dicasts) were substituted for them in the fifth century.

EPHORS. (L 76) The leading magistrates at Sparta, five in number. They held the highest power in the state.

ETESIANS. (D) North-east winds regular in the Aegean in July and August.

EUMOLPIDAE. (I *Panegyricus*, 157) Ancient clan in which the office of the hierophant at the mysteries was hereditary.

GYMNASIARCH. (A 132) Official in charge of a gymnasium, or sports ground, who employed professional trainers, etc., and prepared the runners for the torch race.

HARMOST. (I, *Panegyricus*, 117) A garrison commander, of the kind sent out by Sparta after 404 B.C. to govern states which she had taken over. See sectional introduction to I *Panegyricus*.

HERMAE. (A) Images of Hermes which stood in front of doors and elsewhere throughout Athens, and were regarded as symbols of the god's protection. Their mutilation was thought an act of terrible impiety and an omen of disaster.

JURY. (A 18) The organization of Athenian citizens as juries was called the Heliaea (originally a particular court of appeal). In the fifth century 6000 jurors (dicastae, dicasts) were chosen by lot, but in the fourth all eligible citizens (i.e. over thirty years old) who offered were enrolled and divided into ten sections and the sections allotted to the courts as required, two or more sections being combined, if the case warranted it (see note on A 18). Large numbers and the use of the lot in allocation made it hard to browbeat or bribe a jury, though it may have led to unfair decisions. On the ballot *Panegyricus* see note on L 91.

KERYKES. (A, 128 I, *Panegyricus*, 157) An ancient clan in which the office of torch-bearer at the mysteries was hereditary.

LEITOURGIA. (liturgy, public service) See note 15 on D *Philippic I*. Public services carried out at Athens by the richer citizens and metics, who were compulsorily nominated for the service. The most important of these were the *trierarchia* (equipment of a ship) and the *choregia* (equipment of a chorus for the dramatic or other competitions).

METICS. (Metoeci) (L introduction and 6) Aliens, especially in Athens, more or less permanently resident and given restricted rights and duties in the state.

MONEY. (Athenian) (A 28, D, *Philippic* I, 28) Six obols went to one *drachma*, 100 *drachmae* to one *mina* (mna), and 60 *minae* to one talent.

PARALUS. (D, *Philippic I*, 34, note) The Athenian state galley used for official missions, e.g. for a summons to return to Athens for trial.

PANATHENAEA. (D, *Philippic I*, 35) An annual Athenian festival held near the end of July on the official birthday of Athena, to whom an embroidered robe was offered.

PRYTANEIS, PRYTANEUM. In the Council (q.v.) the fifty members from each tribe in turn served as a working committee for one tenth of the year, the order in which tribes served being chosen by lot, and the chairman again chosen by lot. Members of such a committee were called *prytaneis* (presidents or chairmen), i.e. of the presiding committee for the month.

The Prytaneum, on the north side of the Acropolis, may have been the headquarters of the prytaneis before the Tholos was built for them. It was later used for some homicide cases, but also for some public occasions, e.g. when a dinner was given to a benefactor. Cf. A 46.

STADE. (I, *Panegyricus*, 87) A unit of distance, just over 200 yards, the length of the stadium at Olympia.

STATER. (L 11) A gold coin from Cyzicus equivalent in value to twenty-eight Attic *drachmae*.

STOA, or STOA POIKILE. (A 85) A colonnade in Athens decorated with paintings. Inscribed announcements were posted in it.

STRATEGI. (L 65, A 38) The highest military officers in Athens, after the Polemarch ceased to command the army, the Strategi became also the leading magistrates, military and political power being commonly combined. Outstanding Strategi like Pericles were sometimes elected many times in successive years. They could sit with the Council, but had no special powers in either Council or Assembly.

SYMMORIES. (Committees.) See note 7 on D, *Olynthiac II*, 29.

THESEUM. (A 45) A temple east of the Agora and north of the Acropolis (not that now known as the Hephestiaeum but often still referred to as the Theseum).

THESMOTHETAE. (A 28) The six junior members of the executive body of the nine Archons (q.v.). Their duties were mainly judicial.

THE THIRTY. See sectional introduction to Lysias' *Eratosthenes*.

TRIBES (L 44) were not normal tribal units, but artificially constructed by the constitution of Cleisthenes at the end of the sixth century B.C. for purposes of administration and to prevent the disunion which had persisted in Athens between the ancient divisions of the Coast, the Hill and the Plain.

TRIREME. (D, *Philippic I*, 16) The normal Greek warship.

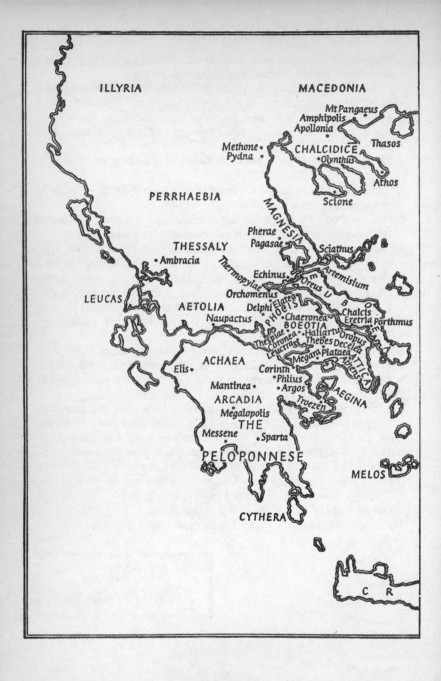

ILLYRIA

MACEDONIA

Mt Pangaeus
Amphipolis
Apollonia

Thasos

Methone
Pydna

CHALCIDICE
Olynthus

PERRHAEBIA

Athos

Scione

Pherae
Pagasae

MAGNESIA

THESSALY

Sciathus

Ambracia

Artemisium

Thermopylae

Echinus

LEUCAS

Orchomenus

Oreus
EUBOEA

Delphi
Plataea
PHOCIS
Chaeronea

Chalcis
Eretria
Porthmus

AETOLIA
Naupactus

BOEOTIA

Thespiae
Coronea
Leuctra

Haliartus
Thebes
Oropus
Decelea

ATTICA

ACHAEA

Megara
Plataea
Athens

Corinth
Elis
Phlius
Argos

AEGINA

Mantinea

ARCADIA

Troezen

Megalopolis

THE

Messene

Sparta

MELOS

PELOPONNESE

CYTHERA

C R

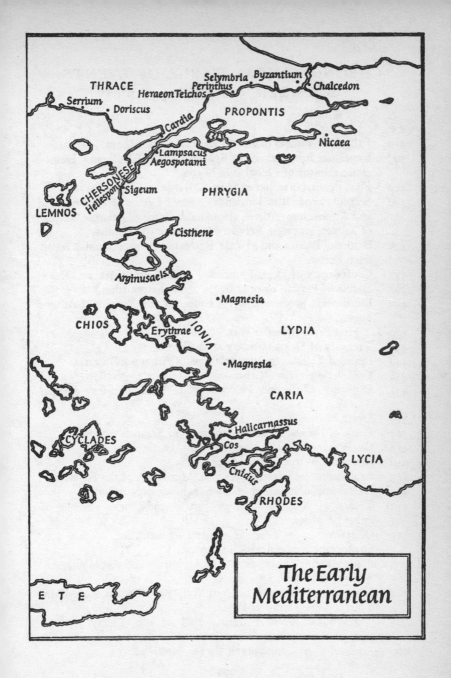

THRACE
Serrium
Doriscus
Selymbria
Perinthus
Byzantium
Chalcedon
Heraeon Teichos
PROPONTIS
Cardia
Nicaea
Lampsacus
Aegospotami
CHERSONESE
Hellespont
Sigeum
PHRYGIA
LEMNOS
Cisthene
Arginusae Is.
Magnesia
CHIOS
Erythrae
IONIA
LYDIA
Magnesia
CARIA
Halicarnassus
CYCLADES
Cos
LYCIA
Cnidus
RHODES
ETE

The Early
Mediterranean

CHRONOLOGICAL TABLE OF EVENTS
BETWEEN 510 AND 336 B.C

B.C.

510   Fall of the tyrants (sons of Peisistratus) in Athens.

507–6 Expulsion from Athens of Spartans under Cleomenes. Democratic reforms of Cleisthenes begun.

490   First Persian invasion of Greece. Battle of Marathon.

480   Second Persian invasion, under Xerxes. Battles of Thermopylae and Artemisium. Athens abandoned. Battle of Salamis. Retreat of Xerxes, leaving a Persian force under Mardonius.

479   Battles of Plataea and Mycale. Retreat of Persians. Ionian revolt from Persia.

477   Confederacy of Delos founded. Fortification of Athens.

468   Defeat of Persian navy at battle of the Eurymedon.

462   Democratic predominance of Ephialtes and Pericles at Athens begins.

459–445 First Peloponnesian War.

454   Treasury of Delos transferred to Athens.

448   Peace of Callias regulates relations of Athens and Persia.

438   Completion of the Parthenon.

431   Outbreak of second Peloponnesian War. Pericles' *Funeral Speech*.

429   Death of Pericles.

421   Peace of Nicias. Athenian recapture of Scione.

418   Greek states again at war. Battle of Mantinea.

416   Athenian destruction of Melos.

415   Athenian expedition to Syracuse. Mutilation of the Hermae.

413   Defeat and destruction of the Syracusan expedition.

412   Treaty of Miletus between Sparta and Persia. Revolt of Athenian allies.

411   Oligarchic *coup d'état* at Athens, constitution of the 400. Democracy restored within the year.

406 and 405 Athenian naval defeats at Arginusae and Aegospotami.

405–4 Athens blockaded.

404   Surrender of Athens. The Long Walls pulled down. Rule of the Thirty. Thrasybulus at Phyle.

403   Thrasybulus seizes Peiraeus. Fall of the Thirty. Lysias' *Against Eratosthenes*.

400   Andocides' trial and speech *On the Mysteries*.

399 Death of Socrates.

397 Conon commander of Persian fleet.

395 Agesilaus of Sparta at war in Persia. Death of Lysander. Athens rebuilding the Long Walls.

394 Confederation of Athens, Thebes, Corinth against Sparta. Corinthian War. Battles of Cnidus and Coronea.

387–6 The King's Peace (Peace of Antalcidas).

384 Formation of the Chalcidian Confederacy.

382 Spartan provocation of Thebes and Athens.

380 Isocrates' *Panegyricus*.

379 Spartan suppression of the Chalcidian Confederacy.

378 Alliance of Athens and Thebes.

377 Second Athenian Confederacy founded.

374 and 371 Peace negotiations, both abortive.

371 Battle of Leuctra. Foundation of Arcadian league and of Megalopolis.

369 Theban operations against Sparta. Messene refounded. Alliance of Athens and Sparta.

366 Thebes seizes Oropus.

364 Orchomenus destroyed by Thebes.

362 Battle of Mantinea. Death of Epaminondas.

359 Death of Perdiccas of Macedon. Philip secures the succession.

358 First victories of Philip over Illyrians, etc.

357 Athens recovers the Chersonese. Philip takes Amphipolis. Revolt of Chios, Cos, Rhodes and Byzantium from Athens (Social War).

356 Phocians seize Delphi. The Sacred War. Philip captures Pydna and Potidaea.

355–4 Social War ended.

353 Philip takes Methone. Demosthenes' *For Megalopolis* and *On the Liberty of Rhodes*.

351 Demosthenes' *Philippic I*.

349 Philip reduces Chalcidice. Alliance of Athens with Olynthus. Demosthenes' *Olynthiacs*.

348 Philip captures Olynthus.

346 Peace of Philocrates. Philip destroys Phocis and presides over the Pythian Games at Delphi. Isocrates' *Philip*. Demosthenes' *On the Peace*.

344 Demosthenes' *Philippic II*.

342–1 Philip in Thrace. Diopeithes sent to the Chersonese. Demosthenes' *On the Chersonese* and *Philippic III*.

340 Philip besieges Perinthus and Byzantium. Naval reforms urged by Demosthenes at Athens.

339 Amphictyonic Council makes war on Amphissa at the instance of Athens.

338 Philip invited into Greece by Amphictyons. Battle of Chaeronea.

337 Pan-Hellenic Council at Corinth.

336 Assassination of Philip. Accession of Alexander.

BIBLIOGRAPHY

History of Greece, J. B. Bury (London, Macmillan).

A History of the Greek World, 479–323, M. L. W. Laistner (London, Methuen).

A History of Greece, N. G. L. Hammond (Oxford).

The Cambridge Ancient History, esp. Vol. VI.

Athenian Democracy, A. H. M. Jones (Oxford, Blackwell).

The Art of Persuasion in Greece, George Kennedy (London, Routledge).

A History of Education in Antiquity, H. I. Marrou, translator G. Lamb (London, Sheed and Ward).

Paideia, Werner Jaeger (Oxford, Blackwell).

Demosthenes, Pickard Cambridge (Putnam).

Demosthenes, Werner Jaeger (University of California Press, Sather Classical Lectures).

Lysias and the Corpus Lysiacum (forthcoming), K. J. Dover (University of California Press, Sather Classical Lectures).